Bognor's Great War Roll of Honour

ALDWICK, BERSTED, FELPHAM, PAGHAM

CLIFF MEWETT

ISBN: 10: 1500853127
ISBN-13: 978-1500853129

'THEY WHOM THIS ROLL

COMMEMORATES WERE NUMBERED

AMONG THOSE WHO, AT THE CALL OF

KING AND COUNTRY, LEFT ALL THAT WAS

DEAR TO THEM, ENDURED HARDNESS,

FACED DANGER AND FINALLY PASSED OUT

OF THE SIGHT OF MEN BY THE PATH OF

DUTY AND SELF-SACRIFICE, GIVING UP

THEIR OWN LIVES, SO THAT OTHERS

MIGHT LIVE IN FREEDOM'

INTRODUCTION

An assassin's bullet in far off Sarajevo on 28 June 1914 seemed a world away from Bognor, an assassin's bullet that would over the next four years affect almost every family in the district. As a result of the assassination of Archduke Franz Ferdinand, Europe became embroiled in war.

On Saturday 1 August, Germany invaded Luxemburg; France and Belgium mobilised and the British called up their Naval Reservists. The following day, Bank Holiday Sunday 2 August, the British weekday daily papers made an unusual Sunday appearance, selling out in hours. In London, crowds of several thousands marched to Buckingham Palace, singing the British and French national anthems and 'cheering wildly' as King George V and Queen Mary came out onto the balcony to receive them. War fever was spreading. On Bank Holiday Monday, Germany declared war on France and issued an ultimatum to Belgium 'requesting' permission to march troops through that country. Belgium refused to allow German troops through her territory, appealing to King George V for assistance. In response, the British Government demanded assurances from Germany that Belgium's neutrality would be respected, they also announced that British naval mobilisation had been completed. Throughout Tuesday 4 August, Britain awaited the German reply, which was due by 11.00 pm that evening. No reply was forthcoming and as eleven o'clock struck a message was sent the Royal Navy, to 'commence hostilities against Germany'. The Great War had begun and the British Expeditionary Force was mobilised. All over the country men aged eighteen and over rushed to the Colours. They were sons, husbands and fathers, living normal lives, working to support their families, who suddenly found themselves in a war, defending freedom, King and Country and protecting their hearths and homes.

Locally, they left a town much smaller than it is today, with fields separating Bognor from Aldwick, Felpham and Pagham. The Bersteds - South, Middle and North - were also separate communities, nestling amongst the meadows, with an unmade track leading to Shripney, passing now long-gone wayside cottages and farms, with a wooden bridge spanning the Rife. Well over one thousand men from the Bognor district fought in the Great War, with around a third of them paying the supreme sacrifice. They are remembered on the Great War Memorial at Bognor's War Memorial Hospital and at South Bersted Church, North Bersted Church, St Mary's Church, Felpham and Thomas A'Becket Church at Pagham. The names on the War Memorials were supplied by relatives of the deceased as the result of an appeal made by the Bognor Council and the Red Cross after the war, no official listings having been maintained locally during the conflict. During my research I have discovered several who were, for one reason or another, not recorded, but I have included them in this book. The Roll of Honour has been presented in real time, as it happened, giving an outline of the war's progress.

Researching this book has taken five years and every effort has been made to ensure its accuracy. The majority of the research has been through the local newspapers of the time, various Regimental and Naval histories, family history websites and the personal records of descendants of the fallen, for which I thank them most sincerely. I would also like to record my thanks to the staff of the West Sussex Record Office at Chichester, for their assistance and expertise during my many visits there and to Joy Fluter, for her time spent proof reading and checking the content.

CLIFF MEWETT

THE
ROLL OF HONOUR

The members of the British Expeditionary Force (BEF) started arriving in France on 9 August 1914 and by the 22 August some 160,000 men had been ferried across the Channel, closely chaperoned by the powerful Royal Navy. Compared to the large conscripted armies of the other countries, the BEF was small in numbers, said to have been described by the Kaiser as 'a contemptible little army'. They were soon in action, suffering heavy casualties during the German advance, which had been rapid in pursuance of the aims of their Schlieffen Plan, the swift defeat of France in the west, before turning their attentions to the Russian forces in the east.

The British Expeditionary Force's first major engagement with the enemy was at Mons, where they attempted to hold the line of the Mons-Conde Canal. Despite being outnumbered they inflicted heavy casualties on the Germans before being forced to retreat. They set up defensive positions at Le Cateau, but on 26 August were heavily attacked and had to withdraw westwards. Having retreated continuously for ten to twelve days and under repeated German attack, the BEF were on the point of exhaustion, when they reached the River Marne, the scene of a further battle. The Germans were now only thirty miles east of Paris and the French Government, expecting the capital to fall, left for Bordeaux. On 4 September the French launched a counter attack and in turning to meet it the Germans opened up a thirty mile wide gap in their lines, between their First and Second Armies. Quick to exploit this, the BEF poured through the gap between the two German armies. Boosted by French Infantry Reservists, who arrived from Paris in a fleet of six hundred taxi-cabs, the German advance was halted and by 9 September they began to retreat towards the River Aisne. This was a significant Allied achievement and ended any German hopes of a swift victory on the Western Front. Casualties were high in the BEF with 12,773 men losing their lives. It was in this battle that the first Bognor casualties occurred.

WESTERN FRONT

Regimental Sergeant Major L2946 William H CLEARE
York Road, Chichester
2nd Battalion, the Royal Sussex Regiment, 1st Division
Killed in Action on 10 September 1914
Aged 40
Buried in Montreuil Aux Lions British Cemetery, France

A regular soldier, the son of Regimental Quarter Master Sergeant and Mrs Cleare of York Road, Chichester, William was born in India in 1874, where his father was serving with 107th Regiment of Foot.

Returning to England, William's father retired to Chichester on his Army pension, whilst by 1891 William (junior) had followed his father and enlisted into the Royal Sussex Regiment. When war was declared the 2nd Battalion, then based in Woking, were quickly mobilized and sent to France in August as part of 1st Division of the British Expeditionary Force. They were soon in action, attempting to stem the German advance towards Paris and fought in the Battle of Marne, before becoming part of the reserve forces for a few days. On 10 September they became the Brigade's advance guard and in heavy rain proceeded through the village of Priez, engaging the enemy who were occupying high ground beyond. Faced with overwhelming German fire power they were forced to retire, then obtaining support from the rest of the Brigade and French troops they drove the Germans back. It was on this day that RSM William Cleare was killed in action.

William, a married man, lived in New Malden, Surrey, close to where his Battalion was stationed in peace time. Quite what his Bognor connection was has not been established, but his name appears on the Bognor War Memorial as the first local casualty of the war. His name is also included on the War Memorials at New Malden, Rumsboldwhyke in Chichester and at North Mundham.

Captain Richard Francis GATEHOUSE
1 Cotswold Terrace, the Esplanade, Bognor
1st Battalion, the Northumberland Fusiliers, 3rd Division
Killed in Action on 13 September 1914
Aged 38
Buried in the Vauxbin French National Cemetery, France

Richard was born the second son and fourth child to George and Fanny Gatehouse, whose family had been brewers and maltsters in Chichester since the early 1800s. They lived in North Street, Chichester and their business was a major employer in the City, with a staff approaching thirty men. On retirement the family moved to Bognor, where George became a JP. Meanwhile, Richard was educated at Charterhouse School as a boarder, subsequently joining the Army as a Second Lieutenant in the West Riding Regiment in December 1897. Promoted to Lieutenant in October 1899 he transferred to the 1st Battalion, the Northumberland Fusiliers, with whom he fought in the South African War, where he took part in many important missions. He was Mentioned in Despatches and received the Queen's Medal with three clasps, followed a year later by the King's Medal with two clasps. He obtained further promotion, obtaining the rank of Captain by 1911. In 1913 he married Evelyn Gardom, at Epsom, Surrey.

When war was declared the 1st Battalion, the Northumberland Fusiliers were in Portsmouth and mobilized immediately, landing in France on 14 August 1914. They fought at Mons and took part in the rearguard action at Le Cateau, before fighting the Battle of the Marne. Captain Richard Gatehouse was initially reported as wounded and missing, before it was established that he had been killed in action on 13 September.

Private L8142 Albert Thomas YEATMAN
Essex Road, Bognor
2nd Battalion, the Royal Sussex Regiment, 1st Division
Died of Wounds on 14 September 1914
Aged 30
Commemorated on La Ferte Sous Jouarre Memorial, France

The second son of William and Hester Yeatman, Albert was well known in Bognor, having worked for some years in the busy International Stores in London Road and then as a railway porter. He became a regular soldier serving with the 1st Battalion, the Royal Sussex Regiment by 1912 and spent some time in India, subsequently transferring to the 2nd Battalion.

Albert was to become one of the earliest war victims when on 14 September his Battalion were ordered to occupy the high ground overlooking Vendresse. Here they captured several hundred German prisoners who, taken by surprise, waved the white flag. Whilst they were being taken into custody other German units opened fire on both the Royal Sussex and their captives, causing many deaths on both sides. Originally reported missing, Albert died that day as a result of wounds received. Albert's name is also included on both the Chichester and St Pancras Church (Chichester) War Memorials.

Private L9956 Ernest KEATES
Copyhold Cottage, Lagness, Sefter, Pagham, Bognor
2nd Battalion, the Royal Sussex Regiment, 1st Division
Killed in Action on 14 September 1914
Aged 19
Commemorated on the Ferte Sous Jourre Memorial

'The parishioners of Pagham are deeply grieved of the news of the death of a young soldier of 'C' Company, 2nd Battalion, the Royal Sussex Regiment. He was only 19 years old and was killed at Vendresse. He has a brother serving in another Battalion of the Royal Sussex'.

Another regular soldier, Ernest Keates, serving with the Royal Sussex Regiment also lost his life that day, whilst supporting an attack on a factory, which 'was found to be held in considerable strength by the enemy'. Ernest was one of eleven children born to farm labourer Charles and his wife Elisa and before enlisting was a farm worker himself. The family had lived at various addresses in Pagham and Lagness.

In the battle, the Royal Sussex were accompanied by the Kings Royal Rifles and supported by the Loyal North Lancashire Regiment. The weather was wet, with a heavy mist, the British meeting 'heavy shell and machine gun fire'. A party from the Royal Lancashire's managed to seize and hold the factory around 1200 hours. Private Keates was killed in that action by a bursting shell 'which wrought such havoc that it uprooted a tree near to where Private Keates and a comrade were standing.'

Bandsman 11558 Jesse William IDE
1 Oxford Street, Bognor
2nd Battalion, the Durham Light Infantry, 6th Division
Killed in Action on 21 September 1914
Age 20
Commemorated on the Ferte Sous Jouarre Memorial, France

The Germans halted their retreat and entrenched themselves on the north bank of the River Aisne. The Allies launched a frontal infantry attack in dense fog, crossing the formidable river using pontoons and partially demolished bridges, only to find when the fog cleared that the Germans were well established on higher ground, where they were able to take a toll on the Allied troops. However, a bridgehead was established and fighting took place on the plateau above it. The Germans counter attacked strongly, being well dug in, deploying machine guns and heavy artillery in defence of their positions. Although the Allies made small advances they could not be consolidated and by 18 September the attack was scaled back and finally abandoned on 28 September, when it became clear that both sides were too well entrenched for any more frontal attack. Trench warfare had begun.

Jesse Ide was born in Nutbourne, Sussex, the eldest son of bricklayer Argo and his wife, Annie. The family lived at Warblington, Emsworth, but by 1911 Jesse had moved to Bognor, where he was known as a 'very useful pianist and a good vocalist'. He decided to take up a musical career in the Army, enlisting at Colchester in 1913 into the Durham Light Infantry. With the outbreak of war his Battalion were sent to France as part of the British Expeditionary Force and Jesse was killed during the above action, on 21 September.

Rifleman 10070 George Alfred SWAIN
10 Chapel Street, Bognor
2nd Battalion, the Royal Irish Rifles, 3rd Division
Killed in Action on 21 September 1914
Aged 20
Commemorated on La Ferte Sous Jouarre Memorial, France

George Swain was born in Bognor, the son of George, who worked for the Urban Council and his wife, Frances; the family then lived at Felpham, before moving to 10 Chapel Street, Bognor. On leaving school after a period as a butchers errand boy, George enlisted at Portsmouth into the Royal Irish Rifles. They were stationed at Tidworth when war broke out and were immediately ordered to France, arriving at Rouen on 14 August 1914. They saw action in the Battle of Mons and at the Battle of the Marne, supporting the Royal Sussex Regiment in the attack on Troyon in which Private Ernest Keates was killed (see above). Seven days later Rifleman George Swain was also killed in action.

Rifleman 3590 Albert Henry HAMMOND
24 Mons Avenue, Bognor
1st Battalion, the Rifle Brigade, 4th Division
Killed in Action on 24 September 1914
Age 30
Buried in the Bucy Le Long Communal Cemetery, France

Albert Hammond was the second son of Edwin, an agricultural labourer and his wife Eliza and was born at Martins Farm, Chichester, spending his childhood in the Halnaker area of Boxgrove. On leaving school he became a domestic gardener and married Sarah Fennell in 1912. He enlisted at Portsmouth into the Rifle Brigade as a regular soldier before the war, his Battalion landing at Le Havre on 23 August 1914, having initially been held back in England to counter the threat of any German landings. With the main Battle of the Aisne over and both sides entrenched, Albert became the third local man to lose his life in as many days, when he was killed in action on 24 September 1914, in one of the many skirmishes which were continually taking place.

THE LOSS OF THE AUSTRALIAN SUBMARINE *AE 1*

The Royal Navy had many local men, both regular and reservists, serving throughout the war and they were also soon in action. The fate of the first local naval casualty is still surrounded in mystery a hundred years later. It involved the loss of the Australian submarine *AE 1* which went missing with all hands.

In 1910, the Royal Australian Navy placed an order for two E Class submarines to be built in Barrow-in-Furness, designated *AE 1* and *AE 2*, the '*A*' standing for Australia. Both vessels were completed and commissioned in Portsmouth, sailing with a British crew on 2 March 1914 for Australia, via Suez and Singapore, arriving in Sydney on 24 May, having completed about two thirds of their journey under their own power and being towed the rest of the way. Three months later when the United Kingdom declared war on Germany, Australia did the same. At that time the submarines were completing a refit in a dockyard at Garden City and shortly afterwards sailed with a combined Australian and British crew as part of a task force which attacked and captured Rabaul, a wireless and coaling station for the German Pacific Fleet. The following day, 19 September 1914, *AE 1* accompanied by the destroyer HMAS *Parramatta*, was ordered to Cape Gazelle to watch for any German Pacific Fleet activity in the Bismark Archipelago and to return in the evening. The two vessels kept in visual contact until mid afternoon, *AE 1* last being seen at 1530 hrs apparently on her way home. HMAS *Parramatta* returned to port, but *AE 1* failed to arrive. Accompanied by HMAS *Yarra*, HMAS *Parramatta* was immediately despatched to search for *AE 1*. They were joined the following day by four other warships, plus local civilian craft. On 19 September 1914, *AE 1* was officially declared lost and to this day no trace of the submarine has ever been found.

Able Seaman 7597 Frederick William WOODLAND
8 Sheepwash Lane, Bognor
HMA Submarine *AE 1*, His Majesty's Australian Navy
Lost at Sea on 19 September 1914
Aged 30
Commemorated on the Plymouth Naval Memorial, England

Able Seaman Frederick William Woodland was the third son of Alfred and Ellen Woodland, of Willowhale Cottages, Coastguard Lane, Pagham. He was an agricultural labourer employed by Willowhale Farm, before joining the Royal Navy, becoming a stoker first class. In 1909 he married Helen Lambeth, the daughter of a carpenter, Napoleon, of 4 Sudley Terrace, Bognor. They settled down in Emsworth where their son, also Frederick, was born. Able Seaman Woodland formed part of the crew that ferried *AE 1* to Australia and lost his life whilst serving in the Australian submarine on 19 September 1914, just six weeks after the declaration of war.

The mystery was soon reported in the Bognor press, highlighted by a letter received by Frederick's wife:

'Much speculation has been caused by the receipt of Mrs Woodland, of a letter from her husband, one of the crew of the Australian submarine *AE 1*. This vessel was returning to Sydney from the coast patrol work when last heard of and she has been officially recorded as lost with all hands since 14 September. The letter, which Mrs Woodland received, bears no date itself, but the postmark is 5 October, with the Sydney impression.

'The contents are of the usual character and the husband says he is alright and his wife is not to worry as his vessel can get under the water when there is anything about. It gives no suggestion of anything unusual having occurred, though it maintains that *AE 1* took part in the operations against the German islands in the Pacific. This particular letter was not stamped, although Mrs Woodland's previous letter had been. She has sent the envelope to the Admiralty. It has been rumoured in Bognor that Woodland's mother, who lives at Bersted has received a cablegram from him, but that was not the case'.

It was Australia's first war loss and the first British built submarine to be lost in the Great War. Able Seaman Woodland was the first Bognor naval casualty of the war.

THE LOSS OF CRUISER FORCE 'C'

Whilst the British Expeditionary Force was fighting on land, the Royal Navy became involved in an action in the North Sea. Since the beginning of the war the Admiralty had maintained a patrol of old Cressy Class cruisers, in support of Harwich-based destroyers, which were tasked with keeping the North Sea clear of enemy torpedo craft and minelayers. The Cruiser Force supported them, noting and reporting enemy war vessels and transport movements. Launched around 1900, the cruisers were quite outdated by the outbreak of war and considered to be vulnerable to any raids by modern German surface ships or U Boats; they were referred to as 'the live bait squadron' by some naval circles and plans were in hand to have them moved to the western entrance of the English Channel. However, before this could take effect the four cruisers HMS *Euryalus*, with a Rear Admiral aboard, HMS *Aboukir*, HMS *Hogue* and HMS *Cressy,* continued with their patrols, running into weather so bad on the 19 September that the Rear Admiral ordered their escort destroyers to return to harbour, leaving the Cruiser Force at sea. On 20 September HMS *Euryalus* also had to return to harbour to take on more coal, leaving the other three cruisers to continue their patrol under the command of Captain Drummond in HMS *Aboukir,* without their destroyer escorts. On the morning of 21 September, HMS *Euryalus* now coaled up, left port to rejoin the others, as did the destroyers, the weather having improved.

Meanwhile Cruiser Force C, continuing their patrol, were unaware that a lone German submarine, *U-9*, was in the area, which positioned herself to attack and just before 0630 hrs fired a single torpedo at HMS *Aboukir*, which struck her port side, causing considerable flooding and loss of engine power. Initially Captain Drummond thought she had hit a mine and signalled the other two ships to close in and assist. However, he soon realized they had been torpedoed and tried to order the other two ships away. The order to abandon ship was given, but only one lifeboat had survived the attack and most of the crew jumped into the sea as she sank twenty five minutes later, leaving hundreds of men swimming in the water or clinging on to pieces of wreckage.

Still thinking that HMS *Aboukir* had struck a mine and unaware of *U-9*'s presence, her sister ships, HMS *Hogue* and HMS *Cressy*, moved in to pick up survivors. Both ships lay dead in the water as they lowered their boats, becoming sitting targets. The *U-9* then fired two torpedoes at HMS *Hogue* and, mortally wounded, she sank in ten minutes with a heavy loss of life. Nobody from Bognor was aboard HMS *Hogue;* however, one Bognorian, was aboard HMS *Cressy* and she was the next target.

HMS *Cressy* was lowering her boats to pick up survivors, but spotted the periscope of *U-9*. Now realising that the three ships had been under submarine attack she fired her guns at the periscope, but to no avail and she tried to make good her escape. However, *U-9* fired two torpedoes at her; one narrowly missed, but the second hit her starboard side. The damage from this hit was not fatal, but a few minutes later *U-9* fired her last torpedo and within fifteen minutes HMS *Cressy* had joined her sister ships under the waves.

There were survivors from the incident, 837 in all, picked up by Dutch merchant ships and British trawlers, but in the two hours that the attack on the ships lasted 1459 men were lost, many of them married Naval Reservists or Naval Cadets, who had been posted to the ships, as they were thought not to be at risk of being involved in any serious action.

The Germans made much of the attack and issued a picture postcard of the incident. Much criticism was subsequently levelled at the Admiralty, for sending mainly inexperienced men in elderly ships that were vulnerable against the more modern German warships.

Stoker First Class 301451 Albert Samuel ROGERS
51 Essex Road, Bognor
HMS *Aboukir* Royal Navy
Lost at Sea on 22 September 1914
Aged 30
Commemorated on the Portsmouth Naval Memorial, Southsea, Hampshire

Albert Rogers was born in Bromley, Kent and lived with his wife in Bognor. He was a stoker on HMS *Aboukir* and like many of the crew, was a Naval Reservist. The *Bognor Observer* reported thus:

'Among the victims of HMS *Aboukir* was a man named Albert Rogers. He was the son-in-law of Mr and Mrs Britton, who have five sons on active service and before the naval catastrophe in which the *Aboukir* was involved, had two son-in-laws in the fighters'.

Assistant Clerk John Verity POORE
HMS *Cressy* Royal Navy
Lost at Sea 22 September 1914
Aged 17
Commemorated on the Chatham Naval Memorial, Kent, England

John Verity Poore was an assistant clerk on board HMS *Cressy* and his name appears on the official casualty listings. John was born in Wandsworth in 1897, the second son of John Poore, a Civil Servant Staff Clerk for the Education Board and his wife, Jessie. Sadly, little is known of him except for a sentence in the *Bognor Observer* to say he had been a local victim. His name does not appear on the Bognor War Memorial.

THE LOSS OF HMS HAWKE

Three weeks after the attack on Cruiser Force C, *U-9* struck again. Her victim this time was another elderly ship, HMS *Hawke*, a 12 gun Edgar Class Cruiser, which had been launched at Chatham in 1891. On 15 October 1914 HMS *Hawke* was engaged with her sister ship, HMS *Theseus*, in operations in the North Sea, both unknowingly being tracked by *U-9*, whose initial attack was upon HMS *Theseus*, which managed to avoid the incoming torpedo. However, seconds later HMS *Hawke* was hit amidships, igniting her magazine, the subsequent explosion ripping the ship apart. She sank within five minutes, the crew managing to get only one boat away, whilst the remainder jumped into the sea or went down with the ship. HMS *Theseus*, under strict Admiralty orders not to pick up any survivors for fear of further losses, abandoned the area, leaving 523 Officers and men to their fate. There were only 48 survivors who were picked up by the Norwegian steamer, *Modesta*. They were subsequently transferred to a British trawler and taken to Aberdeen. Two local men lost their lives on HMS *Hawke*.

Surgeon Gustavus William Musgrove CUSTANCE
St Andrews Lodge, 1 Gloucester Road, Bognor
HMS *Hawke* Royal Naval Division
Lost at Sea on 15 October 1914
Aged 35
Commemorated on the Chatham Naval Memorial, Kent, England

Surgeon Gustavus Custance was one of 14 children born at Colwells, Malvern, Herefordshire, to the Reverend and Mrs Custance. His early days were spent in Herefordshire, where his father was the local vicar and a school chaplain, the family subsequently moving to Bognor.

Gustavus joined the Royal Navy in 1907 as a 'surgeon under instruction' at the Royal Naval Hospital at Haslar, where he studied for two years. In 1909 he was the Ship's Surgeon on HMS *Hibernia*, a battleship of the Home Fleet, serving on her until 1911. From there he joined HMS *Clio* at Hong Kong and went to China. Returning to Chatham in 1912 he was appointed to the Royal Hospital, instructing sick berth staff. He then moved to Plymouth before being 'lent' to the Royal Naval College at Greenwich, whilst he studied for further promotion.

In 1913 he was back at sea, temporarily serving on HMS *Racer*, before joining HMS *Hawke* on the outbreak of war. Surgeon Custance was described as 'a genial and popular Officer'.

Temporary Surgeon James H Digby WATSON
HMS *Hawke* Royal Navy
Lost at Sea on 15 October 1914
Aged 24
Commemorated on the Chatham Naval Memorial, Kent, England

James was the second child and eldest son of Naval Engineer James Watson and his Canadian wife, Eliza and was born in Portsea. Known as 'Bungy', he was a talented rugby forward and played centre for Blackheath, becoming an England international in the 1914 Grand Slam winning team. He joined the Royal Navy as a Doctor/Surgeon and was following a path similar to Gustavus Custance when he lost his life aboard HMS *Hawke*. His name does not appear on the Bognor War Memorial, although the *Bognor Observer* carried a report of his death.

WESTERN FRONT

The Race to the Sea was the name given to the next period of the land war and was the last stage of the mobile warfare on the Western Front. It began immediately after the Battle of the Aisne, as each side extended their lines northwards towards the Channel, in an attempt to outflank the other. During the autumn of 1914 several battles were fought as the Race developed - Artois, La Bassee, Messines, Armentaires and the first battle of Ypres. Each side strove to out-manoeuvre the other, but failed as they both consistently dug in and prepared effective trench defences, the fighting petering out as winter weather began to take effect.

Captain Mervyn Keates SANDYS
Belmont Lodge, Belmont Street, Bognor
2nd Battalion, the York & Lancaster Regiment, 6th Division
Killed in Action on 25 October 1914
Aged 30
Commemorated on the Ploegsteert Memorial, Belgium

The youngest twin son of a well known Bognor military family, Mervyn Sandys' father was Major George Owen Sandys and his twin was a Captain in the Warwickshire Regiment; his mother, Mrs Clarissa Sandys, became active in local affairs. A career soldier, Captain Mervyn Sandys received his first commission in 1903 and served with the Yorkshire and Lancaster Regiment, who were stationed in Ireland at the outbreak of war. The Regiment were hurriedly moved to France, arriving shortly after the first Battle of Marne in mid October 1914 and sustaining their first casualties that month, through German artillery attacks. Captain Sandys died of wounds received from one of these attacks on 25 October 1914.

A memorial window in his memory was placed in St John's Church, London Road, Bognor in 1916. It depicted three figures in three separate lights, Christ in the middle, Courage on the left and Victory on the right, in armour holding a laurel crown. At the foot was the family coat of arms and the dedicated inscription 'In Battle against the Germans'.

The following lines were composed 'in memory of one of Bognor's heroic sons', the first letter of each line spelling out his name:

<blockquote>
'M Mourn we? Aye a nation mourns its brother,
K Kindred souls were ye, each tuned to each,
S Severed! For his Country, Mervyn died,
A Aiding comrades sent forth by their King,
N Never did beat truer heart to their God,
D Dauntless fighting against a cruel foe,
Y You on Earth petitioned keep him here,
S Summoned thither by God, he went'.
</blockquote>

Private L10133 Frederick James RICHARDSON
Holly Oak, 41 Highfield Road, Bognor
2nd Battalion, the Royal Sussex Regiment, 1st Division
Killed in Action on 29 October 1914
Aged 27
Commemorated on the Menin Gate Memorial, Ypres, Belgium

Over the last two days in October, the 2nd Royal Sussex were involved in very hard fighting and subjected to heavy German shelling, during which early in the engagement Frederick Richardson lost his life, shot by a German sniper. Born in Bognor he had enlisted at Eastbourne before the war:

'Among the Bognorians who have made the supreme sacrifice for King and Country is Private Frederick Richardson, on 29 October 1914. He was serving with the Royal

Sussex Regiment and was engaged in the operations at Ypres, when he was picked off by one of the enemy's marksmen and died almost immediately. From the facts gathered by his comrades with him, is that he suffered very little pain'.

That news, reported in the *Bognor Observer* in November 1914, had been forwarded by his mother, following a letter she had received from the War Office, in response to inquiries she had made 'earlier in the month'.

Corporal 44539 Albert AGER
Family Connection, 4 Henry Street, Bognor
2nd Battalion, the Bedfordshire Regiment, 7th Division
Died of Wounds on 1 November 1914
Aged 24

'Mr and Mrs Charles Puckett have received news of the death of Mrs Puckett's brother, Corporal Albert Ager, who died in the Australian Voluntary Hospital at Boulogne. Only three weeks had elapsed from the time he left Southampton for the Front, to the day of his death. He leaves a widow and two children', reported the *Bognor Observer*.

Charles Puckett was a plasterer, who had married Fanny Ager from Bedford in 1908, her brother, Albert, being a regular soldier in the Bedfordshire Regiment. He had enlisted in 1908 and spent his leave periods at Bognor with his sister.

Albert's Regiment was stationed near Pretoria, South Africa, at the outbreak of war and was immediately recalled, arriving at Southampton on 19 September 1914. The Regiment was hastily refitted for European warfare and embarked on SS *Winifredian* at Southampton on 5 October, bound for the Front. After a brief stopover at Dover en route to take on more supplies, they landed at Zeebrugge on 7 October, making their first contact with the enemy eleven days later on the Ypres-Menin Road, where a 'brief skirmish' took place. Over the next few weeks the Battalion fought in the First Battle of Ypres, during which Albert lost his life.

Company Sergeant-Major 8212 Reginald John BAKER
25 Argyle Road, Bognor
1st Battalion, the Seaforth Highlanders, Ross-Shire Buff, attached to
the 2nd Battalion, 4th Division
Killed in Action on 7 November 1914
Aged 36
Commemorated on Le Touret Memorial, France

Company Sergeant Major Reginald John Baker, who was born in Salisbury, Wiltshire, was the husband of Alice Grace Baker. An experienced soldier, Reginald had served many years with the Seaforth Highlanders and had seen action on the North-West Frontier in 1908. With the outbreak of the Great War, the 1st Battalion, who were then stationed in India, were recalled, leaving for France on 21 September and landed at Marseilles on 12 October 1914.

Meanwhile, 2nd Battalion, the Seaforth Highlanders, who had been in France since 23 August as part of the British Expeditionary Force, had sustained heavy casualties including losing their Commanding Officer in the Battle of the Aisne in September. On his arrival in France, Company Sergeant Major Baker was immediately attached to 2nd Battalion, only to be killed in action on 7 November 1914.

Sergeant 7159 Jesse MILLS
109 Collyer Avenue, Bognor
3rd Battalion, the Coldstream Guards, the Guards Division
Died of Wounds on 16 November 1914
Aged 26
Buried in the Grangegorman Military Cemetery, Ireland

'Jesse Mills will be remembered for working for Mr Winter, the butcher in the High Street', wrote the *Bognor Observer*.

Jesse was the son of Jesse and Janet Mills and the brother of George *(see Roll of Honour, December 1915)*. After several years service with the Coldstream Guards, Jesse was demobbed, becoming a reservist, spending seven months in the Isle of Wight Constabulary and stationed at Ventnor, before being recalled to the Colours and going abroad with the Expeditionary Force. Sergeant Mills was wounded and evacuated to the Mater Hospital, Eccles Street, Dublin, where he died on 16 November 1914.

'He was interred with the due honours of his rank, in the Garrison Cemetery; the funeral cortege consisted of a firing party of the Royal Irish Rifles. The band of the Royal Irish Constabulary Depot, in which force he served before joining the army, were in attendance. Following the gun carriage containing the coffin covered with a union ensign were the Sergeants of the Rifles acting as pall bearers, after which marching in double file were a detachment of Officers, NCOs and men. At the cemetery, on conclusion of the burial rites, the firing party and buglers contributed their parting tributes at the graveside'.

Corporal 8105 Walter Thomas AGER
Family Connection, 4 Henry Street, Bognor
1st Battalion, the Hampshire Regiment, 4th Division
Died of Wounds on 23 November 1914
Aged 25
Buried in Trois Abres Cemetery, Steenwerck, Nord, France

Walter Ager was a regular soldier/musician who had enlisted at Sittingbourne, Kent, with the Hampshire Regiment, probably around 1910, when he was based at Aldershot. Born at Dartford, Kent, the eldest son of general labourer Walter and his wife Harriett, the family had connections with Mr and Mrs Puckett, whose address was given as the home of Walter, following his death from wounds and is the same as that for Corporal Albert Ager *(see Roll of Honour, November 1914.)* They were not brothers, but may have been cousins. In any event, the deaths of two close relatives within three weeks or so of each other must have been a devastating blow for Mr and Mrs Puckett so early in the war.

At the outbreak of war the 1st Battalion, the Hampshire Regiment moved from Aldershot to Colchester, before sailing to Le Havre on the SS *Braemar Castle* on 21/22 August. From there they soon found themselves in action at Le Cateau on 26 August. Corporal Ager saw further action in the Battles of Marne, the Aisne and Messines, before succumbing to wounds received at Armentieres, during the First Battle of Ypres.

THE NAVAL BATTLE OF CORONEL

HMS *Good Hope*, a Drake Class heavy cruiser, was laid down in September 1899 and launched in February 1901. She was placed in reserve in 1913, but was re-commissioned at Portsmouth during the Test Mobilisation, just before the outbreak of hostilities and left Portsmouth on 2 August, on her way to join the 6th Cruiser Squadron, as part of the Grand Fleet at Scapa Flow. However, she was almost immediately detached from the main fleet and sent to reinforce the South American Squadron under Rear-Admiral Sir Christopher Craddock, becoming his flagship. At that time it was thought that German liners leaving the United States eastern ports could easily convert themselves into armed merchant cruisers, by installing guns stowed away in their holds and needed therefore to be dealt with. Her job for the first few weeks of the war was to protect British merchant shipping from this threat, as far south as the Falkland Islands, where she and the rest of the Squadron docked at Port Stanley.

For some months the Royal Navy had been searching for the German East Asiatic Squadron under Admiral von Spee, which had been operating in the Pacific. Information had now been received that the Germans were planning to sail into the South Atlantic to prey upon shipping in the British trading routes along the east coast of South America. The Royal Navy South American Squadron consisted of the cruiser HMS *Monmouth*, the light cruiser HMS *Glasgow*, a converted ex-liner the *Otranto* and now the newly arrived HMS *Good Hope*. These ships were no match for the modern German Squadron, which contained five up-to-date cruisers, including the SMS *Scharnhorst* and SMS *Gneisenau*, which could each concentrate six 8.2 inch guns on a single target at once.

Rear Admiral Craddock waited at Port Stanley in the hope of naval reinforcements, but despite his lack of firepower was ordered to seek and attack the German Squadron. On 18 October the British Squadron left Port Stanley to rendezvous with HMS *Glasgow*, which had been sent on patrol earlier to gather intelligence. The British made contact with the Germans at Coronel, off the Chilean coast, just before sunset on 1 November and chose to stay and fight in the failing light, after ordering the *Otranto* to break formation and flee. In difficult seas the engagement began. Using their greater firepower and staying just out of reach of the British guns, HMS *Good Hope* was crippled by SMS *Scharnhorst*'s third salvo and sank with all nine hundred hands.

Able Seaman SS1717/PO Jonathan Jack SAIGEMAN
Ivy Lane, South Bersted, Bognor
HMS *Good Hope* Royal Navy
Lost at Sea on 1 November 1914
Aged 26
Commemorated on the Portsmouth Naval Memorial, Southsea, Hampshire

Jonathan (Jack) Saigeman was born in Littlehampton and the third generation eldest son to have been so named. Both his father and grandfather before him were bargemen on the River Arun, plying between the sea and Amberley. On leaving school, Jack took up employment as a golf caddy at the Littlehampton Golf Club, probably part time, as he also became an employee of the Bognor Gas Works, Argyle Road, as well as being a Naval Reservist. Early in 1914 he married Lillian Osgood from West Ham and they set up home in Bognor. As the war approached he received his call up notice to report to Portsmouth and join HMS *Good Hope*. He lost his life in the Battle of Coronel.

Shortly after being notified of his death Lillian received his last letter. He was worried because he had not heard from her. This was because of his ship's constant movements in the South Atlantic and the Forces post had not caught up with him. The letter Lily received from Jack arrived at Christmas and contained these poignant words:

'I should like very much to get a line from you Lily, the time seems so long to me and I should feel so much better if only I knew that my wife was alright'.

By this time Jack had been dead for nearly two months.

Chief Signal Boatswain William PENNY
Lynette, Tennyson Road, Bognor
HMS *Good Hope* Royal Navy
Lost at Sea on 1 November 1914
Aged 49
Commemorated on the Portsmouth Naval Memorial, Southsea, Hampshire

The name on the Bognor War Memorial has only an initial and the surname is misspelt, which made tracing this man very difficult. His death on HMS *Good Hope* was reported in the *Bognor Observer*, yet his name does not appear on the list of Naval casualties for the Great War. However, the following is almost certainly this sailor's story:

William was born in Benare, Bengal, India in 1864, probably the son of William Penny, who was serving in the Royal Navy. In 1878 at the age of fourteen, William (junior) joined the Royal Navy as a Signal Boy, serving the following year on board the Iron Frigate, HMS *Inconstant*, based at Simonstown, South Africa. Ten years later he was a Chief Yeoman Signaller on HMS *Active*, a corvette. In 1893 he married Ellen Scott from Bognor and they had a daughter, Gertrude in 1897. William was then serving back in Devonport where he now held the rank of Chief Signaller Boatswain on HMS *Prince of Wales*, before joining HMS *Good Hope*, when she was brought out of reserve. He lost his life in the action described above, having served thirty five years in the Royal Navy.

THE BATTLE OF THE FALKLANDS
(The Sequel)

Six weeks later, following the Battle of Coronel, a larger British Squadron, including two Battlecruisers, HMS *Invincible* and HMS *Inflexible*, plus five cruisers, arrived in the Falklands. The following day advance German cruisers were detected heading for the islands, unaware of the British Squadron, and the Battle of the Falklands took place.

On board HMS *Invincible* was Bognorian, Petty Officer Harry Allen *(see Roll of Honour, May 1916)* who gave his account of the battle in a letter published in the *Bognor Observer* in January 1915:

'We only got to the Falkland Islands just in time, as we arrived there on the 7th and fought the battle on the 8th. We were coaling and we had got in about three hundred tons when a German Squadron was sited. HMS Canopus opened fire as she was moored at the entrance and we raized steam and chased the enemy. They did not dream there were two battle cruisers there. We fought for five hours, sinking the Scharnhorst at 4 20pm and the Gneisenau at 6pm. We did not save a soul from the Scharnhorst, but we picked up roughly one hundred and ninety between us (HMS Invincible and HMS Inflexible), from the Gneisenau. We buried 14 the next day at sea, who had died of wounds. We had a good bit of damage done to us but are now being repaired. The big German cruisers concentrated

all their fire on us, for it is the idea in Naval Warfare to sink the Admirals ship first and we have Admiral Sir Doveton Sturdees on board here. He fought a gallant action and we managed to put four German warships to the bottom that day and two colliers, so I am afraid Admiral Von Speed did not do much of a wise thing coming to take the Falklands'.

THE LOSS OF HMS *NIGER*

HMS *Niger* was a minesweeper built in 1892. On 11 November at around 1200 hrs she was operating close to the Deal Light Vessel when she was attacked and sunk by the German submarine *U-12*. The German Navy were now operating from the captured Belgium port of Zeebrugge, HMS *Niger* becoming their first victim. *(Four months later U-12 was shelled, rammed and sunk by the Royal Navy).*

Stoker K5397/PO Charles L BONIFACE
1 Manor Cottages, Felpham, Bognor
HMS *Niger* Royal Navy
Died of Wounds on 11 November 1914
Aged 23
Buried in Deal Cemetery, Kent

The son of bricklayer George and his wife Elizabeth, Stoker First Class Boniface was serving aboard HMS *Niger.* He had been born in Felpham, where the family continued to live, moving at some stage to Greens Cottages, next to the George Inn. The first reports of the loss of HMS *Niger* came from the Admiralty, who announced that all the Officers and 77 men had been saved, with only two men seriously injured. Charles Boniface was one of them, but he died of his injuries in Deal hospital, shortly afterwards, his legs having been shattered by the explosion of the torpedo. Stoker Boniface's funeral took place at Deal, the route from the Infirmary to the Cemetery being lined by large crowds. His coffin was covered with HMS *Niger*'s ensign, which had been rescued by a Petty Officer, just before the warship took her final plunge.

THE LOSS OF HMS BULWARK

HMS *Bulwark*, a London Class battleship, was built in 1902 and served as the Mediterranean fleet flagship until 1907, before being transferred to the Home Fleet, again serving as a flagship until 1911, when she was put into reserve. She was recommissioned and fully manned upon the outbreak of war and was assigned to patrolling with the Channel Fleet, but fears of a possible German invasion saw her transferred to Sheerness, where she lay at anchor in the River Medway estuary. It was here on the morning of 26 November 1914 that she was ripped apart by a powerful internal explosion. Later that afternoon, Winston Churchill, then First Lord of the Admiralty, made the following statement in the House of Commons:

'I regret to say I have some bad news for the House. The *"Bulwark"* battleship, which was lying off Sheerness this morning, blew up at 07 35 o'clock. The Vice and Rear Admirals who were present have reported their conviction that it was an internal magazine explosion which rent the ship asunder. There was apparently no upheaval in the water and the ship had entirely disappeared when the smoke had cleared away. An inquiry will be held tomorrow, which may possibly throw more light on the occurrence. The loss of the ship does not sensibly affect the military position, but I regret to say the loss of life is very severe. Only twelve men are saved. All the Officers and the rest of the crew, whom I suppose, amounted to between 700 and 800, have perished. I think the House would wish me to express on their behalf the deep sorrow with which the House heard the news and their sympathy with those who have lost relatives and friends'.

Able Seaman J22277 Albert John FREEMAN
52 Oving Road, Chichester
HMS *Bulwark* Royal Navy
Lost at Sea on 26 November 1914
Aged 19
Body Recovered and Buried in Woodlands Cemetery, Gillingham, Kent.

Able Seaman Albert Freeman was a son of Richard, a bricklayer and Fanny, a laundress, who lived at Chichester and was born in the City on 11 November 1895. On leaving school he became a baker's assistant, before enlisting into the Royal Navy. Although he lost his life in those few seconds, he was one of the few men whose bodies were recovered. His connection with Bognor has not been established, although his name appears on the Bognor War Memorial. It is also recorded on the Portfield and Chichester War Memorials.

WESTERN FRONT

Captain John Keith CLOTHIER
Innerwyke Manor, Felpham, Bognor
2nd Battalion, the West Yorkshire Regiment, 8th Division
Killed in Action on 7 December 1914
Aged 33
Buried in the Ration Farm Cemetery, La Chaplette D'Armentaires, France

The second son of Henry, a retired Surgeon and Medical Practitioner and Mary Elizabeth Clothier, John was born in Highgate, Middlesex and educated at Highgate School and the Royal Military College, Sandhurst. He was gazetted 2nd Lieutenant and posted to the West Yorkshire Regiment in 1901. John then served in the South African War, earning the Queen's Medal, followed by action in East Africa, where he was 'Mentioned in Despatches' twice in 1910, the year he was promoted to Captain. The Battalion were then stationed in Malta, being recalled to England at the outbreak of war, arriving on 25 September. After a period of re-training and re-equipping, the Regiment moved to France, landing at St Nazaire on 5 November 1914. The Regiment were soon fighting in the Armentaires area, where on 7 December Captain Clothier was killed in action.

Corporal 9793 Frank Alfred BARRETT
3 Claraville, Felpham, Bognor
4th Battalion, the Queens Hussars, 2nd Cavalry Division
Died of Wounds on 10 December 1914
Aged 19
Buried in the Boulogne Eastern Cemetery, France

Henry and Theodosia Barrett were living in Twickenham, where Henry was employed as a Superintendant of Workers at the Singer Sewing Machine Company. Theodosia, two years his senior, was a housewife looking after their four sons, of whom Frank was the second eldest. A move to Felpham subsequently took place, where Henry was then employed as an insurance agent.

On leaving school Frank became a tailor's apprentice, before joining the Queens Hussars in 1912, when he was just seventeen. Prior to the war the Queens Hussars were stationed in Ireland, at Dublin and were moved to France on 6 September 1914. Promoted to Corporal, Frank had been at the Front for a couple of months when he was 'shot in the lung' on 5 November 1914. He was evacuated to the Boulogne Base Hospital where he 'passed peacefully away' on 10 December.

THE LOSS OF THE STEAM TRAWLER *EARL HOWARD*

The contribution made by the men of the Mercantile Marine during the conflict was considerable, with over ten thousand of them losing their lives serving the Country. Locally there were several who paid the ultimate price, the first occurring in December 1914 when the *Earl Howard* was lost. She was one of many Grimsby-based ships to serve with the Mercantile Marine as mine sweepers during the First World War. Whilst steaming 90 miles off Spurn Head she is believed to have struck a mine which caused her to sink immediately, with the loss of nine men, including George Roberts and the 'Skipper'.

Steward George Henry ROBERTS
Steam Trawler *Earl Howard* Mercantile Marine
Lost at Sea on 11 December 1914
Aged 39
Commemorated on the Tower Hill Memorial, London

George was born in Malton, Yorkshire, the son of whitesmith and bell hanger Joseph and his wife Elizabeth, he had an older sister, Jane. Nothing is known of his early life until 1911, when he was lodging in Grimsby and working as a steward, which he continued to do. No connections with Bognor have been established, nor any regarding his wife and family, although his name appears on the Bognor War Memorial.

1915

WESTERN FRONT

Captain Esme Fairfax CHINNERY
Field Place, Horsham, Sussex
The Royal Flying Corps
Killed in a Flying Accident on 18 January 1915
Aged 28
Buried in St Matthews Churchyard, Hatchford, Surrey, England

Quite what the connection Captain Chinnery had with Bognor has not been established, but his name appears on the Bognor War Memorial. He came from a wealthy family, his father, Walter being a member of the Stock Exchange and a Surrey magistrate, while his mother, Alice ran their Park Lane home with a staff of ten. Walter, some years older than Alice, passed away in 1905.

Captain Chinnery was a career soldier, having been gazetted as a Second Lieutenant into the Coldstream Guards in 1910. His eyes, however, looked skywards and in 1912 he entered the Royal Flying Corps with the rank of Flying Officer, gaining his Royal Aero Club Aviators Certificate on 30 April. Promotion in this new service was rapid and by the time war broke out a year later, he had risen to the rank of Temporary Captain with No 4

Squadron. The Royal Flying Corps initially deployed four squadrons to France (No's 2, 3, 4 and 5) with twelve aircraft each, which, with other aircraft in reserve totalled a force of sixty three machines, supported by some nine hundred men. The aircraft, BE2a's, were used in the observation role, but often came into contact with enemy flyers. This happened to Captain Chinnery in early October 1914 when shots were exchanged between him and a German aviator. A little later Captain Chinnery was 'Mentioned in Despatches' for his reconnaissance work.

Life expectancy in the Royal Flying Corps was not great, many pilots being killed, as was Captain Chinnery; although in his case it was not during combat, but whilst a passenger in a French Voisin, with which his Squadron had re-equipped: the aircraft lost height and crashed in Paris not far from the Eiffel Tower.

Captain Chinnery's body was brought back to England for burial.

THE LOSS OF HM SUBMARINE *E10*

Able Seaman 216724 Cranston John IRISH
14 Gravitts Lane, Bognor
HM Submarine *E10* Royal Navy
Lost at Sea on 21 January 1915
Aged 29
Commemorated on the Portsmouth Naval Memorial, Southsea, Hampshire

'News has been received that a young Bognor naval man, Cranston J Irish, has lost his life on naval service under circumstances unknown. Cranston, who was 29 years old had served in the Navy for 12 years and was well known in Bognor and Bersted, where his happy disposition made him very popular with his friends'.

That report in the *West Sussex Gazette* of his mysterious death was clarified a few weeks later, when it was revealed that HM Submarine *E10* had hit an underwater sea mine off Heligoland on 18 January 1914 and as nothing had been heard of her was presumed lost with her crew of thirty one, on 21 January.

The *West Sussex Gazette* reported again:

'The news was received from the Admiralty by Mr William J Irish, of 14 Gravitts Lane, of the death of his brother, Cranston, who lost his life whilst serving on *E10*, one of His Majesty's submarines, on 21 January 1915, in the North Sea'.

William and Cranston were the only sons of Elizabeth, a widow, who brought them up, plus their two sisters, in John Street, Bognor.

DIED AT HOME

Mr Edward HOLDER
2 Caledonian Terrace, William Street, Bognor
National Reservist
Died at Home in January 1915
Aged 43
Buried in the Bognor Town Cemetery, Sussex

Edward 'Ned' Holder was born in Glynde, Sussex and earned his living as a fruit salesman in Bognor, prior to which he had been a car man, delivering mineral waters. He was married to Kate and they had two children. A National Reservist, Edward was mobilized at the beginning of the war. He was subsequently taken ill whilst serving and died at home.

'Military Honours were accorded at the funeral of Mr Edward Holder, a National Reservist, who was very much liked in the town. A firing party from the Hampshire Territorial's attended the graveside. Mr Holder was only 43 and leaves a wife and young family', reported the *Bognor Observer*.

WESTERN FRONT

Lance Corporal G1222 Arthur James HAYES
Woosung Cottage, 69 London Road, Bognor
2nd Battalion, the Royal Sussex Regiment, 1st Division
Killed in Action on 12 February 1915
Aged 18
Commemorated on Le Touret Memorial, France

'Out of the immediate front line areas' for a while in February, the Royal Sussex Regiment sustained 'a steady trickle of losses'. It was during this time that 18 year old Lance Corporal Arthur Hayes lost his life:

'Among the casualties announced on Monday was the death of a young Bognor soldier, Lance Corporal Hayes. His parents received notice that he was killed in action and buried the same day. The War Office stated that they have no further information. Much sympathy is extended to the parents in their bereavement'.

Arthur was born in Hounslow and enlisted in Bognor. He was the only son of James Evett, a surveyor and Annie Hayes, who at one time had run a boarding house in Lyon Street. Arthur is also included on the Arundel War Memorial.

Corporal L6494 Richard John RELF (RELPH)
2nd Battalion, the Royal Sussex Regiment, 1st Division
Killed in Action on 16 February 1915
Aged 31

A regular soldier, Richard was born in Hawkhurst, Kent and although his death was reported in the *Bognor Observer*, his name has been omitted from the Bognor War Memorial. He had enlisted in London, originally into the 1st Battalion, the Royal Sussex Regiment and was serving in India in 1911. Back home in 1914 he married Florence Lloyd in Cranbrook, Kent, close to Hawkhurst, his birth place, shortly before mobilization. He fought in France and Flanders before being killed on 16 February.

THE LOSS OF HMS *BAYANO*

HMS *Bayano*, one of many ships requisitioned in November 1914, was destined to have a short service life. Built for Elders and Fyffes as a 'banana boat', she was converted into an Armed Merchant Cruiser, serving with 10th Cruiser Squadron. Robert was a member of her crew when she left Clyde after her conversion, en route to Liverpool, to 'coal up'. She was attacked by the German submarine *U-27* off Corsewell Point, Galloway, Ireland, in the early hours of 11 March 1915 and sank in under three minutes. Most of the crew were asleep at the time and only a handful survived, whilst 197 of their crewmates, including Able Seaman Robert Hockham, perished.

Able Seaman 217623 Robert William HOCKHAM
17 Southover Road, Bognor
HMS *Bayano* Royal Navy
Lost at Sea on 11 March 1915
Aged 30
Commemorated on the Portsmouth Naval Memorial, Southsea, Hampshire

Robert Hockham was born at Pyecombe, Sussex, a son of James and Alice. James was the village blacksmith, before moving the family firstly to Chailey and then Bognor, by which time James was working for the London, Brighton and South Coast Railway. On leaving school, Robert also joined the railway, working as a porter at Sheffield Park Station, before enlisting into the Royal Navy by 1911 and subsequently joining the *Bayano*.

WESTERN FRONT

The Battle of Neuve Chapelle was a joint British and Indian Corps offensive with the aim of rupturing the German lines and then making a rush for Aubers Ridge. It commenced on 10 March 1915 and as far as the British were concerned, despite bad weather, went well in the early stages, Neuve Chapelle being secured on the first day. On 11 March, fog forced further British attacks and the planned onslaught on Aubers Ridge to be cancelled. The offensive was thwarted by a strong German counter attack on 12 March, which though unsuccessful, did manage to end any chance of further Allied advancement. The campaign was officially abandoned on 13 March, leaving the Allies in occupation of Neuve Chapelle, having gained some two square kilometres of land, at a cost of some thousands of lives: the Germans losses were slightly higher.

Second Lieutenant Arthur Adrian OWEN
Strathmore, Upper Bognor Road, Bognor
1st Battalion, the Royal Warwickshire Regiment, 4th Division
Killed in Action on 13 March 1915
Aged 19
Buried in the Royal Irish Rifles Graveyard, Laventie,

Arthur Owens family moved to Bognor from London where their business interests were in the City. After serving time with the Officers Training Corps, Arthur was gazetted into the Royal Warwickshire Regiment, which was stationed at Shorncliffe, Kent, at the outbreak of war. The Regiment landed in France on 22 August 1914, having been held back from the original British Expeditionary Force in case of a German landing. On arrival in France they were immediately in action in the earlier battles already described. Arthur Owen lost his life on the last day of the Battle of Neuve Chapelle.

Second Lieutenant Harold John STRONG
2nd Battalion, the East Surrey Regiment, 28th Division
Killed in Action on 13 March 1915
Aged 29
Buried in the Locre Churchyard, Belgium

The 2nd Battalion, the East Surrey Regiment, took part in a subsidiary action in support of the Battle of Neuve Chapelle, commencing on 13 March 1914, when they attacked the German positions at Spanbroek Molen. This was one of a series of actions designed to prevent any sudden massing of reinforcements by the enemy to the main battle. The attack was planned to commence just after dawn, but owing to thick fog it was mid afternoon before the East Surreys could advance, during which Second Lieutenant Harold Strong was killed.

Harold Strong was born in Chertsey, Surrey, the second son of Robert Bennett Strong, a hairdresser and his wife Linda. The family moved to Harwich, Essex, in the 1890s and Harold's father passed away in 1904.

Harold was a regular Officer, having attended the Royal Military School of Music, Twickenham and becoming a Bandmaster whilst serving in India before the war. His Bognor connection has not been established, although his mother remarried and may have then moved to Bognor.

THE SECOND BATTLE OF YPRES

The Second Battle of Ypres was the only major attack launched by the German forces on the Western Front in 1915, marking their first large scale use of poison gas. It commenced on 21 April and lasted until 25 May, the first engagement taking place at Gravenstafel Ridge on 22 April.

Private 9851 John RUSSELL
The Lodge, Middleton, Bognor
1st Battalion, the Dorsetshire Regiment, 5th Division
Died of Wounds on 22 April 1915
Aged 26
Buried in the Poperinghe Old Military Cemetery, Belgium

Born in Beaminster, Dorset, one of the eight children of John and Elizabeth Russell, the family moved to Middleton, where John (junior) followed his father in becoming a carter on a farm at Felpham, before enlisting at Chichester into the Dorsetshire Regiment.

At the outbreak of war, 1st Dorsetshire were stationed at Mullingar in Ireland and were moved to France, arriving there on 16 August 1914. They took part in the Battles of Mons, the Aisne and the Marne. There then followed a quick move north to Flanders, where they also fought in the Battle of La Bassee and the first Battle of Ypres. After this they became firmly entrenched, the winter being spent in a purely defensive role. However, a German build-up had been taking place and a surprise attack by them on 22

April heralded the start of the Second Battle of Ypres. Private John Russell's war ended that day when he died of wounds.

From 24 April until 5 May the fighting continued around the village of St Julien. During this engagement a further four local soldiers lost their lives.

Private 8616 William Edward HEWITT
5 Gravitts Lane, South Bersted, Bognor
2nd Battalion, the Royal Scots Guards, 3rd Division
Killed in Action on 28 April 1915
Aged 31
Buried in the Kemmel Chateaux Military Cemetery, Belgium

The Royal Scots Guards were the most senior Scottish Regiment and arrived in France as part of the BEF on 14 August 1914. Having taken part in the early battles, January 1915 found them in action at Givenchy and Cuinchy. The Second Battle of Ypres was six days old when William lost his life.

'We regret to record the death of another Bognorian killed in action at the Front, Private Hewitt of the Scots Guards', wrote the *Bognor Observer*. 'The sad intelligence reached his wife last week. In addition of his widow, he leaves a little boy of five or six to mourn his death'.

William was born in Bognor, where his father, John, was a farm labourer; his mother, Anne, passed away whilst William was still a lad. Prior to enlisting in Bognor, William had married Ellen and was employed as a domestic gardener.

Gunner 62766 Frederick John LITTLECHILD
3 Victoria Cottages, Bersted Street, South Bersted, Bognor
43rd Brigade, the Royal Field Artillery
Killed in Action on 2 May 1915
Aged 22
Buried in the Duhallow ADS Cemetery, Belgium

'A well known young Bognor man, Frederick John Littlechild, the second son of Mr and Mrs Littlechild, is numbered amongst the fallen. The gallant young Britisher was only 22 years of age'.

Corporal Frederick John Littlechild, who served in the Royal Field Artillery, fell at the Second Battle of Ypres on 2 May 1915. His death was described in a letter from one of his Officers to his parents a few days later:

'It is my painful duty to write to inform you that your son was killed in action near Ypres this afternoon, 2 May. He was on duty at the telephone from my Headquarters to one of the batteries. The battery position was very heavily shelled by eight inch howitzers and a shell burst at the mouth of the dug out where he was working. He and three others were in the dugout and when we had extricated them we found two were quite dead and your son and another were still living, but very badly wounded. Your son lived for about an hour and was partially conscious. His chum, Driver Pearce, who was with him when he died, is also writing to you. Two doctors were in attendance at once and remained with him until he died, but he was beyond hope. He was a good lad and died at his post'.

Frederick was born in Bognor, where his father Edwin was a baker in North Bersted and had bought up eight children with his wife Eliza. It seems likely that Frederick was already serving in the Royal Field Artillery before the war commenced.

Lance-Corporal 9893 Thomas (Andrzejewski) Andrew PACE
Woodford House, Upper Bognor Road, Bognor
1/5th Battalion, the London Regiment, 4th Division
Died of Wounds on 4 May 1915
Aged 31
Buried in the Poperinghe Old Military Cemetery, Belgium

'Another local man has to be added to the list of killed, in the death of Lance Corporal Thomas Andrew Pace, the son of the late Mr H Pace. He answered at once his Country's call and joined the London Rifle Brigade last August. As Lance Corporal he left for the Front in January 1915 and was continually in the trenches until the Battalion was ordered to take part in the recent great Battle of Ypres. During that dreadful slaughter, in which his Battalion lost one hundred and twenty men out of one hundred and eighty, Lance Corporal Pace was wounded and taken to a Field Hospital where he died the following day, 4 May 1915'.

Born and bought up in Kensington, Thomas, the son of Mr Henry Pace, Barrister at Law and his Polish wife, Sophie, had also qualified as a Barrister. He was the brother of Captain Henry Pace, *(see Roll of Honour, August 1915)*.

Lieutenant William Edward Brymer SCHRIEBER
1 Marine Parade, Bognor
Motor Transport Section, the Canadian Army Service Corps
Died of Wounds on 4 May 1915
Aged 31
Buried in the Haringhe (Bandaghem) Military Cemetery, Belgium

'The younger son of Colonel and Mrs Schrieber, William was educated locally at Holyrood House School, followed by Radley College. In 1908 he emigrated to Canada and at the outbreak of war volunteered for the Canadian forces, receiving a commission in the Motor Transport Section, Divisional Ammunition Park, Canadian Army Service Corps. He was sent to France as part of the Canadian Ammunition Party Expeditionary Force and died of wounds received in action on 4 May 1915. He leaves a widow, Gabrielle and two sons, in Canada'.

The Canadians were heavily involved in the Second Battle of Ypres and suffered greatly from the first use of poison gas by the Germans. Lieutenant Schrieber's roll was in the re-supply of ammunition to the Front line.

William Schrieber was born in Wexford, Ireland where his father was serving, the family moving to Bognor by 1891 and taking up residence at 1 Albert Road, where they employed two servants and had a school governess as a boarder. They later moved to Marine Parade.

THE BATTLE OF AUBERS RIDGE

The Battle of Aubers Ridge was fought as part of the Ypres offensive and its outcome hit Bognor hard.

Seven weeks after the Battle of Neuve Chapelle failed to get as far as Aubers Ridge, another attempt was set for 9 May, in which the 2nd Battalion, the Royal Sussex Regiment was heavily involved. As part of the British 1st Division, the 2nd Royal Sussex Regiment and 1st Northants were the first to go over the top at 0530 hrs on 9 May 1915, as the southern pincer in a movement against the German positions at Richebourg.

The object of the attack was to gain the high ground the Germans were occupying in the Aubers Ridge sector, thereby relieving the pressure on the French forces. The Germans were well dug in with many machine guns covering the vast open ground that the British would have to cross to reach them. The British artillery bombardment commenced at 0530 hours., but failed dismally to breach the German barbed wire entanglements. The

1st Division advanced, only to be met with the murderous machine guns untouched by the British bombardment.

'Heavy machine gun fire cut down the British, even on their own ladders and parapet steps, but the men continued to press forward as ordered'.

This letter appeared in the *Bognor Observer* a week or two later, written by an 'unknown Officer of the Regiment' and it refers to heavy losses in 2nd Battalion, the Royal Sussex Regiment. It continued:

'We embarked on a desperate enterprise. By the merciful power of God I got through safely. I cannot say too much, but there has never been such a day. After a bombardment by our guns on the German trenches, the good old Sussex went forward like one man, only to be met by a fire from the gunners, which simply mowed our men down like rabbits. The barbed wire in front of the trenches was not cut by our shrapnel as had been planned and we were caught up like rats in a trap. I cannot express myself as I would like to, but it was perfect hell. We had fourteen Officer and five hundred and eighty men casualties. Luckily our Colonel was not touched, nor our Adjutant. Though we were unable to take the trenches and had to retire, we got through and all our men were heroes, for they enabled others to go through us and reap the honour and glory. What were left of the Sussex were sent back to have a rest. It had been "hell let loose", the boys stuck to it and were mown down like corn'.

The 2nd Battalion, the Royal Sussex Regiment suffered horrendous losses, many being killed as they clambered out of their trenches and crossed open ground, the survivors being pinned down in No Man's Land. The following day the offensive was ended. The British lost over 11000 men, amongst whom were over five hundred and fifty men from the Royal Sussex Regiment, including six from Bognor, South Bersted and Pagham.

Private G1151 Walter Ernest ARBEN
8 Essex Road, Bognor
2nd Battalion, the Royal Sussex Regiment, 1st Division
Killed in Action on 9 May 1915
Aged 18
Commemorated on Le Touret Memorial, France

When war was declared, Walter Arben, the youngest son of Mrs Ruth Shrubb, was living with his elder brothers, George and James and his only sister Mabel. They had moved from West Ham, where his father had been a dockyard labourer and lived for a while at 13 Gainsborough Road, Bognor. Walter, on leaving school, was a fishmonger and a

National Reservist who joined the Royal Sussex Regiment, landing in France early in August 1914. Private Walter Arben, was just 18 when he lost his life.

Private G4615 Maurice Henry BLACKMAN
25 Nyetimber, Pagham
2nd Battalion, the Royal Sussex Regiment, 1st Division
Killed in Action at Richebourg L'Avoue on 9 May 1915
Aged 23
Commemorated on Le Touret Memorial, France

Maurice Blackman had enlisted into the Royal Sussex Regiment in November 1914. He was a farm labourer who was born at Coldwaltham, Sussex, the son of John, a carter on a farm and his wife Ellen, a laundress. He was the brother of Frederick *(see Roll of Honour, September 1918)*. Part of his childhood was spent at Poling, where his father worked at the time, before the family moved to Pagham. Maurice became a National Reservist, subsequently joining the Royal Sussex Regiment.

Private S1663 Joseph William COOTE
Chalcraft Cottages, Chalcraft Lane, North Bersted, Bognor
2nd Battalion, the Royal Sussex Regiment, 1st Division
Killed in Action at Richebourg L'Avoue on 9 May 1915
Aged 27
Commemorated on Le Touret Memorial, France

The eldest son of Joseph and Elizabeth Coote, Joseph (junior) was born in Boxgrove where his father was an agricultural labourer. By 1901 the family had expanded and had moved to Rose Green, where Joseph (senior) was employed as a cowman. A further move to North Bersted followed, where father was still a cowman and Joseph (junior) was employed as a farm labourer. At some stage Joseph (junior) became an Army Reservist who was called up into the Royal Sussex Regiment. He was killed in action at Richebourg L'Avoue on 9 May 1915.

Private G1150 Benjamin Harry IDE
7 Gainsborough Road, Bognor
2nd Battalion, the Royal Sussex Regiment, 1st Division
Killed in Action at Richebourg L'Avoue on 9 May 1915
Aged 22
Commemorated on Le Touret Memorial, France

Benjamin Ide was a son of fisherman Benjamin and his wife Charlotte. He was employed as a 'domestic groom gardener' before he enlisted at Bognor into the Royal Sussex Regiment and was also killed in action on 9 May 1915.

A letter from one of his chums, Private H F Linfield, was sent to his parents a few days later. He was seemingly unaware of his death:

'I am exceedingly sorry to have to write to you to say that Harry has been wounded in the head, but not very badly I believe. He was standing at our port hole when a beastly great shell came in just in front of the hole and blew it to pieces. It was a wonder he was not hurt any more. I do not know whether he has been able to write to you to tell you about it so I thought I would write in case he has not. I am sorry he has left me for I found him one of the best fellows to get on with and I can assure you he is a great credit to the name Ide. I am longing for this war to end so that everyone can settle down to a peaceful life'.

Private G1471 James PATTEN
Pagham
2nd Battalion, the Royal Sussex Regiment, 1st Division
Killed in Action at Richebourg L'Avoue on 9 May 1915
Aged 32
Commemorated on Le Touret Memorial, Pas de Calais, France

James was born in Compton, Somerset and had moved to Sussex by 1901, lodging with his older brother Joseph and his family at Green Lane, Upmarden. Before the war he was living in Lagness when he enlisted into the Royal Sussex Regiment. James was also killed in action on 9 May 1915, 'a day of heavy losses'.

Private G1210 Sidney Arthur EDE
6 Retort Cottages, Ivy Lane, South Bersted, Bognor
2nd Battalion, the Royal Sussex Regiment, 1st Division
Died of Wounds on 10 May 1915
Aged 20
Buried in the Chocques Military Cemetery, Pas de Calais, France
Commemorated on the Family Grave in Bognor Town Cemetery

Born in South Bersted, Sydney was the eldest son of bricklayer Charles and his wife Kate Ede; he had one brother and three sisters. The *Bognor Observer* reported his death:

'An old member of the Church Lads Brigade at Bognor, Private S A Ede, the 2nd Battalion, the Royal Sussex Regiment has died at the Front on 10 May, from wounds received the preceding day.

'The news came to his mother last week in a letter from the Chaplain, who stated he was in no pain and passed peacefully away. The Colonel of the Regiment came to inquire of him, but it was too late.

'The deceased, who was twenty years old, was among those who enlisted at Bognor after a recruiting meeting at the Queens Hall, last September and he went to the Front early in January. He was formerly a Sergeant in the Church Lads Brigade, in which he received a long service medal and prior to joining in September he was employed by Mr Hother, as a grocer's assistant in his shop at Bersted Street'.

THE SECOND BATTLE OF YPRES
(continued)

Second Lieutenant George Biddulph RAYNER
24 Birchington Road, Kilburn, West Hampstead, London
2nd Battalion, the Gloucester Regiment, 27th Division
Killed in Action on 12 May 1915
Aged 31
Buried in the Bedford House Cemetery, Ypres, Belgium

George Rayner was born and grew up in West Hampstead, where his father was an insurance agent; he died whilst George was still at school, leaving his widow Anastasia as the head of the family of twelve children, of whom eight survived. Both George and his younger brother Gerard worked for stockbrokers. George enlisted into 3rd (Reserve) Battalion, the Essex Regiment, based in England. At some point he was transferred to 2nd Battalion, the Gloucester Regiment and saw service with them in France where he met his death. A local connection has not been established, although his name does appear on the Bognor War Memorial.

Lieutenant John Holland Ballett FLETCHER
Aldwick Manor, Upper Bognor Road, Bognor
1/7th Battalion, the London Regiment, 5th Division
Died of Wounds on 15 May 1915
Aged 35
Buried in the Bethune Town Cemetery, France

The only son of Mr W H B Fletcher, JP and Mrs Agnes Caroline Fletcher, Lieutenant Fletcher had studied law, achieving a Master of Arts at St John's College, Cambridge University, becoming a Barrister at Law, Inner Temple. He was also a member of the West Sussex County Council and lived part of his early life in the Steyne, Worthing, where his father owned considerable land in the Broadwater area.

An Officer in the Territorial's, John served with the London Regiment and was sent to France early in 1915, to the trenches around the villages of Fleurbaix and Festubert. In May 1915 a large attack was launched, the 7th Londoners being tasked to remain in support and await orders to join in. These orders never came, but all day and on subsequent days the Germans laid down a heavy artillery barrage on the front line British trenches and during one such bombardment John Fletcher was wounded. Despite being swiftly evacuated to a military hospital for Officers in Bethune, he was too badly wounded to be saved and died soon afterwards. The *Bognor Observer* commented:

'Lieutenant John Fletcher was a promising Barrister, well known in the Sussex Courts and whose last appearance professionally being made in uniform. For some years he had practised as a Barrister and often appeared at Crown cases at the Quarter Sessions. In that capacity it was noticed that if he erred at all it was always on the side of mercy for the accused. When staying with his father in Bognor, he was also identified with the Constutional Club'.

Private 684 Cyril Ernest PERRY
North Somerset Yeomanry
Killed in Action on 13 May 1915
Aged 28
Commemorated on the Menin Gate Memorial, Ypres, Belgium

Cyril Perry was the son of 'gold' jeweller Thomas and his wife Florence and was born in Marylebone, London. Much of his childhood was spent in Sussex, the family living at East Preston and Worthing, before returning to London. The youngest of three sons, Cyril was educated at a boarding school in Margate, Kent, becoming a land surveyor and enlisting at East Grinstead as a Territorial in the North Somerset Yeomanry, opting for Imperial Service abroad at the outbreak of war. The Somerset Yeomanry was mobilized at Bath in August 1914, after which they were moved to Sussex. Detached from their Brigade, they were moved independently to France in October 1914. 13 May 1915 was a black day for the North Somerset Yeomanry, the Regiment suffering heavy losses whilst defending a German attack near Bellewarde, Ypres. It was in this attack that Cyril Perry lost his life.

Private 9574 Arthur Edwin JONES
12 Ockley Road, Bognor
2nd Battalion, the South Staffordshire Regiment, 2nd Division
Killed in Action on 18 May 1915
Age 26
Commemorated on Le Touret Memorial, France

Arthur Edwin Jones had for some years before the war worked for Mr Yeates, the fishmonger in Manor Place, Bognor. The son of Mrs Burton, Arthur enlisted at Woolwich into the South Staffordshire Regiment. He was killed in action at Richebourg, the news coming as a particular shock to his mother 'who, until she was notified by the War Office had no idea that her son was at the Front'.

Private Arthur Jones had three brothers also serving, two in the Royal Navy and the other in the Royal Field Artillery. They all survived the war.

Guardsman 11485 William Charles BAXTER
Bruntlands, the Grove, Felpham
The Scots Guards, the Guards Division
Died of Wounds on 19 May 1915
Aged 20
Buried in the Chocques Military Cemetery, Pas de Calais, France

William, was the son of William (senior), the chief Officer of His Majesty's Coastguard Station at Felpham and his wife Ann. Born in Caithness, Scotland, William volunteered at the outbreak of war, enlisting into the Scots Guards in London on 3 October 1914. After training he was sent to France in April 1915 and just a month later died at the 1st Casualty Clearing Station of wounds received in action the previous day. The Scots Guards had been in action that month at both Aubers Ridge and Festubert.

DIED AT HOME

Private 5975 Ernest PARKER
Home Address, 50 Coleman's Street, Brighton
9th Queens Royal Lancers, 1st Cavalry Division
Died at Home at 24 May 1915
Aged 44
Buried in the Wandsworth (Earlsfield) Cemetery, London

Living in Bognor, whilst employed as an attendant on Bognor Pier, Ernest enlisted into 9th Queens Royal Lancers, 1st Cavalry Division. He had previously served in South Africa with 14th Hussars. He was known as the 'Lonely Lancer', because he had few relatives, only a mother who lived in Brighton. Having been badly wounded, he made light of his injuries, which he described in a letter to a friend 'as the result of a small parcel sent over by the Germans'. Brought back home, he died of heart failure at Balham Red Cross Hospital on 24 May 1915, as a result of wounds received in action.

DIED OF ILLNESS

Petty Officer 210094 Rupert William MATTHEWS
Outram House, Outram Road, Felpham, Bognor
HMS *Barham* Royal Navy
Died of Disease on 30 May 1915
Aged 30
Buried in St Mary's Churchyard, Felpham, Bognor

Rupert Matthews was born in Barton Cliffs, Hampshire, the son of agricultural labourer Thomas and his wife Caroline. A regular sailor, Petty Officer Matthews was sent to Scotland, to join the new Queen Elizabeth Class Battleship, HMS *Barham* after she was launched in 1914, as a member of her pre-commissioning crew. Whilst serving there he 'died of disease', five months before she was commissioned. The *Bognor Observer* covered his funeral:

'An impressive scene was witnessed at Felpham on Thursday afternoon when with Naval Honours, Petty Officer Rupert William Matthews of HMS *Barham* was laid to rest in the village churchyard. The deceased, who was only 30 years of age and had seen thirteen years of service, was well known in this district and was very popular. The body had been conveyed to Felpham from Scotland, the deceased having died at Clyde Bank. The coffin was shrouded in a Union Jack. The funeral was attended by the Coastguards and local Sea Scouts, the Hampshire Regiment providing the firing party'.

Rupert Matthews joined the Royal Navy at the age of 17. He met and married Florence Taylor, the daughter of a Felpham fisherman, Hiram Taylor, in 1912.

GALLIPOLI

The Gallipoli Campaign was a disaster. Turkey, Germany's ally, had attacked Russia and was thrown back with a large loss of life. Russia appealed to Lord Kitchener for assistance and a British landing with French support in the Gallipoli Peninsula was decided upon. Had it been successful, Egypt, which had already been subject to a Turkish attempt to seize the Suez Canal, would have been safe and Russia would have a warm water seaway to export much needed wheat to the Allies and in turn to receive arms and ammunition. The campaign commenced with British naval actions in February 1915 and ended in a complete withdrawal of Allied forces in January 1916. It was particularly devastating in terms of losses relating to troops from Australia and New Zealand, the 25 April, Anzac Day, still commemorated in those countries as they remember the anniversary of their disastrous landings. The Gallipoli Campaign ended in January 1916, when the Allies withdrew. Seven Bognorians, both Navy and Army, lost their lives in this campaign.

THE LOSS OF HMS *GOLIATH*

HMS *Goliath* was built at Chatham Dockyard in 1900, one of six Canopus Class battleships in service. She spent her early years in Chinese waters, followed by duty in the Mediterranean, being mothballed in 1913.

It is likely that First Lieutenant Arthur R G Beal joined HMS *Goliath* when she was brought out of reserve in August 1914, as Fleet Paymaster. Sent to the Dardenelles in 1915, HMS *Goliath* survived damage from attacks on her on 25 April and 2 May, but her luck ran out on the night of 13 May, whilst on duty providing artillery support for the forces at Gallipoli. Unseen, the Turkish destroyer *Mauvenet-I-Milet* slipped through the fog, gently running with the current, evading two British destroyers, to close in on HMS *Goliath*. Manned by a mixed German/Turkish crew the *Mauvenet-I-Milet* fired three torpedoes, two of which hit the *Goliath* simultaneously, causing her to capsize immediately. There was no time to launch her life boats and a third torpedo struck her turret as she was lying on her beam ends. She then rolled over completely and within minutes sank by the bows, taking five hundred and seventy of her seven hundred strong crew with her. The crew of the Turkish ship were all presented with gold watches by the Sultan in person, for their successful mission.

First Lieutenant Arthur Reginald George BEAL
HMS *Goliath* Royal Navy
Lost at Sea on 13 May 1915
Aged 51
Commemorated on the Chatham Royal Naval Memorial, Kent, England

Petty Officer Beal was a long term serving sailor and had been born in Waterlooville, Hampshire. In 1901 he was a Paymaster based at Portsmouth. He married his wife, May, who was the daughter of Robert Morris, the retired Chief Cashier of the London and South Western Railway Company.

Corporal Frederick Charles CLARK
Nyewood Lane, Bognor
2nd Battalion, the Hampshire Regiment, 2nd Division
Killed in Action June 1915
Aged 25

Frederick Clark was born in Eastbourne in 1890 where his father was employed as a coachman. Little information has surfaced about his early life, his family having moved to Bognor in the meantime.

By 1911 Frederick was serving with the Hampshire Regiment in South Africa and India, returning to England in December 1914. His Battalion spent some time at Romsey and Stratford upon Avon, before moving to Warwick in February 1915, in preparation for deployment to Gallipoli. They sailed from Avonmouth on 29 March for Egypt and then Cape Helles, where they landed on 25 April 1915. The landings were chaotic but initially, largely unopposed. However, without definite further orders the landing force entrenched to await instructions. Soon Turkish forces appeared and what might have become a quick advantage degenerated into stalemate. During this period Lance Corporal Frederick Clark lost his life.

His name does not appear on the Bognor War Memorial, although his death was reported in the *Bognor Observer:*

'Mr and Mrs Fred Clark, of Nyewood Lane, have received official notification that their eldest son, Corporal Frederick Charles Clark, was killed in action during operations in the Dardenelles. He was 25 years old and a single man'.

Lieutenant, the Honourable Maurice Henry Nelson HOOD
28 Norfolk Square, Hyde Park, London
Hood Battalion, the Royal Naval Division
Killed in Action on 7 June 1915
Aged 34
Commemorated on the Helles Memorial, Gallipoli

A member of the aristocracy, the Honourable Maurice Hood was born in Chard, Somerset, the only son of Lieutenant Colonel W Hood, of the Somerset Yeomanry and Lady Maria Hood; they were otherwise known as Viscount and Lady Bridport of Bognor.

Their family home was in Grosvenor Gardens, Westminster, where they employed a large household - two lady's maids, two nurses, a nursery maid, two housemaids, a kitchen maid, a scullery maid, a butler and two footmen. In 1908 Maurice married his wife, Ellen Rose Kendall Hood, their son Rowland being born two years later.

A member of the Royal Navy Volunteer Reserve, Maurice became part of the large surplus of manpower mobilised for the Royal Navy. Winston Churchill, the then First Lord of the Admiralty, took the decision to use these men to form battalions of Naval Brigades, who joined the Marines, to form the composite Royal Naval Division of soldiers. Subsequently, the Division was sent to the Dardanelles and landed at Cape Helles. Maurice was reported missing in June 1915, his death not being confirmed until October when it was reported in the *Bognor Observer*:

'The only son of Lord and Lady Bridport, of Bognor, who together with his young widow, will have the sympathy of a large circle of friends'.

Private 8092 Edward Wilfred KENT
27 Steyne Street, Bognor
2nd Battalion, the Hampshire Regiment, 2nd Division
Killed in Action on 6 August 1915
Aged 24
Commemorated on the Helles Memorial, Gallipoli

Born at Fishbourne, Edward was the youngest son of bricklayer's labourer Henry and his wife Mary Jane Kent. By 1911 he had enlisted at Chichester into the Hampshire Regiment. With the outbreak of war, the Regiment was hurriedly brought home from an eight month deployment in India and was initially destined for France, but this was changed to Gallipoli in March 1915. Prior to sailing, the whole Division was reviewed by the King in a march past.

On 16 March 1915 the Regiment sailed from Avonmouth, arriving in Egypt two weeks later. From there they sailed on the *'River Clyde'* to Gallipoli, landing at Cape Helles on 25 April. Here the *'River Clyde'* was grounded some forty yards from the beach and was met with 'devastating fire', inflicting terrible losses as the men attempted to row ashore. For a while, those who had managed to make land were stranded on the beach in the face of the Turkish machine guns. A little later the guns of three British Battleships silenced the Turks. Those Hampshire's ashore with the Dublin's and Munster's took the cliff and the Turkish fort at the top of it, thus allowing the *'River Clyde'* to release the remainder of the troops. They then held the positions at Cape Helles, under constant fire, until they withdrew in January 1916. Six months after Private Edward Kent was killed in action.

Captain Henry Joseph PACE
Woodford House, Upper Bognor Road, Bognor
Royal Marine Artillery
Died at Home on 7 August 1915
Buried in the St Mary's Roman Catholic Cemetery, Kensal Green, London

'Many Bognorians will regret to hear of the death of Captain Henry J Pace, of the Royal Marine Artillery, whose family have been residents of Bognor for a good number of years. He died of enteric on 7 August 1915 whilst attached to the Royal Naval Division at the Dardanelles. At the beginning of the war he was in hospital at Haslar, but in December, whilst still convalescing, he accepted an offer to join a naval expedition to Belgium, where he served for two months at Nieuport. In February he was recalled and sent for duty to the Mediterranean forces'.

Captain Harry Pace, who was also a Russian-speaking interpreter, died at the home of his parents on 7 August 1915. His funeral took place with full military honours at the Church of Our Lady of Victories, Kensington 'in the presence of a large assembly'.

(Captain Henry Pace was the brother of Lance Corporal Andrew Pace, see Roll of Honour May 1915).

Lance Corporal William G GREGORY
1 Bungaree Villas, Neville Road, Bognor
8th Battalion, the Duke of Wellington's Regiment
Killed in Action on 28 September 1915
Aged 22

William was born in Newbury, Berkshire. Details of his young life are sketchy, but it would seem that his mother was widowed early in her married life and subsequently remarried a few years later. By 1911 William was lodging in Bognor and working for Messrs Hawkes and Son as a grocer/clerk. An athlete, he had many friends within Bognor's sporting circles, as well as having 'a great love of music.' He enlisted into the Duke of Wellington's Regiment, which was raised at Halifax in August 1914 and sailed to Gallipoli in July 1915. Two months later William was killed in action. The *Bognor Observer* wrote:

'His kindly disposition earned him many friends and his success at games won him fame in sporting circles. He was a music lover and sportsman who played hockey, representing Bognor, football and enjoyed swimming, excelling in them all'.

His name does not appear on the Bognor War Memorial.

DIED AT HOME

Sergeant Trooper Albert WILSON
Felpham, Sussex
The Sussex Yeomanry
Died at Home in November 1915
Aged 28
Buried in St Mary's Churchyard, Felpham, Bognor, West Sussex

Albert Wilson does not appear on the Bognor or Felpham War Memorials, but on the Yapton Memorial, the village in which he was born. A member of the Sussex Yeomanry, he went to Gallipoli with his Regiment and was repatriated immediately 'because of illness'. He died of pneumonia and dysentery at the Netley War Hospital, Southampton. His body was bought home to Felpham where he was buried, the Hampshire Regiment providing the firing party.

Prior to enlisting Albert was lodging at the Fox Inn, Felpham, before marrying and living with his wife in the village. He was employed as a carpenter by Mr Thomas Start, the builder and was well known and respected in the district. So far as is known he was the first local casualty in the Sussex Yeomanry.

GALLIPOLI

Lance Corporal 2853 Stanley Cyril NARRAWAY
West Street, Bognor
2/2 Battalion, the London Regiment, Royal Fusiliers, attached to the Royal Naval Division
Killed in Action on 11 December 1915
Aged 20
Buried in the Redoubt Cemetery, Helles, Gallipoli

Stanley was born in Leyton, Essex, the only son of Stanley, a stock exchange clerk and his wife Florence, who was born in Bognor. Their only other child was a younger daughter, Lucy. The family were fairly well off and lived at Wallington, Surrey where they employed a servant. On leaving school, Stanley was working as a bank clerk before enlisting into the Royal Fusiliers, who were attached to the Royal Naval Division and landed in Gallipoli on 25 April 1915. Stanley survived most of the campaign, but was killed in action a couple of weeks before his Battalion were evacuated. His Bognor connections came from his mother's family, where her sister operated a dress making business.

WESTERN FRONT

Private G426 George Thomas MERRITT
25 Essex Road, Bognor
7th Battalion, the Royal Sussex Regiment, 12th Division
Died of Wounds on 3 July 1915
Aged 25
Buried in the Bailleul Communal Cemetery Extension, France

Felpham born and bred, George had worked for Messrs L and F Jacobs at the Argyle Nurseries, before becoming a policeman. He married in the summer of 1911 and enlisted at Chichester into the Royal Sussex Regiment at the beginning of the war. At the time of his death he was serving north of Armentaires. The first weeks of July saw his Battalion operating numerous working parties, large and small, improving the state of their trenches and it was whilst he was thus engaged he lost his life at the hands of a sniper.

'We regret to announce another Bognor casualty with fatal results - Private G T Merritt, serving with the Royal Sussex Regiment, having died of the injuries he sustained, while on the lookout, from the trenches, in the Western Theatre of the war on 1 July. He was shot through the lungs, another Bognor man, Ted Caiger, of South Bersted, being with him at the time. He is also stated to have been picked up by another Bognor man, named Robinson and conveyed to hospital'.

In a letter to his widow, the Chaplain states that her husband was 'brought in rather badly wounded' and in order to be on the safe side he administered the Sacrement. He had improved at the time of writing and had asked him to tell his wife that his thoughts were ever of her and their two young children.

Private Merritt's death was also referred to in a letter home written by a comrade, Private Eddie Stares, of London Road, Bognor, in which he added these words of comfort:

'We have had quite enough casualties for trench work, among them Private Merritt and it might be pleasing to the relations to know what great respect is shown to the dead and how nicely and becoming the graves are kept up, with an artificial cross, with full particulars on it, done by our own sign writer, a fitting tribute to our fallen heroes'.

Lieutenant Colonel Bertram Georges Reginald GORDON DSO
Canonbury House, Esplanade, Bognor
2nd Battalion, the Gordon Highlanders, 7th Division
Killed in Action on 20 July 1915
Aged 35
Buried in the Dernancourt Communal Cemetery, France

One of two brothers, both serving Officers with the Gordon Highlanders, who were killed within three months of each other *(see Roll of Honour, Second Lieutenant Robert Gordon, September 1915)* Lieutenant Colonel Bertram Gordon DSO had previously been injured.

The 2nd Battalion Gordon Highlanders were regular soldiers who were in Egypt at the outbreak of war and returned to Southampton on 1 October 1914, moving to Lyndhurst to join 20th Brigade, 7th Division. The following week on 7 October they landed at Zeebrugge to assist in the defence of Antwerp, but arrived too late to prevent the city falling, taking up defensive positions at bridges and road junctions to aid in the retreat of the Belgian Army. The Division suffered heavy losses in the first Battle of Ypres. By February 1915 they had been reinforced to fighting strength and fought in the Battles of Neuve Chapelle, Aubers, Festubert, Givenchy and Loos. It was during the Battle of Bazentin, on the Somme, that Lieutenant Colonel Gordon DSO lost his life.

DEATH OF A VETERAN

Quarter Master Sergeant SD2182 John James MAY
Swansea House, West Street, Bognor
12th Battalion, the Royal Sussex Regiment, 39th Division
Died at Home on 22 July 1915
Aged 52
Buried in the Bognor Town Cemetery

A long serving veteran, Sergeant Major John James May moved to Bognor in 1912 and commenced training 'difficult young boys', with the result that there had been no police cases 'to show that his boys had been in any trouble at all'. The boys were of all religious sects and they attended Sergeant May's classes after school on Tuesdays and Thursdays. There they were given physical training, taught fencing and boxing and had the opportunity to play musical instruments. On 29 July 1913, Sergeant May's 'Bognor Boys' had their first parade and marched through the town, complete with their band and 'gave a good impression'; the band then entertained on the Pier. In this capacity Sergeant May made 'a host of friends, not only in Bognor but throughout West Sussex and became acquainted with all classes'. His 'troop of my boys' evolved into a semi military youth band and in June 1915 they held a practice with the Bognor Town Band.

'So successful was the result that it is hoped that the combination of forces would make a really good band shortly'.

Sergeant May never saw the fruits of his labours, for he was taken seriously ill and succumbed to pneumonia a few weeks later, on 22 July 1915.

A well known Bognor figure prominently identified with the Unionist Party and a member of the Constitutional Club, he had retired from the Royal Sussex Regiment on a pension, having completed twenty one years' service. Prior to that he had served with 18th Hussars and had fought with them at Ladysmith. He became an instructor in No 1 Company of the Volunteers and when they were disbanded in 1908 he joined the new Territorial's. He continued his valuable service, becoming an instructor with the Middleton School Cadets. Although he had relinquished his association with the Territorial's, the outbreak of war found him ready to offer his services, aged 51, being one of the three 'old soldiers' who had helped with the requisitioning of horses. He then re-enlisted into 12th Battalion, the Royal Sussex Regiment.

Sergeant May was given a full military funeral, the 9th Hampshire Regiment providing the firing party. Royal Sussex Regiment Sergeants acted as pall bearers, with a 'score' of Sergeants from 12th Battalion in attendance. The Reserve Band of the Cavalry Regiment played and 'the procession from the deceased's home to South Bersted Church was of a most impressive character, the Band playing the Dead March en route'.

(Sergeant May was the father of Lance Sergeant George May, see Roll of Honour, 30 June 1916).

Private R2080 Harry Stanford SIMMONS
East Road, Selsey
The Kings Royal Rifles
Killed in Action on 30 July 1915
Aged about 27

Harry Simmons was born in Burgess Hill, Sussex, but became well known in Bognor as the manager of the International Stores in London Road, where he was employed in the four years leading up to the war. He enlisted in Bognor. The report of his death appeared in the *Bognor Observer* in August 1915:

'The sad news has reached Bognor this week of the death in action of Private Harry Simmons of the Kings Royal Rifles. For three or four years he was manager of the London Road Branch of the International Stores, joining Kitcheners Army in September last. He was about 27 years of age and was engaged to Miss Vincent *(Jessie Vincent, a dress maker, aged 26)* of Lyon Street, who we understand has been informed of his being killed in action at Hooge on 30 July'.

Private Harry Simmons' name does not appear on the Bognor War Memorial.

Lance Corporal G1049 Harry BARRON
15 Norman Terrace, Longford Road, Bognor
7th Battalion, the Royal Sussex Regiment, 12th Division
Died of Wounds on 5 August 1915
Aged 34
Buried in the Cite Bonjen Military Cemetery, Armentieres

Harry Barron was born in Murrow, Cambridgeshire, subsequently moving to Bognor, where he lived with his wife Annie and their three children. He enlisted at Chichester into the Royal Sussex Regiment. From the barracks at Chichester, the Battalion was moved to Colchester, becoming part of 12th (Eastern) Division. October 1914 found them at Shorncliffe, moving into Folkestone in December, where they stayed for three months. In March 1915 the Battalion were moved to Aldershot and thence to France, arriving at Boulogne over the two days of 31 May and 1 June.

In the period of build up to the Battle of Loos and now having achieved the rank of Lance Corporal, Harry was killed. At the time his Battalion was in Reserve, although they were continually harassed by rifle fire, which led to the deaths of a number of men. One of his Officers, Lieutenant Towers, wrote to Mrs Barron:

'Since the Battalion came to France, Corporal Barron has done splendid service for us and by his keenness and personal example, had made his section one of the best in the Regiment. He was killed when helping his Officer in a dangerous but necessary bit of work at night in front of the trenches. The whole of the Company, both Officers and men, will miss him. Corporal Barron was buried by the Church of England Chaplain at Armentieres'.

Private 15039 William MERRITT
55 Essex Road, Bognor
7th Battalion, the Bedfordshire Regiment, 18th Division
Killed in Action on 10 September 1915
Aged 21
Buried in the Dartmoor Cemetery, Becordel-Becourt

The second of three sons born to Mr and Mrs Merritt, on leaving school William became an errand boy, his family living in Ockley Road at the time. His father had died whilst William was still at school, his mother making ends meet as a charwoman.

William enlisted in Lambeth into the Bedfordshire Regiment in September 1914. In July 1915 they moved to France and Flanders, embarking on the *SS Onward* at Folkestone, arriving at a rest camp at Boulogne, where they stayed for several weeks musketry training, route marching, bayonet fighting and generally preparing for a move to the Front, which took place on 23 August. Over the next fortnight the Regiment engaged the enemy on a number of occasions and on 10 September Private William Merritt was killed in one such incident.

Private 9117 Edward BURNAND
Flansham Lane, Felpham
1st Battalion, the Hampshire Regiment, 4th Division
Killed in Action on 13 September 1915
Aged 19
Buried in the Crouy Vauxtrot French National Cemetery, France

Born in St Pancras, Chichester, Edward Burnand moved with his parents to Flansham Lane, Felpham, before living with his cousin, who was in the Royal Navy and his family in Portsmouth. Here Edward was employed as a boot repairer and errand boy. He then became a regular soldier, enlisting at Winchester into the Hampshire Regiment at Aldershot. On the night of 21/22 August 1914 they embarked at Southampton onto two ships, the *Braemar Castle* and the *Cestrian*, destined for Le Havre.

Arriving in France, they were immediately moved to the east, de-training at Le Cateau and were marched six miles to help cover the retreat from Mons. Faced with overwhelming forces, they moved into position south west of Cattenieres, where they engaged the enemy and helped to foil the German plan to cut off that part of the British Expeditionary Force. Forced to withdraw, they had to leave their wounded behind and by the end of the engagement had lost around two hundred men.

In the Spring of 1915 they fought in the Second Battle of Ypres and later on 12 September the Battalion was poised to go on the offensive over a river which had to be crossed. This battle raged until 15 September, Edward Burnand sadly losing his life in the early stages, on 13 September.

The notification letter his parents received from his Commanding Officer stated:

'It is with extreme regret that I have to let you know of the death of your son, who was killed in action beside me on Sunday afternoon, 13 September 1914. One consolation to you is to know that there was never a cheerier, brighter lad and that he met a gallant death, whilst making an attack upon the enemy. All his comrades in the Company wish to express their heartfelt sympathy to you in your bereavement. His name will live long in the memory of those who were with him'.

THE BATTLE OF LOOS

The Battle of Loos commenced on 25 September 1915, a major British offensive mounted on the Western Front and the first large scale use of volunteers signed up for Kitchener's Army. The objective was to capture the town of Loos, which was the British task in a combined Anglo-French larger offensive known as the 3rd Battle of Artois. Referred to sometimes as the Big Push, the opening day was fairly successful, with inroads being made into German territory despite heavy casualties, but with reserves being held well to the rear, further progress was limited.

The actions on the Hohenzollern Retreat took place during the Battle of Loos. This was a strongly defended strategic German fortification which provided all round defensive observation. The assault on this also commenced on 25 September 1915 when the British captured it, only to lose it again two days later in a strong German counter attack. When the Battle subsided on 28 September, the British had retreated to their starting positions.

The situation remained little changed until a fresh British attack on 13 October ended in the loss of over three thousand Officers and men in a very short time. The Battle ended on 18 October; a further assault was considered for early November, but abandoned due to heavy rains and German shelling.

Lance-Sergeant 8130 Arthur Thomas HOMER
Bognor Road, Lagness, Pagham, Bognor
2nd Battalion, the Royal Berkshire Regiment, 8th Division
Killed in Action on 25 September 1915
Aged 27
Commemorated on the Ploegsteert Memorial, Belgium

Born at Portfield, Chichester, Arthur Homer was the second son of Noah, a farm carter and his wife Ann and the older brother of Charles *(see Roll of Honour, October 1918)*. On leaving school Arthur became an agricultural labourer, before enlisting into the Royal Berkshire Regiment as a regular soldier, serving in India prior to the war. His Battalion was recalled, arriving in the United Kingdom on 22 October 1914. Three weeks later they were sent to France, landing at Le Havre on 5 November. Arthur was killed in action in Belgium on 25 September 1915.

Second Lieutenant William IRELAND
39 London Road, Bognor
2nd Battalion, the Royal Sussex Regiment, 1st Division
Killed in Action on 25 September 1915
Aged 33
Commemorated on the Loos Memorial, Pas de Calais, France

Second Lieutenant William Ireland was 'killed instantaneously whilst leading his men against a German position' on the first day of the offensive. He was an experienced soldier, who only days before had been commissioned, having been a regular Sergeant-Major in the 1/6 Cyclist Battalion, the Royal Sussex Regiment and had fought all through the South African War.

In a letter to his widow, Eva, Lieutenant Colonel Green expressed the sympathy of all ranks in her great loss. He continued:

'Your husband was killed gallantly leading his men against a German position. He is buried with his brother Officers about a mile east of Vermelles. We shall miss your husband very much and the Battalion lose in him a very useful, gallant Officer. For myself, I felt that I had lost a friend of many years standing'.

The *Bognor Observer* wrote:

'Yet another Bognor Officer has been killed and one who was most popular among his confreres'.

Private G1469 George Herbert KING
31 Essex Road, Bognor
2nd Battalion, the Royal Sussex Regiment, 1st Division
Killed in Action on 25 September 1915
Aged 22
Commemorated on the Loos Memorial, Pas de Calais, France

'Special Constable King has lost his eldest son Private George King of the Royal Sussex Regiment, who was killed in action at the Battle of Loos, on 25 September 1915. He has another five sons serving'.

George King's father was at one time the Angmering policeman, where George was born. The family moved to Felpham, to where his father had been transferred before retiring and becoming a wartime Special Constable. Before enlisting George was employed as an assistant to Mr R Winter, the butcher, of 49 High Street, Bognor.

Private G1216 Leonard SQUELCH
7 West Cottages, West Hampstead, London
9th Battalion, the Royal Sussex Regiment, 24th Division
Killed in Action on 25 September 1915
Aged 20
Commemorated on the Loos Memorial, Pas de Calais, France

Born and raised in West Hampstead, London, the son of William, a police constable, on leaving school Leonard became an errand boy. His connection with Bognor has not been established. However, it is known that he enlisted in the town into the Royal Sussex Regiment in September 1914. Early training took place at Portslade and Shoreham, continuing until August 1915, when on the last day of that month the *SS La Marguerite* took them away from England, arriving at Le Havre the following day. Further training in trench digging, musketry, bomb throwing and endless route marches took place over the next few weeks, before they were moved to the front for the Battle of Loos.

All day on 25 September, the 9th Sussex were held in readiness, whilst reports were filtering back that all the attacks on the German lines made that day had been repulsed. Finally, close on midnight, the order came to advance on a large and conspicuous slag heap known as 'Fosse 8' and hold it 'at all costs'. This they did, despite the fact that the men had been at readiness all day and by now had run out of food and water. But casualties were high, sixty five Officers and men losing their lives, including Private Leonard Squelch, in his first action.

Corporal 28626 Thomas VENUS
Nyetimber Village, Pagham
No 102 Company, the Royal Garrison Artillery
Died of Wounds on 25 September 1915
Aged 28
Buried in the Lijssenthoek Military Cemetery, Belgium

Thomas was born in Pagham, the son of George, a cowman and Elizabeth Venus. When he left school he took employment as a farm labourer, before enlisting into the Royal Garrison Artillery in 1908. He served for a few years in Malta, moving to the Western Front early in the war and then fought at Hooge, where he received the wounds from which he died.

Captain Bernard Henry HOLLOWAY
Craigwell House, Aldwick
9th Battalion, the Royal Sussex Regiment, 24th Division
Killed in Action on 27 September 1915
Aged 27

Bernard, the son of Sir Henry and Lady Holloway, had been born in Clapham, London. He was educated at the Leys School, Cambridge, where he excelled at sport, representing Cambridge against Oxford at both Association and Rugby Football. He enlisted into the Royal Sussex Regiment and in February 1915 the local press recorded his promotion to Captain, describing him as 'that well known Cambridge cricketer, a fine sportsman and a thorough gentleman'.

The *Bognor Observer* reported his death in December 1915:

'The death at the Front of Captain Holloway will be felt by many admirers in various parts of the County. A young man not yet 30, Captain Holloway was best known in Sussex as a cricketer, who had played County cricket. For some years whilst living at Aldwick he was one of the best players in the Bognor Cricket Club and he used annually to take eleven of his own on tour, 'Holloways XI' was a familiar name on the cricket field. He was also a fine athlete and a keen sportsman in other directions and before the war he was expected to enter into a legal career, for which he had been training. He made an ideal Officer and leader of men and had he lived would have probably adopted the Army as his profession. He went through his training as an Officer and went to the Front, where some of the first men he met in the trenches were men he had known on the cricket field back home. He was a fine tall man and it appears that just as his Company was being relieved in the trenches during the big fighting in September, he was killed by a sniper'.

Captain Alistaire Hillyar Darby CHAPMAN
Kilhendre, Ellesmere, Shropshire
1st Royal Dragoons, 3rd Cavalry Division
Killed in Action on 27 September 1915
Aged 33
Buried in the Noeux Les Mines Communal Cemetery

Little is known of this Officer who was probably a regular soldier. He served with 1st Dragoons in 3rd Cavalry Division and was killed in action on 27 September 1915.

No Bognor connections have been established, although he is listed on the Bognor War Memorial.

Sergeant G3245 John Charles BONIFACE
2 Police Cottages, Station Road, Bognor
9th Battalion, the Royal Sussex Regiment, 24th Division
Killed in Action on 28 September 1915
Aged 17
Commemorated on the Loos Memorial, Pas de Calais, France

John Boniface (junior), was the eldest son of John, a Police Constable serving with the Bognor Constabulary and his wife Ada. Before moving to Bognor, PC Boniface served at Chichester and had also been the village policeman in Funtington. John (junior) had a younger sister and two brothers and on leaving school became a drapers assistant and errand boy.

It would appear that when he enlisted into the Royal Sussex Regiment he was possibly underage. The 9th Battalion was raised at Chichester in September 1914 as part of Kitchener's New Army and moved first to Portslade in December 1914 and then on to Shoreham in April 1915. During this period the Battalion often took part in recruitment marches around Sussex. A final move within the UK took place in June 1915 to Woking in Surrey, before being posted to France, landing at Boulogne on 31 August 1915, where within a few weeks the Battalion was fighting the Battle of Loos.

The 9th Royal Sussex were committed to the battle, breaking through the German lines on the second day, 26 September. Two days later Private Boniface was killed, during one of the many attacks and counter attacks. At the time of his death Private Boniface was recorded as being just 17 years old!

Lieutenant Robert Charles Lowther GORDON
Canonbury House, the Esplanade, Bognor
8th Battalion, the Gordon Highlanders, 7th Division
Died of Wounds on 30 September 1915
Aged 36
Buried in the Wimereux Communal Cemetery, France

A man who 'will be well remembered in Bognor for the keen interest he took in the fishermen of the town, in the organisation of the annual regatta and whose amiable and pleasing disposition brought him a host of friends, who will deeply regret his death', was the *Bognor Observer's* tribute to Lieutenant Robert Gordon.

Robert Gordon, a keen cricketer and member of the Bognor Cricket Club, was born in Stroud, Gloucestershire. He enlisted into the Gordon Highlanders and 'died of wounds' in the Base Hospital at Boulogne, less than three months after his brother Bertram was also killed *(see Roll of Honour, July 1915)*.

Private G2744 William Edgar KINGMAN
2 Buckingham Place, the Steyne, Bognor
8th Battalion, the Royal West Surrey Regiment, 24th Division
Died of Wounds on 19 October 1915
Aged 25
Buried in the Lijssenthoek Military Cemetery, Belgium

One of five serving brothers, four of whom had joined the Royal Navy, Private Kingman had before the war 'been employed in two of Bognor's busiest shops, Mr Wade's, the butchers and Mr Staley's, the drapers'. Before enlisting he lived with his widowed mother, who ran an apartment house in the Steyne. His late father had worked for the Merchant Taylor's Company.

William was well known in Bognor when he enlisted at Deptford into the Royal West Surrey Regiment and was sent to France. On 19 October 1915 he was so badly wounded in his 'arms and back' that he died a short while afterwards. He was 'buried in a soldiers cemetery, a wooden cross being erected over his grave'.

Private G623 James Edward SQUIRES
The White House, Shripney
7th Battalion, the Royal Sussex Regiment, 12th Division
Killed in Action on 20 October 1915
Aged 21
Commemorated on the Loos Memorial, Pas de Calais, France

James Squires lived with his parents William, a farm labourer and Mary, growing up in a farm cottage at Shripney. The second of eight children and their eldest son, on leaving school he was employed by Mr Hogben, of Shripney Farm. James enlisted into the Royal Sussex Regiment at Bognor and in the autumn of 1915 was fighting near Loos. On 14 October, his Battalion occupied the trenches at Hulluch, where they remained for a week, carrying out much needed work on both the trenches and wiring, under occasional heavy German shelling. On 20 October 1915, the Battalion were moved out by motor bus, but at some stage during that day James was killed, whilst attacking a German trench with a bombing party. The 20 October was also the day his Battalion were issued with their first tin helmets.

Private GS180 Edward (Teddy) GEORGE
Seafield, Felpham
7th Battalion, the Royal Sussex Regiment, 12th Division
Killed in Action on 6 November 1915
Aged 30
Commemorated on the Loos Memorial, Pas de Calais, France

Thomas George had been a long serving sailor and at the outbreak of war was retired on his Royal Navy pension, living with his wife Emily. They had eleven children, one of whom, Edward, was also a Special Reservist, who enlisted at Chichester into the Royal Sussex Regiment. Prior to enlisting, Edward jnr. worked for Mr W Harfield and the Bognor builder, Mr Thomas Start.

In November 1915, the 7th Royal Sussex were occupying part of the Hohenzollern Redoubt and were involved in the grisly task of burying bodies, which had laid there since the fighting a week or two earlier. The weather at the time was very wet and the trenches were knee deep in mud. Whilst this work was being carried out there were periods of heavy German shelling, during which, on 6 November, Private Edward George lost his life.

PALESTINE

The decision by Turkey, taken in October 1914, to enter the war on the side of the Germans, prompted the despatch of British and Indian troops to protect the vital oil supplies at Abadan. This they achieved within a few weeks and made further progress to the town of Kut-al-Amara, from where they anticipated a final march into Baghdad, a hundred miles or so further north.

On 31 May 1915 the Regiment took part in the successful advance North of Kurna, capturing Amara using long canoes called 'ballums' which they punted across marsh land. This success was followed by the Battle of Es Sinn in which Kut-el-Amara was occupied at the end of September. The ultimate aim was to take Baghdad, as well as to protect British oil supplies. However, three weeks later, from 22 to 24 November these successes were reversed in the Battle of Ctesiphon, with very heavy losses amongst Officers and men. After this the Division fell back to Kut, the Oxford and Buckinghamshire Regiment fighting a rearguard action all the way. Plans to retreat further south were cancelled in order to hold the town and tie up as many Turkish forces as possible, repulsing an attack and inflicting very heavy casualties on the enemy.

Private 2817 Leonard Stephen KNAPTON
1/4th Battalion the Dorsetshire Regiment, 15th Indian Division
Died of Wounds on 10 October 1915
Aged 31
Buried in the Basra War Cemetery, Iraq

'His many old friends in Bognor have heard with regret of the death of Private Knapton, of 2nd Battalion, the Dorset Regiment, which occurred on 10 October 1915. He died from wounds received in action near Kut-el-Arnarah in the Persian Gulf on 28 September'.

Leonard was born in Yeovil, Somerset, the second son of George and Amy Knapton who ran a grocers business in the town. The family moved to Dorset, where Leonard spent a lot of his childhood, becoming an office boy on leaving school. Shortly afterwards he enlisted into the Dorset Regiment, did his time and was discharged, subsequently moving to Bognor. When war broke out Leonard re-enlisted at Dorchester into his old Regiment, having recently married a Southampton lass, Elsie Lambert.

The *Bognor Observer* paid the following tribute to him:

'He will be remembered as a good footballer and athlete. He was a member of the Bognor Cycling Club and was for some time employed by Messrs. Hawkes and Son, grocers. On the outbreak of war he joined the 1/4th Dorset's one of the first to volunteer for active service and proceeded to India'.

The 2nd Battalion, the Dorset Regiment were stationed in India, at Poona in August 1914 and were moved to Mesopotamia in November as part of the Indian Expeditionary Force.

We will return to the Mesopotamian Campaign a little further on.

DIED AT HOME

Staff Sergeant H PINCHES
Rosslyn Cottage, Felpham
2nd Battalion, the Grenadier Guards
Died at Home on 18 December 1915
Age Unknown
Buried in St Mary's Churchyard, Felpham, Bognor

'On 20 December 1917 military honours were accorded the funeral of Staff Sergeant H Pinches, of the 2nd Battalion Grenadier Guards, who passed away on 18 December at home. The deceased had served with the Colours and Reserve for nine years and was one of the 'Contemptibles', being in one of the drafts sent to France in 1914. He went through Mons and other battles and was invalided home in 1915, having contracted TB. For more than a year he was employed at the Norman Thompson Flight Works as a telephonist, but having caught a cold he was confined to his bed for a fortnight before the end came. The Chief Officer and a number of Life Guards formed a Guard of Honour. An impressive address was given at the graveside by the vicar who also thanked the lifeguards for their honour paid to the Sister Service. Messrs Reynolds and Co carried out the funeral arrangements'.

Guardsman 12217 William Bertram NORTON
Sunnyside, Canning Road, Felpham
3rd Battalion, the Coldstream Guards
Died at Home on 15 December 1915
Aged 21
Buried in St Mary's Churchyard, Felpham, Bognor

William was the second child and eldest son of Albert, a carpenter and his wife Francis and was born in Havant, Hampshire. His family moved around a lot during his childhood - Gosport, Portsmouth and Bosham - before settling in Felpham. On leaving school, William became an apprentice to his father, before joining the Coldstream Guards. He was wounded in 1915 and sent home, where he died just before Christmas.

Private SD847 Byron SNOOK
Victoria Cottage, Sea Road, Felpham
11th Battalion, the Royal Sussex Regiment
Died at Home on 29 December 1915
Aged 28
Buried in the St Mary's Churchyard, Felpham, Bognor Regis, West Sussex

Byron was the eldest son of Henry, a market gardener and his wife Emma. He had three brothers, *(see Arthur Snook, Roll of Honour, May 1918)* and one sister and was born in Brighton, after which the family moved to Felpham. On leaving school, Byron became an errand boy and then a butcher, before enlisting at Bognor. He died of pneumonia at Whitley Camp and was bought home for burial.

'The loss of this young man is keenly felt in the neighbourhood where he was well known, having been before he enlisted, employed by Mr Rickie, the butcher, of London Road. A military funeral was accorded on Tuesday afternoon (4 January 1916) when six members of his Battalion acted as pall bearers'.

WESTERN FRONT

Private Harry ROE
Cecil Cottage, 9 Parramatta Terrace, Ockley Road, Bognor
2nd Battalion, the Duke of Cornwall's Light Infantry
Missing on December 1915 presumed Killed in Action
Aged 20

The name Private H Roe appears on the Bognor War Memorial, but no other details are recorded. Research indicates that he was Private Harry Roe, whose death was reported in the *Bognor Observer* in April 1916:

'News has been received that Private Harry Roe, of the Duke of Cornwall's Light Infantry has been killed in France. He had spent his twentieth birthday in the trenches and had been reported missing in December 1915. Before enlisting he had obtained an appointment in the Civil Service under the National Health Commissioners. Mr Roe had relatives and friends in Bognor, who will be saddened to hear of his death'.

Private G591 Robert John LITTLE
Address Unknown
7th Battalion, the Royal Sussex Regiment, 12th Division
Killed in Action on 28 December 1915
Aged 33
Buried in the Guards Cemetery, Windy Corner, Cuinchy, France

A former 'valued member, very active and very willing', of the Bognor Fire Brigade, Robert 'Bob' Little enlisted into the Royal Sussex Regiment. In mid October 1915, the 7th Battalion were occupying trenches in the Hohenzollern Redoubt, 'where conditions were very bad, trench mortar and shelling activity on both side was very heavy and the state of the trenches owing to the excessive rains being indescribable'.

A glowing tribute to the pluck and coolness of Private Robert Little was paid to him by his Lieutenant, RT May, to his sister:

'I am very sorry to have to tell you that your brother, No 591 Bob Little, was killed by a sniper yesterday. He was shot through the head and though lived for as hour or so afterwards. I am sure he was totally unconscious and could have felt no pain. He was always as cool and cheerful in the worst and most dangerous trenches, as I imagine he was at home. In fact he lost his life doing an action which showed his pluck and coolness. After a mine explosion, our trench was badly blocked by the parapet falling in at a point where there were several bomb boxes. Some of these were put on and off the parapet out of the way, whilst the fallen sandbags and dirt were cleared away. Your brother was one of the party working there. A bullet struck one of the bomb boxes and it started smoking. Needless to say this looked and was extremely dangerous, as if the box had caught on fire the bombs would have exploded. The Officer shoved the box a little way over the parapet, but this was not good enough for your brother. He reached up to throw it away still further, but in doing so exposed himself and was shot by a sniper. The fact that the box did not, as it happened, catch fire, does not in the least to my mind detract from the coolness of his action. I expect you know that your brother had been my servant ever since I joined the Battalion. I can assure you he will be badly missed by all the Officers in the Company, as he was always cheerful and did twice as much work as anybody else. Personally I had come to regard him as a most reliable friend, rather than as a servant and one that would do any job for me if he possibly could.

'He was buried at a soldiers' cemetery at Givenchy, a Chaplain from another Battalion reading the burial service, as ours was sick. If ever you care to have the exact position pointed out to you please let me know. His grave will of course be marked by a cross with his name and Regiment on it. I enclose your brother's cap badge with sympathy for you and your brother and sisters in your loss.

'PS. Your parcel of food arrived, so I told the other servants to share it out. I hope this meets with your approval'.

Corporal G819 George MILLS
45 Chapel Street, Bognor
7th Battalion, the Royal Sussex Regiment, 12th Division
Died of Wounds on 31 December 1915
Aged 18
Buried in the Bethune Town Cemetery France

'By the death of Corporal George Mills, of the Royal Sussex Regiment on New Year's Eve 1915, who died in France of wounds received two days earlier, Mr and Mrs Mills have now lost their two sons in the Country's cause *(see Jesse Mills, Roll of Honour, November 1914)*. George, who was 18 years of age, was wounded in the head by the explosion of a hand grenade. He had been in the Army for about 16 months, having enlisted a month after the war began'.

The *Bognor Observer* commiserated with the family:

'Poor Mrs Mills, who has been anxiously awaiting news of her son, Corporal George Mills, who had been wounded in France, has now had the official news from the War Office that the young man has died of his wounds. Mrs Mills has now lost both of her sons. Another Bognorian, Sergeant Read of Essex Road, was with him when he was killed:

"I was sorry when he got hit, I was close to him at the time and came home on leave the same night as it happened and informed his mother about it", he told the Observer.

1916

WESTERN FRONT

Lance Corporal G434 Charles John WATSON
3 Gordon Terrace, Felpham, Bognor
7th Battalion, the Royal Sussex Regiment, 12th Division
Died of Wounds on 2 March 1916
Aged 29
Buried in the Bethune Town Cemetery, France

A territorial soldier, Charles Watson, the 30 year old son of Mrs Fanny Watson, left his employment at Messrs Reynolds, to 'patriotically join the National Reserve'. Whilst serving with the Royal Sussex Regiment, he sustained wounds to which he succumbed on 2 March 1916, aged 29. The 7th Battalion had a well earned restful time in January, returning to the Front on 11 February.

'Things hotted up on 2 March', when the Germans opened up a barrage of heavy trench mortars, field guns and howitzers, followed by a 'great deal of close quarter bomb fighting'. It was during this attack that Lance Corporal Watson was killed.

Rifleman R17478 Cyril James Turner WHITE
Lynwood, Sturges Road, Bognor
2nd Battalion, the Kings Royal Rifle Corps, 1st Division
Died of Wounds on 12 March 1916
Aged 31
Buried in the St Sever Cemetery, Seine-Maritime, France.

Cyril was born in Islington, London, the son of Robert Quintas, an accountant with the railway and his wife Esther Miriam White, being their fourth child and second son.

At some stage Cyril became a regular soldier. He served in 1st Rhodesian Regiment Kings Royal Rifles, with General Botha in the South Africa War and in German South West Africa in 1914. His Regiment was sent to France where, whilst now serving in the 2nd Battalion, he died of wounds at the 1st Stationary Hospital at Rouen on 12 March 1916, aged 31.

Captain George Maria Joseph Alphonsus GRISEWOOD
The Den, Upper Bognor Road, Bognor
11th Battalion, the Royal Sussex Regiment, 39th Division
Died of Pneumonia on 27 March 1916
Aged 26
Buried in the Merville Communal Cemetery, Bethune, France

The Grisewood family lived at the Den, the house being owned by Lieutenant Colonel Harman Grisewood, a retired Army Officer. He was a friend of Colonel Lowther who created Lowthers Lambs, or the Southdowners, three Battalions of volunteers who eventually became the 11th, 12th and 13th Battalions, the Royal Sussex Regiment.

Harman Grisewood had five sons, one of whom, George, had previously served in the Grenadier Guards before emigrating to Australia. When war was declared he quickly returned and re-enlisted into 11th Battalion, the Royal Sussex Regiment. On re-enlisting he had taken 'an active part' in the recruiting of 'The Southdowns' and spoke on many occasions at rallies on the pier and 'other places in Bognor where recruiting meetings were held'. He was for six months the Adjutant and temporarily held the rank of Major. He served in France and Flanders with the Expeditionary Force from 20 February 1915 and died at the Front of pneumonia.

Lance Corporal G1211 George William Pratt VERION
South View, North Bersted, Bognor
9th Battalion, the Royal Sussex Regiment, 24th Division
Killed in Action on 28 March 1916
Aged 26
Buried in the Ration Farm Cemetery Annexe, Belgium

'He is missed by us all and his influence was always great and always for the good', wrote Captain ES Rogerson, of Lance Corporal George Verion of the Royal Sussex Regiment, who has died from a sniper's gunshot wound to the head.

His mother received the news in a letter from the Captain, who says he was killed at 1915hrs on 28 March. He continued:

'He had gone in a moment, without pain, to our great home above. His body lies in a little soldiers cemetery behind the lines, where it was put in its last resting place by a Church of England Chaplain. At the head is a wooden cross, that sure and certain sign of our Saviour's death for us and a very certain guarantee of our all meeting again in the near future. It happened in the Front Line trenches. He was shot in the head, but there was no disfigurement and he lay looking so peaceful and quiet. I am sorry Mrs Verion. He was the best Lance Corporal I had and was absolutely straight'.

Mrs Verion also received a letter from the Chaplain in which he said the Lance Corporal died 'as an Englishman should die for his Country'.

Lance Corporal Verion had many friends in North Bersted and formerly worked for Mr Booker, at the South Bersted Post Office. March had been a very quiet month for his Battalion, bitterly cold with periods of heavy snow. Most of the month had been spent on working party duties, with four days route marching, once the weather had cleared. The last week had been particularly quiet, even so four men, including Lance Corporal Verion fell victim to enemy activity. He was the younger brother of Horace *(see Roll of Honour, March 1918)*

Private SD782 William Thomas CARTER
29 Essex Road, Bognor
11th Battalion, the Royal Sussex Regiment, 39th Division
Died of Wounds on 24 May 1916
Aged 21
Buried in the Gorre British and Indian Cemetery

Formerly a member of the Church Lads Brigade, William would have paraded many times in Bognor playing the side drum. He was the eldest son of William Carter, a domestic gardener and general labourer from Fareham and his Yapton-born wife Elizabeth, who was employed as a laundress. William had a younger brother and two sisters. Born in Fareham, William was employed as a grocery apprentice prior to enlisting at Bognor.

The *Bognor Observer* 28 June 1916 reported:

'Among recent Bognorians to make the extreme sacrifice last week was Private Carter, whose parents reside in Steyne Street. He was a member of the Sussex Regiment, his father receiving the following letter from his Commanding Officer:

'I venture to offer you my deep and respectful sympathy for the sad loss of your son. As his Company Commander I can assure you he was an excellent soldier, well beloved by all the Officers, NCO's and men. He met with the wound that caused his death when actually in No Man's Land. He was an excellent soldier and good companion and I personally feel his loss, as such splendid soldiers as he proved to be are not always to be found, believe me'.

THE BATTLE OF JUTLAND

The Battle of Jutland was the largest naval battle in history, fought over two days, 31 May to 1 June 1916, near Jutland, Denmark. It had been anticipated, since the declaration of war, that at some stage the British Grand Fleet and the Imperial German Navy High Seas Fleet would clash. The German Fleet was insufficient in number to engage the entire British Fleet and had planned to lure out, trap and destroy a portion of it, as part of the German strategy for breaking the British naval blockade of the North Sea. British intelligence, however, had learned that a major naval operation was likely and took the initiative when Vice-Admiral Beatty attacked the German battle cruiser force on 31 May, before their submarine 'pickets' were in position, thus upsetting their plans to divide and conquer the British Fleet.

The two fleets and some two hundred and fifty ships commenced an epic dual on the afternoon of 31 May, which was to last all night. The result was somewhat inconclusive; the British lost more ships and men, whilst the German surface fleet escaped back to their home port and were effectively neutralized. The *Bognor Observer* commented on the largest loss of local sailors in the war to date:

'Twelve local men lost their lives in the battle, along with a number of men from Chichester, Littlehampton, Arundel and the surrounding villages'.

THE LOSS OF HMS *INVINCIBLE*

HMS *Invincible* was the first battle cruiser to be built by any country. Launched in 1907, she was commissioned into the Home Fleet in March 1909. When war broke out she was completing a major refit at Portsmouth and declared 'operational' on 14 August 1914, joining the 2nd Battle Cruiser Squadron and seeing action a fortnight later in the Battle of Heligoland Bight, sinking the German light cruiser *Anadine*.

HMS *Invincible* was then part of a strong squadron sent to the South Atlantic to seek the German fleet and avenge the British losses in the Battle of Coronel *(see Jonathan Saigeman, Roll of Honour, November 1914)* and to prevent the Germans destroying the Falklands Radio Station at Port Stanley.

Following temporary repairs at Port Stanley, HMS *Invincible* then made for Gibraltar, where she was dry-docked for more permanent repairs, which took about four weeks. She then set sail for England to join the Grand Fleet in February, after having her worn out guns replaced.

In April 1916, in response to the German Navy's bombardment of Lowestoft and Yarmouth, the 3rd Battle Cruiser Squadron was sent to find the German ships but failed to locate them in heavy weather. However, during the sortie, the *Invincible* was rammed by a patrol yacht, the *Goissa*, causing considerable damage to her side which led to flooding and she was forced to limp back independently to Rosyth for repairs which took about four weeks. Seaworthy by the end of May, the 3rd Battle Cruiser Squadron were assigned to the Grand Fleet for gunnery practice. However, events overtook these when on 30 May the entire Grand Fleet was put to sea in response to the expected sailing of the German Grand Fleet: the long anticipated sea battle between the two mighty fleets was poised to commence.

In the ensuing battle Rear Admiral Hood's flagship, HMS *Invincible*, went to the rescue of the signals cruiser HMS *Chester* just before 1800 hrs, hitting and disabling the German light cruiser *Wiesbaden*, which with three others had been pounding away at HMS *Chester* for some while. HMS *Invincible*, along with HMS *Lion* and HMS *Inflexible*, then turned their attentions to the German Admiral Hipper's flagship SMS *Lutzow*, together with the SMS *Derfflinger* and SMS *Seydlitz*. HMS *Invincible* hit the SMS

Lutzow twice below her waterline, which ultimately sank her. Then at 1830 hrs HMS *Invincible* became a clear target in the evening light, receiving three hits each from the doomed SMS *Lutzow* and SMS *Derfflinger*, one of which penetrated *Invincibles*'s turret, causing the magazine to explode, splitting her in two halves; she sank in less than two minutes. Of her compliment of one thousand and thirty one Officers and men only five crew members survived.

Petty Officer First Class 188226 Harry ALLEN
HMS *Invincible* Royal Navy
Lost at Sea on 31 May 1916
Aged 36
Commemorated on the Royal Naval Memorial, Southsea, Hampshire

Harry Allen's mother lived at Chichester, whilst Harry himself, a regular sailor, is shown in the 1901 Census as registered at the Portsmouth Naval base serving upon one of Her Majesty's ships as an Able Seaman. By the war he had married and was living at Southsea, close to the Naval Base, with his wife Emma Bessie. Harry was serving as a Gunnery Instructor on the battle cruiser.

Able Seaman 194248 Leonard BAILEY
2 Willowhale Farm Cottages, Pagham, Bognor
HMS *Invincible* Royal Navy
Lost at Sea on 31 May 1916
Aged 34
Commemorated on the Royal Naval Memorial, Southsea, Hampshire

Also serving on HMS *Invincible* was Leonard Bailey. He was born on 20 February 1882, one of a large family of five boys and five girls, all of whom lived with their father, Thomas, who was a shepherd and a widower. By 1901 Leonard was in the Royal Navy serving on HMS *Majestic*, eventually joining the battle cruiser HMS *Invincible*. By now he had risen to the rank of Petty Officer (Able Seaman on War Memorial) and was living in Eastney, Portsmouth, with his wife Lucy, close to the Naval Base.

Able Seaman Robert 'Bobs' SMITH
HMS *Invincible* Royal Navy
Lost at Sea on 31 May 1916
Age Unknown
Commemorated on the Royal Naval Memorial, Southsea, Hampshire

Robert 'Bobs' Smith's name appears on the Bognor War Memorial, but no information regarding him has come to light other than the fact that he was lost on HMS *Invincible*. Even that is a mystery, because his name does not appear on the official casualty listings.

THE LOSS OF HMS *DEFENCE*

HMS *Defence*, a Minotaur class armoured cruiser which had been launched in 1907. She had an active career, serving initially with the 1st Cruiser Squadron before escorting the Royal Yacht *Medina* on a cruise in 1912. The outbreak of hostilities saw her operating in the Mediterranean, being involved in a chase after the German warships, the *Goeben* and *Breslau*. Ordered to the South Atlantic in revenge for the loss of the HMS *Good Hope*, she eventually returned to home waters as the Flag Ship of the 1st Cruiser Squadron.

It was during the Battle of Jutland that HMS *Defence* met her end. On 31 May 1916 the Squadron were steaming some miles ahead of the main battle fleet, when accompanied by HMS *Warrior* they steamed across the line of some British battle cruisers to attack German light cruisers, including the SMS *Wiesbaden*. The visibility was not good at the time and both British ships came under attack from the German battle cruisers SMS *Derfflinger* and SMS *Lutzow,* whose positions had been hidden by smoke and mist. HMS *Warrior* was badly damaged by SMS *Derfflinger* but managed to escape. HMS *Defence* was not so lucky; hit by successive salvos from SMS *Lutzow* she 'blew up in spectacular fashion'. Broken in half and enveloped in flame she quickly sank. The entire compliment of 903 sailors lost their lives in those few seconds.

Gunner Herbert James COOPER
South Bersted Street, South Bersted, Bognor
Royal Marine Artillery
HMS *Defence* Royal Navy
Lost at Sea on 31 May 1916
Aged 18

Herbert, was the second son of Herbert Cooper (senior), a farmer and his wife, Mary Ann. He grew up in South Bersted, attending the local school before enlisting into the Royal Navy around the time war was declared.

THE LOSS OF HMS *QUEEN MARY*

HMS *Queen Mary*, 'the most beautiful ship the Royal Navy possessed', was part of the Grand Fleet. Having seen earlier action at the Battle of Heligoland Bight, she returned from a refit, rejoining the 1st Battle Cruiser Squadron and fought at the Battle of Jutland.

Fitted with the new Pollen gunnery control system, she was soon in the thick of it, firing full broadsides and badly damaging the German warship SMS *Derfflinger*. She then turned her attention to SMS *Seydlitz*, which, although thought to be slowly sinking, struck back at HMS *Queen Mary*, which sustained hits on one of her turrets and another causing her forward magazine to explode. This was followed by more explosions as HMS *Queen Mary* listed to port and then sank.She was the second British battle cruiser to blow up under fire at Jutland and the largest British warship to be sunk by German gunnery throughout the war. Of her crew of one thousand two hundred and sixty six Officers and men, only twenty one survived.

Stoker First Class K16824 Francis William FARLEY
3 Cross Cottages, Bedford Street, Bognor
HMS *Queen Mary* Royal Navy
Lost at Sea on 31 May 1916
Aged 25
Commemorated on the Portsmouth Naval Memorial, Southsea, Hampshire

Francis William Farley, a Stoker 1st Class, aged 25, was the son of Richard and Mary Farley. On leaving school Francis became a baker's assistant before joining the Royal Navy.

First Stoker K17647 Joseph PARSLOW
Madras Villa, Highfield Road, Bognor
HMS *Queen Mary* Royal Navy
Lost at Sea at the Battle of Jutland on 31 May 1916
Aged 21
Commemorated on the Portsmouth Naval Memorial, Southsea, Hampshire

Living at Madras Villas, Highfield Road, Bognor, Joseph was the youngest son of bricklayer William and his wife, laundress Elizabeth, who had five other children, two boys and three girls. Joseph was born in Middlesex, where his father worked as a navvy, the family moving to Bognor whilst he was still a schoolboy.

It is not clear when Joseph joined the Royal Navy - it may have been in 1911. However, he was serving with the Grand Fleet on HMS *Queen Mary* at the Battle of Jutland, losing his life when the cruiser was sunk during that engagement.

THE LOSS OF HMS *BLACK PRINCE*

Launched on 4 November 1904, HMS *Black Prince*, a Duke of Edinburgh armoured cruiser, became part of the Grand Fleet and fought in the Battle of Jutland. During the course of the engagement HMS *Black Prince,* in company with HMS *Defence* and HMS *Warrior,* came under attack, HMS *Defence* was sunk and HMS *Warrior* disabled. HMS *Black Prince* had a rough time and during the engagement had become detached and out of touch from the Grand Fleet, which had taken a different direction. Alone, she headed for a line of battleships which were dimly visible in the far distance, only to receive a German recognition flash. She had unwittingly headed for a line of larger, powerful German vessels. Hopelessly outnumbered, she tried to escape by turning, but by now was totally exposed by the brilliant searchlights of four German warships, SMS *Thuringen*, SMS *Ostfriesland*, SMS *Nassau* and SMS *Friedrich der Grosse,* which battered her from stem to stern, disabling her guns before she could fire a shot. Now out of control, HMS *Black Prince* drifted past the German ships, who continued to fire at her; an eye witness account from a member of the crew aboard HMS *Spitfire* later described the scene:

'I saw a few hundred yards away on our starboard quarter what appeared to be a battle cruiser on fire steering straight for our stern. To our intense relief she missed our stern by just a few feet. She tore past us with a roar and the very crackling and heat of the flames could be felt. She was a mass of fire from fore-mast to main-mast on decks and between decks. Flames were issuing out of her from every corner. At first she appeared to be a battle cruiser as her funnels were so far apart, but it afterwards transpired it was the unfortunate *Black Prince* with her two central funnels gone. Soon afterwards, just after midnight there came an explosion from the direction in which she had disappeared'.

HMS *Black Prince* was lost with all hands, thirty seven Officers and 820 men.

Petty Officer Stoker 283821 Henry HELLYER
3 Elm Grove, Bersted, Bognor
HMS *Black Prince* Royal Navy
Lost at Sea on 31 May 1916
Aged 38
Commemorated on the Portsmouth Memorial, Southsea, Hampshire

Petty Officer Stoker Hellyer aged 38, lost his life along with the rest of the ship's company. He was born in Bognor, the son of fisherman William and his wife Isabella, living in Norfolk Street, before the family moved to 2 Hamburg Cottages, Chichester Road. By 1901 Henry was serving in the Royal Navy as a stoker.

Yeoman Signaller 202833 William Alfred BULBECK
Burnham Avenue, Bognor
HMS *Black Prince* Royal Navy
Lost at Sea on 31 May 1916
Aged 24

William was born in Bognor in 1882 to Isaac, who was a carpenter and Wesleyan local preacher and his wife Martha. Isaac was born in Pagham and married Martha Ann Whittington from Bognor in 1873. In 1891 the family were living at 25 West Street, next to the Wheatsheaf Inn. William was their sixth child and third son.

The 1911 Census shows William as a Leading Signalman in the Royal Navy and living with his sister Constance Bell and her family in Portsmouth. He married Elizabeth Jane Staples from Fulham, London in the spring of 1915 and they made their home in Burnham Avenue, Bognor, by which time he was probably serving on HMS *Black Prince*.

(Possibly) Seaman Charles HOMER
HMS *Black Prince* Royal Navy
Lost at Sea at the Battle of Jutland on 31 May 1916
Aged 24

This sailor's name does not appear on any of the local War Memorials, or the official casualty listing of those who lost their lives on HMS *Black Prince*. The only trace of him appears in the *Bognor Observer*'s report of the Battle of Jutland:

'Another Bognor sailor on the *Black Prince* was named Homer, who was to have been married within a few days'.

Able Seaman J22253 Alfred Ernest NEWBURY
11 Scott Street, Bognor
HMS *Black Prince* Royal Navy
Lost at Sea on 31 May 1916
Aged 19
Commemorated on the Portsmouth Naval Memorial, Southsea, Hampshire

The name on the War Memorial for this man is wrong, being listed as Albert, when it was in fact Alfred. The *Bognor Observer* report of his death, reproduced below, also gives it as Albert. However, the Bognor Council handwritten listings for the War Memorial prepared in 1919 gives his name as Alfred, as do the 1911 and 1901 Census returns and the Naval Casualty listings for the Great War.

'The son of Mr and Mrs Newbury of 11 Scott Street, Bognor, Able Seaman Albert Newbury lost his life with the sinking of HMS *Black Prince*, at the Battle of Jutland'.

Alfred was born in Ashbourne, Staffordshire on 1 October 1897, the youngest of Ernest and Ann Newbury's four children. At some stage during the Edwardian years the family moved to Bognor where Alfred continued his schooling. How he spent his first years after leaving school has not come to light - he may have followed his father into gardening or joined the Royal Navy as a boy. In any event 1916 found him serving on board the ill fated *Black Prince* on which he lost his life.

Leading Seaman 223542 Walter Alfred SIMMONDS
Bedford Street, Bognor
HMS *Black Prince* Royal Navy
Lost at Sea on 31 May 1916
Aged 29
Commemorated on the Portsmouth Naval Memorial, Southsea, Hampshire

Scott Street lost its second resident serving on HMS *Black Prince*, being Leading Seaman Walter Simmonds. The son of Samuel and Fanny, a laundress working from home, Walter was born in Bognor on 2 February 1887. His father died when Walter was a young child and his mother then married John Hopkins, a naval pensioner some years her senior and he may have guided Walter into serving in the Royal Navy. Prior to that, on leaving school, Walter worked as an assistant in an Oil and Colour Stores in Bognor.

THE LOSS OF HMS *SHARK*

HMS *Shark*, a four year old Acasta class destroyer, was one of four ships who counter attacked the Germans attacking the British Third Battle Cruiser Squadron. Capable of thirty two knots she led this attack, but was hit and disabled. Her Captain, badly wounded, having had his leg shot away, continued to direct the fire from the only gun left working, for which he was awarded a posthumous Victoria Cross. HMS *Shark*, although subjected to heavy fire herself, continued firing 'until she sank with her colours flying'. Following the order to 'abandon ship' only thirty of her crew managed to escape.

Able Seaman J12295 Reginald WADE
Outram House, Felpham, Bognor
HMS *Shark* Royal Navy
Lost at Sea on 31 May 1916
Aged 21
Commemorated on the Portsmouth Naval Memorial, Southsea, Hampshire

Amongst the casualties was Able Seaman Edward Wade, who was born on 10 March 1895 in West Kirby, Cheshire. Little is known of his childhood, but in 1911 he and his brother Neville were boarding at Outram House in Felpham. Two other boarders were Naval Pensioners, the house being owned by Thomas and Annie Humphrey. When Edward was killed his next of kin was listed as his mother, Mrs Elizabeth Jane Ayre, c/o a London solicitor.

THE DEATH OF LORD KITCHENER AND THE LOSS OF HMS *HAMPSHIRE*

Part of the Grand Fleet, HMS *Hampshire,* a Devonshire Class armoured cruiser, had spent her early days operating in the English Channel and the Mediterranean before being transferred to the China Station, where she stayed until the outbreak of war. Recalled to home waters at the end of 1914 she joined the Grand Fleet and fought at the Battle of Jutland on 31 May 1916. Returning to Scapa Flow she was immediately withdrawn for a 'diplomatic' mission to Russia. This voyage was 'top secret', as the *Hampshire* was carrying no less a personage than Lord Kitchener, the British Commander in Chief and Secretary of State for War. At the time it was felt that our Russian allies were 'wavering' and Lord Kitchener's mission was to persuade the Czar and his Generals to remain in the war. Any Russian/German settlement would release thousands more German troops to the west to face the British and French.

Leaving Scapa Flow and accompanied by two destroyers, HMS *Hampshire* and her escorts ran into a fierce summer storm. Unable to maintain speed, the two destroyers were signalled to return to port, whilst HMS *Hampshire* struggled on. At 1940 hrs 'an explosion shook the whole ship'. HMS *Hampshire* had hit a mine, believed to have been laid by the German submarine *U47* and sank within fifteen minutes, taking Lord Kitchener with her.

Further information on this incident was the subject of an article published in the *Bognor Post* ten years later, on 14 August 1926, by another local man, Stoker Walter Charles

Farnden of Lake Lane, Barnham.   He was one of only twelve survivors of HMS *Hampshire* and his graphic account of the sinking is reproduced here:

'On Saturday 3 June, the "Hampshire" steamed into Scapa Flow, was coaled up and moored to a buoy close to the "Iron Duke". On the following Monday, 5 June, Lord Kitchener and his retinue came aboard and orders were given to leave harbour at   5 30pm in the evening. The ship was under sealed orders but the buzz soon spread to the effect that the destination was to be Archangel. Promptly at 5 30pm the "Hampshire" slipped her moorings and proceeded out of harbour accompanied by her escorts, the destroyers "Unity" and "Victor". By this time a gale which had prevailed all day had shifted from the north-east to north and was rapidly increasing in violence. The destroyers, almost as soon as they were in the open, found it difficult to keep up with the cruiser in the teeth of the gale and consequently they were ordered to return to port, as they only delayed the "Hampshire".

'At 7 30pm I was on watch in the port engine room when a terrific explosion occurred and immediately the ship was plunged into darkness. There was no panic and we all remained at our posts until the order was given to abandon ship. By this time the vessel was down at the bows and was sinking rapidly. When I got on deck Officers and men were standing by their appointed stations. Tremendous seas were running at the time and one boat that I saw lowered from the davits was immediately smashed to pieces against the ship's side. My station was the No 3 Caley float and after we had assisted in getting the other two floats away we launched our own. There were fifteen or twenty men in the float including myself and by the time we had picked up one or two from the water we were overcrowded. Fortunately for us the current set towards the shore, but it was a terrible ordeal being adrift in those surging seas at the mercy of the wind and waves. About midnight, after four of the most dreadful hours I have ever spent in my life our float was dashed against the rocks near Stromness and a large wave washed me over the side. In the ordinary course of events I cannot swim, but I swam that night and eventually reached a rock and dragged myself ashore. I saw the float again hurled towards the rocks and three of my companions made a jump for it and succeeded in reaching the shore. The remainder were too exhausted to help themselves and perished in the waves when the float overturned. Dazed and shaken I rested awhile, but when I attempted to stand I found that I had lost the use of my legs and I had to crawl until I regained sufficient strength to walk to the nearest cottage. I knocked them up and explained what had happened and they gave me some warm clothing and put me to bed. They afterwards searched the coast and discovered some more survivors. It transpired that six men had been saved from the second float and two from the first making twelve in all'.

Able Seaman J7559 William Arthur FREEMAN
52 Oving Road, Chichester
HMS *Hampshire* Royal Navy
Lost at Sea on 5 June 1916
Aged 23
Commemorated on the Portsmouth Naval Memorial, Southsea, Hampshire

William Freeman, the brother of Albert *(see Roll of Honour, November 1914)*, was born on 18 January 1894 to bricklayer Richard and his laundress wife, Fanny. Educated at the Central Boys School in Chichester, on leaving he took up employment as a gravel digger in the Chichester pits close to his home. He had been in the Royal Navy since 1910 and had only been home once in that time, on special leave to see a brother who was visiting from Australia, where he had lived for five years. Both William and his brother Albert also appear on the Portfield War Memorial at Chichester.

WESTERN FRONT

Private G4214 George William BRIDGER
4 Manor Cottages, Felpham, Bognor
9th Battalion, the Royal Sussex Regiment, 24th Division
Killed in Action on 17 June 1916
Age 21
Buried in the Ration Farm Annexe Belgium

The 9th Battalion the Royal Sussex Regiment was formed in Chichester from Kitchener's volunteers in September 1914. All the original volunteers were given a 'G' prefix in front of their numbers. George Bridger was one such man and would have taken part in the training and recruitment marches in the Brighton area, before the Battalion was moved first to Portslade in December 1914 and then Shoreham the following April. This was followed by a further move to Woking, Surrey in June 1915. Until then, the 9th Battalion had only served in England, but that was soon to change. In August 1915 they landed at Boulogne and a few weeks later were fighting in the Battle of Loos in which they suffered heavy losses.

June 1916 found them experiencing an 'unusually quiet period' until the seventeenth when 'the Germans decided to liven up the situation'. This took the form of three separate gas attacks accompanied by some heavy shelling and machine gun fire. These attacks accounted for fifteen Royal Sussex men including one local soldier.

George Bridger was born in Petersfield, Hampshire, to George (senior), a carter on a farm and his wife Edith. Part of his childhood was spent at Pulborough, before the family moved to Court Hill, Slindon, by which time George was an assistant farm carter. From Slindon they moved to Felpham from where George enlisted at Chichester.

EGYPT

Private TF3312 Cecil LUFF
Baldhorns Cottages, Faygate, Rusper, Sussex
4th Battalion, the Royal Sussex Regiment, 53rd Division
Died of Wounds on 28 June 1916
Aged 23
Buried in the Alexandria (Hadra) War Memorial Cemetery, Egypt

Cecil was born in 1883 at Plaistow, near Kirdford, Sussex and was a son of Edward and Elizabeth Luff, who were farm workers. According to the 1871 Census Edward was a farmer of 190 acres who employed three men and two boys at Fernhurst. Ten years later he was a stockman on a farm at Plaistow, but by 1901 was described as a cowman, a position that Cecil also occupied on leaving school. The family appear to have worked on several farms in the area, from Rusper to Tortington, near Arundel. Edward passed away in 1911 and Elizabeth moved to East Grinstead. However, Cecil enlisted at Bognor. Following his death in 1916 Elizabeth, his next of kin, was still living in East Grinstead and Cecil's name appears on the East Grinstead War Memorial as well as that of Bognor.

A Territorial soldier, Cecil was sent to Egypt, sailing on the *'Ulysses'* from Devonport on 17 July 1915 to join the Mediterranean Expeditionary Force, arriving at Alexandria eleven days later. The following week they sailed for Gallipolli, disembarking at Sulva Bay on 8 August. Cecil survived the five months in Gallipolli before the Battalion were withdrawn to Egypt in December. He died in the Alexandria Military Hospital on 28 June 1916. It may have been from wounds received in the Gallipolli fighting.

Private G8128 George Joseph DENYER
1 Ivy Cottages, Ivy Lane, South Bersted, Bognor
2nd Battalion, the Royal Sussex Regiment, 1st Division
Killed in Action on 30 June 1916
Aged 31
Buried in the Maroc British Cemetery, Pas de Calais, France

George was the youngest and seventh son of thirteen children born to bricklayer James and his wife Sarah. He had attended South Bersted School and before volunteering had made his living as a brick maker's labourer.

'THE DAY THAT SUSSEX DIED'

The blackest day of the Great War for many families of soldiers in the Bognor area was 30 June 1916, as no less than eleven local men, all volunteers, were killed in action. In all, the Royal Sussex Regiment lost a total of seventeen Officers and 349 men killed in action, with a further 1100 wounded or missing. This was the Battle of the Boars Head, which lasted less than five hours; so great was the sacrifice that 30 June 1916 is remembered as 'The Day That Sussex Died'.

In 1914, Lieutenant Colonel Claude Lowther, MP recruited and raised three 'pals' Battalions, comprising of men, all volunteers, from all over Sussex. Their training took place at Cooden Camp, near Bexhill, which was specially constructed by him for that purpose. Known as Lowther's Lambs, or the Southdowners, they also became dubbed 'pals' Battalions, evolving into the 11th, 12th and 13th Battalions of the Royal Sussex Regiment. When their training was completed they moved to France in March 1916, serving in the Fleurbaix and Festubert sectors, before taking over the trenches at Richebourg.

In early June 1916, the Southdown Battalions were pulled back for rest and recuperation, amid rumours of a large scale attack being planned, in which they were to play a key part. The Battle of the Boars Head was a 'holding attack', a diversionary action to make the German High Command believe that this was to be the location of the major offensive planned for 1916, thereby preventing them from moving troops south to the Somme, some fifty kilometres away, where the actual main offensive was to take place. The Southdown's Battalions were chosen to lead this diversionary attack; the 11th would lead with the 12th on its right and the 13th in reserve.

Lieutenant Colonel Harman Grisewood was the Commanding Officer of 11th Battalion and lived at the Den, Upper Bognor Road, Bognor, who, on seeing the plans for the assault, was convinced it would be a failure, declaring:

'I am not sacrificing my men as cannon fodder'.

For this he was sent on leave, his son, Second Lieutenant Francis Grisewood, remaining with the 11th Battalion. Lieutenant Colonel Grisewood had recently suffered the death of another of his three sons, George, *(see Roll of Honour, March 1916)*, which had affected him badly. Concerned that Colonel Grisewood's comments and removal might affect the morale of 11th Battalion, the roles of the 11th and 13th were reversed.

The 12th and 13th Battalions assembled at 0130hrs on 30 June and waited whilst an artillery bombardment took place at 0250hrs. Fifteen minutes later the first wave left the trenches and started across No Man's Land, but soon ran into trouble. A smoke cloud, planned to mask the British advance, drifted right across the front and made it impossible to see only a few yards ahead, resulting in all sense of direction being lost and devolving the attack into small bodies of men unsure as to where to go. Despite this some of the Royal Sussex reached the German trenches having bombed and bayoneted their way through, but they were small in number. In retaliation the Germans threw everything at them and for nearly three hours the Sussex Battalions faced an enormous barrage of fire, before the order to withdraw was issued.

Following their sister Battalion, the 11th, carrying ammunition, bombs, water and stretchers, were also forced to withdraw, the No Man's Land being littered with great numbers of dead and wounded men, who could not be recovered until darkness fell late in the evening. The 13th Battalion, who led the attack, were virtually wiped out.

That day proved to be the costliest in terms of lives lost that the Lowthers Lambs suffered throughout the whole war, impacting on many Sussex communities whose men folk volunteered together, only to die together. The local men were:

Sergeant SD657 Albert Edward CUTLER
South Stoke, Sussex
Southdown's Battalion, the Royal Sussex Regiment, 39th Division
Killed in Action on 30 June 1916

Although this soldier was not a local resident, he was well known in the town as 'a smart young Police Officer' who had served in Bognor for some considerable time. When war was declared he enlisted at Bognor, fighting and dying alongside many local men. His death was reported in the *Bognor Observer*.

Private SD1331 Peter FULLER
The Nook, Felpham, Bognor
12th Battalion, the Royal Sussex Regiment, 39th Division
Killed in Action on 30 June 1916
Aged 26
Buried in the Cabaret Rouge British Cemetery, France

One of seven children born to farm labourer George and his wife, Charity, Peter was born in Sea Lane, Ferring. At this time Peter's father was employed as a shepherd. Peter volunteered at Bognor into 12th Battalion, Royal Sussex Regiment and was reported as missing on 30 June 1916. The next six months must have been the worst his parents had experienced, as they did not know whether he was missing, dead or possibly a prisoner of war. It was not until January 1917 that they received notification he had been killed in action on that day.

Second Lieutenant Francis J M GRISEWOOD
The Den, Bognor
11th Battalion, the Royal Sussex Regiment, 39th Division
Killed in Action on 30 June 1916
Aged 34
Commemorated on the Loos Memorial, Pas de Calais, France

The second of Lieutenant Colonel Harman Grisewood three sons, Second Lieutenant Francis Grisewood had emigrated to Australia a few years earlier, where he was a mining engineer and owned a large ranch. On the outbreak of war he returned to England immediately and was gazetted into 11th Battalion, the Royal Sussex Regiment, becoming the Adjutant and later the Field Works Officer. In that fateful attack, Francis was one of seventeen Officers killed in action. He was buried where he fell.

Sergeant SD769 George Edward MAY
Alverton, Linden Road, Bognor
11th Battalion, the Royal Sussex Regiment, 39th Division
Killed in Action on 30 June 1916
Aged 20
Buried in the St Vaast Post Military Cemetery, Richebourg, France

The son of Sergeant and Mrs Sophia May, George (junior) was born in India where his father was serving as a 'rough riding Sergeant' with 18th Hussars *(see Roll of Honour, July 1915)*. The report of his death did not reach Bognor until the following month.

'It is stated that Sergeant George May, the son of the late Sergeant Major May has been killed in the recent fighting. He was in one of the Southdown's Battalions that lost heavily. His father was well known in Bognor, where he resided at Swansea House and organized the Bognor Boys'.

Private SD819 Arthur Thomas MITCHELL
Laburnam Cottages, North Bersted, Bognor
11th Battalion, the Royal Sussex Regiment, 39th Division
Killed in Action on 30 June 1916
Aged 18
Commemorated on the Loos Memorial, Pas de Calais, France

Brothers Arthur and William Mitchell enlisted together and carried consecutive Army numbers. The sons of Mr and Mrs Mitchell, they both served with 11th Battalion the Royal Sussex Regiment.

Arthur was reported missing on 30 June 1916. His brother, William, said at the time that they were together until that day, but then 'by a stroke of bad luck' they were parted before the attack began and Arthur had not been heard of since. In July, William sent a letter to the *Bognor Observer*, announcing his belief that Arthur had been killed a month before his 19th birthday, but this was not confirmed until 30 December 1916.

Lance-Corporal SD4233 Albert Frederick PAIGE
2 Church Cottages, South Bersted, Bognor
13th Battalion, the Royal Sussex Regiment, 39th Division
Killed in Action on 30 June 1916
Aged 28
Buried in the St Vaast Military Cemetery, France

The son of Mr and Mrs Paige and the husband of Alice, Alfred Paige enlisted into 13th Battalion, Royal Sussex Regiment. Alfred was initially reported missing, but his wife soon learned that he had been killed 'by a bayonet wound to the heart'.

A letter from his Captain stated:
'He died while bravely attacking the German trenches. He was a fine man and on the way to promotion'.

Second Lieutenant Lewis Atkins PRIOR
c/o Tresco, Sudley Road, Bognor
13th Battalion, the Royal Sussex Regiment, 39th Division
Killed in Action on 30 June 1916
Aged 34
Commemorated on the Loos Memorial, Pas de Calais, France

Little has been gleaned from the records regarding Lewis Prior. It appears that before the war he was serving in North Borneo as a Constabulary Officer, returning in 1915 to enlist. Lewis was then commissioned into 13th Battalion, the Royal Sussex Regiment and betrothed to Miss Mackenzie, of Sudley Road. In July 1916 his sister received the following letter:

'It is with great regret I have to tell you your brother is missing and that there is absolutely nothing known as to his fate. When we attacked the enemy on 30 June it was rather dark and we captured part of his trenches. The last anybody saw of your brother, was just after the capturing of the enemy first line and he was then lost sight of in the darkness and confusion and was never seen again. He was a most gallant Officer and one whom we can ill spare'.

Lance-Corporal SD3225 Henry Charles SCOTT MM
15 Steyne Street, Bognor
13th Battalion, the Royal Sussex Regiment, 39th Division
Killed in Action on 30 June 1916
Aged 34
Buried in the St Vaast Military Cemetery, France

Henry Scott lived with his wife and two children and worked for Messrs Reynolds & Co of the High Street. The only son of general labourer William and his wife Eliza, of Belmont Street, Bognor, Henry grew up in St John's Street with his three sisters and enlisted at Bognor in December 1914. Lance Corporal Scott soon made his mark, being awarded the Military Medal for erecting wire entanglements and cutting the German wire for a raid on the succeeding night; he was engaged in this work with an Officer for nearly four hours, at great risk. As a result of the work the raid was successfully achieved with the loss of only a few wounded and none killed. Henry Scott did not live to receive his Military Medal, which was forwarded to his widow, or to hear of his promotion to Lance Corporal.

Back in Bognor his widow received the following letter from Major Roberts, of the Royal Sussex Regiment:

'I have just seen that your husband has been killed in action. I am sure you will forgive me writing to you but I must write to tell you how grieved I was to hear of his death and also to tell you of the high respect I had for his personal qualities as a soldier. It may interest you to know that on three occasions your husband was in my Platoon and on three occasions we went out on reconnaissance together. He proved to be perfectly cool and absolutely without fear and so was of the greatest assistance. I am also glad to hear that his gallantry has been officially recognized, though it is bitter luck to know that he did not receive his well merited reward. On this occasion your husband and I were again together and spent the whole night cutting the enemy's barbed wire and you can judge the nature of the work when I mention that the enemy's sentry group were within twenty feet of us the whole time and we could hear them coughing and talking. Only the long grass saved us from being discovered. On the next night when we raided the enemy your husband's good spirits quite buoyed us all up and made us feel confident in ourselves, while the enemy's trenches were entered and I had the misfortune to be wounded. I remember that Private Scott helped in carrying me to our trenches again. It is for these reasons that I have written to tell you how very sorry I am and ask you to accept my sincere sympathy in your loss'.

Private SD3015 Albert SMITH
Address Unknown
13th Battalion, the Royal Sussex Regiment, 39th Division
Killed in Action on 30 June 1916
Age Unknown
Buried in the Cabaret Rouge British Cemetery, France

Albert Smith was born in Bognor and enlisted in Chichester into 13th Battalion the Royal Sussex Regiment. On 23 July 1916 he was reported as missing, but he had in fact been injured and died of his wounds received on 30 June 1916.

Private SD3260 Herbert Edwin Thomas WALTERS
2 Limmer Lane, Felpham, Bognor
13th Battalion, the Royal Sussex Regiment, 39th Division
Killed in Action on 30 June 1916
Aged 28
Buried in the Cabaret Rouge British Cemetery, France

The second son of Ephraim and Sarah Walters of North Bersted, Herbert was born in Pagham and lived in Felpham with his wife, Emily and their young son, also Herbert. A bricklayer, Herbert was employed by the Railway Company before volunteering in 1914.

Lance Corporal SD1772 Robert Henry LUCAS
Laburnam Cottages, North Bersted, Bognor
12th Battalion, the Royal Sussex Regiment, 39th Division
Died of Wounds on 1 July 1916
Aged 23
Buried in the Merville Communal Cemetery, France

Robert was born in Brighton, the eldest son of Robert and Mary Lucas. His father was a bricklayer and although some years older than his wife, he became a widower. Robert (junior) was their third child and the eldest of three sons, who on leaving school was a milk roundsman in Brighton. By 1914 he was living in the Bognor area having married local girl, Lily Keates. When war was declared, Robert enlisted in Bognor into the Royal Sussex Regiment and rose to the rank of Lance Corporal. Lily received a letter from him which Robert had written a week or two earlier, describing how he had met up with his brother 'and the other Bognor Boys' one night:

'They all seemed to be in good health and spirits, but would like to be back in dear old Bognor again', he wrote.

Robert was destined never to see Bognor again; in fact, although his wife did not know it at the time of receiving the letter, Robert was already dead, succumbing to wounds received the previous day in that horrendous battle.

THE SOMME

The Somme had been planned following discussions in December 1915, in which the Allies agreed on a concerted offensive against the Germans. This was to be the Anglo-French contribution, intended to create a rupture in the German line which would be followed by a decisive blow; instead it became an indiscriminate slaughter from the start. When the whistles blew and British troops climbed out of their trenches and began walking slowly towards the German lines their machine guns opened up and the casualties mounted. The Allied artillery which for a week previously had pounded the German positions with around one and half million shells had failed to break their defences; the Germans stayed underground and waited for the attack. When it came they simply left their bunkers, set up their positions and opened fire. The British suffered catastrophic losses and as the summer weather turned to an autumn quagmire and with the onset of winter the Somme Offensive ground to a halt. During the Offensive many separate battles were fought and over fifty local men lost their lives on the Somme, with many more wounded.

Private G7230 William James SKEITES
Chapel Cottage, Flansham, Felpham
9th Battalion, the Royal Sussex Regiment, 24th Division
Killed in Action on 2 July 1916
Aged 22
Buried in the Dranoutre Military Cemetery, Belgium

The son of farm labourer James and Annie Skeites, William had seven brothers and sisters and was born in Flansham, Felpham. On leaving school he joined his father working as a labourer on a local farm, before enlisting at Bognor into the Royal Sussex Regiment. William was killed in action on the Somme on the second day of the battle.

Lance Corporal G617 John Edward NEW
Woodbine Cottage, Upper Bognor Road, Bognor
7th Battalion, the Royal Sussex Regiment, 12th Division
Killed in Action on 7 July 1916
Aged 17
Commemorated on the Thiepval Memorial, France

John New was born and bought up in Felpham. His father, Robert, was a farm carter, whilst his mother looked after their four children, of whom John was the youngest. The family at some time moved into Bognor. On leaving school John became a gardener, but enlisted early in the war, although he was almost certainly underage.

The 7 July was a hard day for the 7th Royal Sussex, attacking the village of Ovilliers. The Germans were aware of the impending attack and launched a heavy artillery barrage before the Sussex went 'over the top'. Although they achieved two of their three objectives, the Battalion suffered their highest number of deaths for any single day of the war. Lance Corporal John New was initially reported missing, but letters home from his comrades gave every reason for his family to fear he had been killed, which was confirmed a few days later.

Lance Corporal G1594 Charles Edmund CAIGER
Bersted House, South Bersted, Bognor
8th Battalion, the Royal Sussex Regiment, 18th Division
Killed in Action on 13 July 1916
Aged 28
Commemorated on the Thiepval Memorial, Pas de Calais, France

The Caiger family hailed from Walberton and later Aldingbourne, where in the 1840s two brothers were talented flint and brick builders and were responsible for several buildings which still stand today in Woodgate, notably the original Woodgate Railway Station and the Prince of Wales Public House. Charles' father Alfred, was born in Westergate and after marrying Ellen evidently moved to Newhaven, possibly due to military service, where Charles was born in 1889. Charles was the eldest of four children; he had two brothers, Edwin and James and a sister, Ellen. The family had moved to South Bersted by the late 1890s, where Alfred became a chimney sweep, a business which was still thriving at the outbreak of war, when Charles was his assistant. Charles had been a choir boy at South Bersted Church and was a founder member of the South Bersted Cricket Club; he was also well known in Bognor as a member of the Ancient Order of Foresters and the Buffaloes. He enlisted at Worthing into the Royal Sussex Regiment, his Battalion arriving in France in July 1915.

After the initial attack on 1 July, his Battalion enjoyed a few days welcome rest at a safe distance from the fighting, before going into action again on 13 July 1916. Their task was to capture Trones Wood and consolidate a line to link up with the French. This they did and this was where 'he met his death in the glorious advance in which the Battalion bore a noted part'. It was another day of heavy casualties, the Battalion War Diary recording 'three Officers and twenty four men killed, with eighty five wounded and eight missing'.

Gunner 62238 Cecil Stanley JONES
Crescent Cottages, South Bersted, Bognor
20th Trench Mortar Battery, the Royal Garrison Artillery
Died of Wounds on 14 July 1916
Aged 34
Buried in the Bognor Town Cemetery, West Sussex

Stanley Jones had married a daughter of Mary Wheatland, Bognor's famous bathing machine lady. They had two children and Stanley was working as a gardener for Mrs

Daubney, of The Mulberries, Bersted Street, before enlisting and serving with the Royal Garrison Artillery. He died of wounds in Netley Hospital, Southampton on 14 July 1916, having been evacuated from the battlefield. His Death Certificate reveals just how badly wounded he was, his cause of death being:

1) Gunshot wounds to the right and left arm, right buttocks and right leg amputated.
2) Septicaemia.

His funeral service took place from home, his widow and young family leading the sad procession from South Bersted Church where the first part of the service was held 'in the presence of a large number of sympathisers', to Bognor Cemetery, where Gunner Jones was laid to rest.

Lieutenant John Doria HAVILAND
The Dutch House, Campbell Road, Bognor
10th Battalion, the Royal Fusiliers, 18th Division
Killed in Action on 16 July 1916
Aged 34
Buried in the Heilly Station Cemetery, France

The only son of John Haviland, a solicitor and Bognor County Councillor and his wife, Helen, John (junior) was born in Northampton, where his father was practising. He grew up with his three sisters, looked after by a Governess; the family also employed three servants. The 1911 Census shows John living as a boarder at Torrington Square, Bloomsbury, London, his occupation being shown as a 'gentleman'.

At the outbreak of war John re-enlisted into the Royal Fusiliers, City of London Regiment, having previously served in the Boar War. He was wounded and invalided home as reported in the *Bognor Observer:*

'He sustained a stomach wound in October 1915 whilst fighting with one of the new regiments of that Battalion. We understand that the wound is not of a serious nature and the Lieutenant hopes to be well again shortly. He served with the mounted cavalry in the last Zulu Campaign in South Africa'.

After a period of compassionate leave in 1916, following the sudden death of his father, he returned to the Front.

'He could not have returned to duty more than a few days 'ere he met his own death', lamented the *Bognor Observer*, 'killed with a bayonet thrust near the heart. He was a fine man and on his way to rapid promotion. The double bereavement of a family so well known and respected in the town has evoked the greatest sympathy'.

John was killed in action on 16 July 1916, his Commanding Officer writing to his mother thus:

'I take the first opportunity to write and offer you my deepest sympathy on the death of your gallant son, my dear friend and brother Officer. From the very first he showed extraordinary ability, judgement and daring, his loss is quite irreparable. What must it be to you? I was greatly distressed when he left me in September and rejoiced in his return. Since then he has been invaluable. He practically lived outside the wire and kept watch on every movement of the enemy. In an attack yesterday he was wounded in the hand, I ordered him to the rear, but he declined to go and remained with his men under severe fire. He was eventually hit in the right lung and was brought to me. He asked to see me and we talked for ten minutes and I told him I appreciated everything he had done. As usual he was gloriously plucky and uncomplaining and was then carried off to the rear where he was well looked after. I may say he received immediate attention and every care at once, his wounds being dressed in my presence. I grieve to tell you that he died this morning, 16 July, mourned by everyone in the Battalion. He was a splendid and gallant soldier of whom England may well be proud of. He was among the very best and bravest and is buried at Heilly, about three miles south west of Albert'.

Lance Corporal G3224 Albert Edward WILLIAMS
Aldwick Lodge Cottage, Aldwick Road, Pagham
4th Battalion, the Royal Fusiliers
Killed in Action on 18 July 1916
Aged 30
Commemorated on the Thiepval Memorial, the Somme, France

The son of Pritchard and Mary Williams, Albert was born in Pagham, his father being employed as a stockman/domestic servant, who died in 1902. Albert was the youngest of three sons, he also had four sisters. On leaving school Albert also became a stockman. Albert volunteered in 1914, enlisting at Barnet into the Royal Fusiliers, City of London Regiment, losing his life on the Somme.

Private G6950 Sidney Edgar BROWN
4 Franklin Terrace, Highfield Road
2nd Battalion, the Royal Sussex Regiment, 1st Division
Killed in Action on 23 July 1916
Aged 22
Commemorated on the Thiepval Memorial, Pas de Calais, France

Frederick, a railway ganger and his wife Charlotte Brown had eleven children, seven of whom died in infancy. The surviving four were two girls and two sons, Horace *(see Roll of Honour, May 1917)* and Sidney, who both gave their lives for their Country. Sidney was four years older than Horace and was employed by Webster and Webb at their printing works in Lennox Street, where he was 'very esteemed by his employer and fellow employees'. He enlisted into the Royal Sussex Regiment in May 1915 and fought at the Battle of Loos, where he was seriously wounded and following lengthy hospital treatment was sent back to Bognor for convalescence.

Having recovered, he rejoined his Regiment at the Somme where the British attempted to capture the Munster Alley communication trench. A 'tremendous bomb fight took place, but on the day only a small section of trench had been secured'.

Sidney, aged 22, fell that day.

Private 45588 William George GIBBS
Lilianet, Belmont Street, Bognor
The Royal Army Medical Corps
Died on 26 July 1916
Aged 25
Buried in La Neuville British Cemetery, Corbie, France

William was one of three sons born to Bognor Urban Councillor, George William and Mrs Ada Gibbs. The family had moved from Norwood in Surrey. Prior to enlisting at Chichester into the Royal Army Medical Corps, William lived with his wife Ethel Mary in Guildford, where he was employed as a stationer's assistant. He is reported to 'have died' on 26 July 1916.

Private SP2417 Randolph Spencer LOIBL
West Bognor
The Royal Fusiliers
Died of Wounds on 28 July 1916
Aged 21

Randolph was born in Maida Vale, Paddington in 1896. The 1901 Census shows that he was living with his four sisters and older brother in the care of an aunt and five servants, two of whom were nurses, plus a parlour maid, housemaid and cook. The family, obviously wealthy, sent Randolph to Cranleigh School, Surrey as a boarder. On leaving school he went to Canada, returning on the SS *Scotian* in September 1914, his occupation, according to the passenger listings being a farmer. He then enlisted into the Royal Fusiliers. At some stage his family moved to Bognor, his sisters living in Aldwick and soon became established entertainers, giving many performances in aid of wounded soldiers.

Randolph's death was reported in the *Bognor Observer* in August 1916:

'Among those who have suffered bereavement are the Misses Loibl of West Bognor, whose brother was killed in action on 28 July. Much sympathy will be felt for the young ladies who have worked zealously in theatrical entertainment on behalf of war charities and in entertaining wounded soldiers'.

Private Randolph Loibl's name does not appear on the Bognor or Pagham War Memorials.

Sergeant G F YOUNG DCM
18 Council Cottages, Bognor
The Royal Sussex Regiment, Battalion Unknown
Killed in action in August 1916
Age Unknown

The brother of Mrs Sharpe, of 18 Council Cottages, Bognor, Sergeant Young 'had fought his way in most of the big engagements on the Western Front'. Serving with the Royal Sussex Regiment, Sergeant Young had received rapid promotion due to his 'kindness as an NCO and his bravery and ability in the field. He was leading his Platoon in his usual way when he was killed'.

Sergeant Young had previously been awarded the Distinguished Conduct Medal for Gallantry in the Field at Loos. He had joined up at the outbreak of war and was killed in action in August 1916, after having just returned to the Front, following a rest break at home. His three brothers were also doing their bit.

Private GS182 Ernest Henry SHAWYER
Meka Cottage, South Bersted, Bognor
7th Battalion, the Royal Sussex Regiment, 2nd Division
Killed in Action on 1 August 1916
Aged 36
Commemorated on the Thiepval Memorial, France

Ernest Shawyer and his twin brother, Edward were the second sons of Albert and his wife, Charlotte. At the time of his birth the family were living in Bedford Street, Bognor, before moving to Meka Cottage, South Bersted. His mother was employed at some time as a laundress, whilst his father was a groom and coachman. Ernest was one of the first to volunteer and enlist at Chichester into the Royal Sussex Regiment, on 12 August 1914, his Battalion moving to France in May 1915, experiencing considerable fighting during that year and the start of 1916. During a period away from the Front in May, the Battalion suffered from an outbreak of measles and many men were inoculated. Ernest was killed on the Somme, in the fighting for Mouquet Farm, almost two years to the day that he enlisted. At the time the Battalion were occupying trenches to the east of Pozieres and on 1 August suffered a number of casualties from both shell and sniper fire, of which Private Shawyer was one.

Private 8158 William Richard NORRIS
4 Sea Road, Felpham, Bognor
2nd Battalion, the Hampshire Regiment, 29th Division
Died of Wounds on 9 August 1916
Aged 26
Buried in the Lijssenthoek Military Cemetery, Belgium

The son of Richard and Edith Norris, Richard jnr, a regular soldier, had enlisted at Bognor into the Hampshire Regiment before 1911. The 2nd Battalion were moved to France in March 1916, landing at Marseilles and proceeding to the Western Front. Three months later they were taking part in the Somme Offensive, where on 9 August William died from wounds.

A letter from Captain W L Archer, the Church of England Chaplain at 3rd Canadian Casualty Clearing Station, dated 10 August, gave his parents details of his death:

'You will have already received the sad news of the death of your son William, of the Hampshire Regiment. It was to our hospital that he was bought after the gas attack on

Tuesday night, but from the first it was evident that nothing we could do would save him. Very soon he passed away, almost unconscious, to the rest he so bravely earned. We have laid his body away at our Cemetery on the Poerinlgle-Boeschepe Road where his grave will be marked with a cross. I know how sad you will be, but even in your sorrow you will be proud to remember how bravely your boy gave himself in devotion to his Country and for its sake. His life is not thrown away it is given in a worthy cause. Please accept my very sincere sympathy'.

Lance Corporal G2842 Bernard George LAMPARD
Lyon Street, Bognor
9th (Service) Battalion, the Essex Regiment, 12th Division
Died of Wounds on 13 August 1916
Aged 28
Commemorated on the Thiepval Memorial, France

Born in Lenham, Maidstone, Kent, Bernard and his brother and sister were initially bought up by their grandparents; however, by 1901 Bernard had been placed in the Infant Orphanage in Wanstead, Essex. On leaving there he became a book keeper, living as a boarder in Clapham, London. At the outbreak of war Bernard enlisted into the 9th Battalion the Essex Regiment, in which County he had spent a lot of his childhood, the Battalion being formed at Warley in August 1914. After training at Shorncliffe and Aldershot, the Battalion landed at Boulogne on 31 May 1915. Four Battalions of the Essex Regiment fought at the Somme, where Lance Corporal Lampard died of wounds.

Although he was registered to an orphanage, later information states he was the son of Mr and Mrs Bernard Lampard of Lyon Street, Bognor.

Gunner 555 Charles STRUDWICK
5 Market Street, Bognor
1/1st Wessex Heavy Battery, the Royal Garrison Artillery
Died at Home on 14 August 1916
Aged 20
Buried in the East Dean Churchyard, Sussex

'Charles Strudwick joined up at the commencement of the war and was wounded in the leg and sent home to hospital. He had only been back at the Front a few weeks. He is in the Field Hospital at Calais'.

Having recovered he rejoined his unit and was again reported wounded in July 1916, this time in the head and was invalided home, where he passed away a few weeks later.

Private L 9064 Hugh Frank BEER
Clyde Road, Felpham, Bognor
2nd Battalion, the Royal Sussex Regiment, 1st Division
Killed in Action on 17 August 1916
Aged 21
Commemorated on the Thiepval Memorial, France

Hugh, *(related to Frank Beer, see Roll of Honour 4 October 1917)* the son of general labourer, Francis and his wife Clara, was a regular soldier who had been was serving with the Royal Sussex Regiment since 1911. In 1915 he wrote the following letter home:

'We have just finished a month's rest after a glorious advance and are now in the trenches again. We are all quite happy here and none the worse for the mud. Mr Shippam, of St John's Terrace, Highfield Road and I have just been looking at your last week's edition *(Bognor Observer)* and are both very sorry to hear about Sergeant Wilson. There are several Bognor fellows out here and I am sure the people at home have not forgotten them. We have been running up and down the trenches all day trying to dodge the German shells, but there were no casualties, the shells went all wide. At present the boys are singing to a mouth organ, so you can guess we are not downhearted, but still hoping the war will end. This is both mine and Mr Shippams second time out here. We have just had a very good experience of shell fire, seventeen of us were told to draw rations and water. We got to the appointed place and just as we were coming away they started to shell us, there was a general stampede for ten minutes. Luckily no one was hit and we all got back safely'.

It was not long after that letter that Hugh was wounded, when a shell shattered his knee in April 1915 and he was invalided home. He was back with his Regiment the following year and was subsequently killed in action at Bazentin le Petit on 17 August 1916. On that day the Germans made 'a determined counter attack' in which they used flame throwers and hand grenades. Casualties amongst the Royal Sussex numbered some thirty men killed on that day.

Second Lieutenant Evelyn BLECK
33 Bedford Gardens, Camden Hill, London
The Machine Gun Corps
Killed in Action on 18 August 1916
Aged 20
Buried in the Guillemont Road Cemetery, Somme, France

Second Lieutenant Evelyn Louis Bleck, of the Machine Gun Corps, was the eldest son of Edward Charles Bleck, CMG, librarian and keeper of the papers at the Foreign Office and his wife Helen Laura Bleck, the daughter of the late Captain Stuart Ogilvy. He was educated at Middleton School, Bognor and Marlborough, where he obtained his school colours for rugby, football and hockey. From there he was due to go to King's College, Cambridge, had the war not intervened.

At the outbreak of war Evelyn obtained a commission in the East Surrey Regiment, subsequently transferring to the Machine Gun Corps. A brother Officer wrote to his parents:

'Your boy has done consistent good work with the Company ever since he joined us. He was hit by a shell while getting to his position. He was awfully unlucky and the Company will find it hard to find another Section Commander so calm and brave, so thoughtful to his men, so painstaking and keen as your son'.

Private G7752 William John JONES
Flansham Lane, Felpham, Bognor
9th Battalion, the Royal Sussex Regiment, 24th Division
Killed in Action on 18 August 1916
Aged 20
Commemorated on the Thiepval Memorial, France

A son of 'jobbing gardener' Frederick and Ruth Jones, William was one of seven children. He was born at Oving and enlisted in Bognor into the Royal Sussex Regiment. On 17 August 1916, the 9th Battalion were involved in an attack on the village of Guillemont, alongside 7th Northamptonshire's, the 9th Sussex due to follow up in a further attack at 0500hrs the next day. However, events did not go as planned, with the Northamptonshire's losing heavily in hand to hand fighting, causing 9th Sussex to be called in a day early as reinforcements, taking considerable casualties. The following day further British reinforcements were drafted in and 9th Sussex were withdrawn, having lost nearly two hundred men, including Private William Jones, who was initially reported as missing.

Private L945 Sidney OAKMAN
Lawrence Villa, Canada Grove, Bognor
2nd Battalion, the Royal Sussex Regiment, 1st Division
Killed in Action on 18 August 1916
Aged 26
Buried in the Maroc Cemetery, Pas de Calais, France

A soldier in the Royal Sussex Regiment, Private Oakman was attached to 107th Field Company the Royal Engineers. Sidney Oakman was born in Hastings and enlisted at Arundel. His wife received the following letter from Captain E Bryde of the Royal Engineers:

'It is with great regret that we hear of the death of your husband. He had been working under me for a very short time, but had done good work with another section and he will be greatly missed by his comrades. He was killed instantaneously so that he suffered no pain. He was hit by a rifle grenade, just as he was coming out of a dugout, in a very well protected part of the front line. He was buried at night in a graveyard about a mile behind the Front and his grave will be numbered and registered and as well as the official cross we shall erect another. About thirty of his comrades attended the funeral as well as myself and the service was read by a Chaplain of the Middlesex Regiment. It was an occasion fitting for the burial of a soldier killed in action at the dead of night, with the bullets singing overhead, but quite still. As soon as the service was over a heavy bombardment started for many miles along the Front. We all offer you our sincerest sympathy in your bereavement. 'Your Country is proud of the men who give up their lives for it and prouder still of the wives who give their loved ones to make the greatest sacrifice for King and Country'.

Sidney had married his wife, Phyllis, in the spring of 1913 and at the beginning of the war was called up as a Reservist and had been in France since August 1914.

Second Lieutenant Harold Charles PAWSEY
40 Alexandra Park Road, Muswell Hill, London
1/4th Battalion, the Suffolk Regiment
Killed in Action on 18 August 1916
Aged 38
Buried in the Caterpillar Valley Cemetery, France

Serving with 4th Suffolk Regiment, Harold Pawsey's death was reported in the *Bognor Observer* as follows:

'It is with much regret we have to report the death of Second Lieutenant Harold Pawsey, who was killed in action on 18 August 1916, whilst leading his men towards the German trenches. Mr Pawsey was a man of singularly charming manner and his death will be deeply felt by a large circle of friends and acquaintances in Bognor. He leaves a young wife and three sons'.

His Colonel wrote to his wife confirming Harold's death:

'D Company, of which he was serving, took heavy casualties. Harold, his Company and another were the only portions of the force to enter the German trench where they, however, could not remain unsupported. He was gallantly leading his men into action when he was killed by a bullet. He died without pain, his last words to his Sergeant were 'carry on'. He died the death of a hero fighting for those he loved best'.

Harold's roots went back to Suffolk, where his father, Arthur was a ship repairer in the 1880s and 90s. Before enlisting Harold was a colliery agent and lived with Beatrice, his wife and their two young sons, Donald and Owen, in a large ten roomed house in London. His connection with Bognor has not been established.

Second Lieutenant Stewart Francis HUMPHREYS
Cottesmore, Gordon Avenue, Bognor
14th Battalion, the Royal Fusiliers
Killed in Action on 26 August 1916
Aged 24
Buried in the Thistle Dump Cemetery, High Wood, Longueval, France

At the outbreak of war Second Lieutenant Humphreys enlisted with the Sussex Yeomanry, in the ranks, but after a year in France was sent home for his commission in the Royal Fusiliers. During his training he was sent to Ireland to help quell the Dublin Rebellion. He had only been back in France a few weeks when he was killed on 26 August 1916. A letter to his parents explained:

'During a very difficult task the Battalion had to perform, of clearing the ground, he was shot, whilst cheerfully encouraging his men. It is hard that he should fall, as in him we have lost one of our promising young Officers'.

Stewart's father, William, was a property surveyor, a career that Stewart was also following when the war intervened. He was Mentioned in Despatches a few weeks before his death.

Sergeant Andrew PATTERSON
Address Unknown
The Scots Guards, the Guards Division
Killed in Action on 26 August 1916
Aged 34
Buried in the Poperinghe New Military Cemetery, Belgium

Bognor policeman Andrew Patterson went back to his roots by enlisting into the Scots Guards. Having spent a short while back in Bognor on leave in July 1916, Andrew returned to the Front and was killed in action a few weeks later on 26 August. No other information has come to light for Sergeant Patterson.

Private G508 George GARDNER
2 The Villas, Linden Road, Bognor
9th Battalion, the Royal Sussex Regiment, 24th Division
Killed in Action on 31 August 1916
Aged 27
Commemorated on the Thiepval Memorial, Pas de Calais, France

'The village of Shripney must be proud of the heroic death of Private George Gardner, who was previously in the employ of Mr Edward Hogben when he volunteered at the outbreak of war', wrote the *Bognor Observer* in February 1917. It had taken nearly six months for his death to be confirmed.

Private Gardner was born in Tonbridge, Kent, the son of laundryman, George and the late Mrs Gardner, of Shripney and had enlisted at Chichester. His heroic actions were described in a letter to his father from his Platoon Commander:

'It is with deepest regret I have to announce to you the death of your son, killed in action. It was on the morning of the 31 August 1916, about noon, when a formidable attack was launched by the Prussian Guard against our line, which gave way and the Huns broke through. Your son was in my Platoon, which was in support and we were called upon to reinforce. Your son was the first ready and the first over the top, his courage inspiring others who were hanging back. We took up position in front of the charging enemy and held them up until reserves came up. In the meantime your son was sniped through the head and his death was instantaneous. He was buried where he fell by the Platoon Sergeant and a little cross marks the place where a brave man fell. The deeds of these heroic little bands of men, in all not more than eighty of them, who held up more than 500 of the enemy, should go down in the annals of history. I enclose his pocket book and a postal order for the amount of 10 shillings, which was found on him in French money. Again let me condole with you for the loss of such a son, a man who was always popular in the Platoon and who died such a glorious death'.

The operation described above accounted for thirty men killed and eighty wounded.

Sergeant L10063 James Greenwood HORNIBROOK
2 St Catherine's, Felpham, Bognor
8th Battalion, the Royal West Kent Regiment
Killed in Action on 1 September 1916
Aged 21
Commemorated on the Thiepval Memorial, France

'News has been received of the death in action of Sergeant James Greenwood Hornibrook, of the Royal West Kent Regiment, who lived at Felpham. He had been in the regular Army and had fought in many of the big engagements of the war on the Western Front', reported the *Bognor Observer.*

'He was very brave and capable and at the same time very modest and unassuming', wrote his Lieutenant. 'He was the first man in the Company I should have thought of if any special work had to be done and I should have complete confidence in his carrying it out well. I believe he would have gone far if he had been spared'.

James Greenwood was the stepson of retired Naval Lieutenant Francis Hornibrook and his wife, Priscilla. A baker's errand boy, on leaving school James enlisted at Chichester into Royal West Kent Regiment.

(Step brother of Sergeant Cornelius Hornibrook, see Roll of Honour, September 1916)

Second Lieutenant Thomas Campbell TATE
Richmond Road, Bognor
12th Battalion, the Royal Sussex Regiment, 39th Division
Killed in Action on 2 September 1916
Aged 23
Buried in the Coin British Cemetery, France

Second Lieutenant Thomas Tate died in hospital in France on 2 September, of wounds sustained. He refused a Commission at the beginning of the war but rather to serve in the ranks with the East Surrey Regiment, rising to the rank of Corporal. In May 1915 he was gazetted into the Royal Sussex Regiment.

'Many people in Bognor will be pleased to hear of the promotion of Corporal TC Tate from the East Surrey Regiment, to Second Lieutenant in the Royal Sussex Regiment. He is the son of William Tate, one of Bognor's best known and respected townsmen and a former Chairman of the Urban Council'.

His first action with the Royal Sussex took him to Ireland to help quell the troubles there. From there he was posted to France and on 1 September took part in a major attack involving 11th, 12th and 13th Battalions Royal Sussex Regiment in the area of Beaumont Hamel and Beaucourt-sur-L'Ancre. The attack ended in a withdrawal costing several hundred lives. Second Lieutenant Thomas Tate was seriously wounded and died the following day in hospital.

Private 21021 James BONIFACE
Kent Cottage, Essex Road, Bognor
8th Battalion, Royal Berkshire Regiment, 18th Division
Killed in Action on 3 September 1916
Age 38
Commemorated on the Thiepval Cemetery, France

James, the fourth son of Robert and Fanny Boniface, was born in South Bersted, the family living in Sheepwash Lane. At the time Robert was a gardener before eventually becoming the landlord of the Queen Victoria Inn in Bersted Street. Having attended South Bersted School, James joined his brother Robert and family in Birmingham, where he worked in a timber yard before moving back to Bognor. He lived with his wife and family in Essex Road.

James enlisted into the Royal Berkshire Regiment, which was formed at Reading in September 1914. Following training at Salisbury Plain and back at Reading the Battalion moved to France in August 1915. During the next twelve months they suffered heavy casualties, fighting in France, Flanders and then the Somme, where Private James Boniface was killed in action.

Corporal SD1225 George Leno FARLEY
17 Ockley Road, Bognor
12th Battalion, the Royal Sussex Regiment, 39th Division
Died of Wounds on 4 September 1916
Aged 27
Buried in the Couin British Cemetery, France

A Bognorian, George Farley was the son of William, a bricklayer and his wife Mary and grew up in Scott Street. When war broke out he enlisted at Bognor into the Royal Sussex Regiment in 1914, leaving his wife and two young children at home. It was there that Mrs Farley learned of the death of her husband in 1916. He suffered horrific wounds fighting on the Somme, from which he died, his left arm having being blown off and the whole of his left side 'terribly injured'.

A letter from his Commanding Officer arrived a few days later:

'I am sorry to say that your husband Corporal Farley died of wounds received in an attack on 4 September. His loss is a heavy one for all the Company. He was a most excellent soldier and I had, shortly before his death, recommended him for promotion to Corporal. He died a gallant death and I am deeply sorry to lose him'.

Sergeant 6150 Cornelius G HORNIBROOK
2 St Catherine's, Felpham, Sussex
2nd Battalion, the Royal Munster Fusiliers, 1st Division
Killed in Action on 8 September 1916
Age 22
Commemorated on the Thiepval Memorial, France

Cornelius Hornibrook *(step brother of James Greenwood Hornibrook, see Roll of Honour, September 1916)* was born in Cork, Ireland and enlisted at Kinsale into 2nd Battalion the Royal Munster Fusiliers. Before enlisting he lived with his mother, Priscilla at 2 St Catherine's, Felpham. His father, Francis, a retired Royal Navy Officer, passed away shortly before the outbreak of war. On leaving school Cornelius had become an errand boy, before working for Mr Dadswell, the engineer, at his premises in 56 High Street, Bognor.

Sergeant Hornibrook was killed on the Somme on 8 September 1916. In a letter to his mother his Commanding Officer paid 'a high tribute to his abilities as a soldier'. Sadly his mother never read those words of comfort, for she had passed away 'while the Sergeant was fighting'.

Sergeant SD3052 William George YEATMAN
Odessa Cottage, Sheepwash Lane, Bognor
13th Battalion, the Royal Sussex Regiment, 39th Division
Died of Wounds on 12 September 1916
Aged 38
Buried in the Coin British Cemetery, France

William Yeatman lived with Alice, his wife and their three children. Like his brother Albert (*see Roll of Honour, September 1914*) William also worked in the International Stores, before enlisting and was 'well known and esteemed by his friends'.

He died of wounds received on 12 September 1916. During the week of his death his Battalion had been engaged in improving their front line trenches and repairing them, where heavy rains had caused them to collapse. All this was whilst they were under heavy trench mortar fire along with gas attacks. His widow, Alice, received the following notification of his death:

'I am sorry to tell you that your husband, Sergeant Yeatman, was wounded and bought into this hospital today. He was very severely wounded in the abdomen and there was very little hope for his recovery. Everything possible was done for him and he had an operation, but he died later in the afternoon. He did not suffer much pain and his operation eased him a great deal, I am sorry, please accept my deepest sympathy in your great loss. His only message to you was not to worry. I don't think he realized he was dying, as he really slept away. He will be buried in the Military Hospital for British Soldiers'.

Private 114839 Wilfred Arthur LEMMON
1 High Street, Bognor
5th Canadian Mounted Rifles
Killed in Action on 15 September 1916
Aged 27`
Commemorated on the Vimy Memorial

Wilfred Lemmon, the fifth son of Frank and Sarah, the well known drapers of 15 London Road, was killed at the Front. He had enlisted into the 5th Canadian Mounted Rifles and was killed in action on 15 September 1916. He was formerly an apprentice to Mr Newton, the ironmonger of London Road, but emigrated to Canada about 1912. On the outbreak of war he immediately lined up and was in the trenches at Ypres, when the Canadians lost some ground to the Germans and where he lost many of his chums, but he came through that ordeal unscathed. He was the brother of Signalman Frank Lemmon (*see Roll of Honour, January 1918*).

Private A AGER
Canadian Forces
Killed in Action on 15 September 1916
Aged 34

Two years to the day that Mrs Puckett of 4 Henry Street, Bognor, had received news of the death of her brother Walter, (see *Roll of Honour, November 1914*) the sad news was conveyed to her that her other brother had lost his life whilst serving with the Canadian Forces. She received the news in a letter from Private Ager's widow in Canada. Private Ager had enlisted in Ontario soon after the death of Walter in 1914 and had been at the Front since June 1916. He left a widow and five children aged three to eleven in Canada to mourn his loss.

Second Lieutenant Thomas Frederick STONES
London Road Buildings, Bognor
10th Battalion, the Royal West Kent Regiment, 41st Division
Killed in Action on 17 September 1916
Aged 19
Buried in the Longueval Road Cemetery

The only son of Mr H Stones, Thomas enlisted into Royal West Kent Regiment. He was killed on 17 September 1916, aged 19 'by a shell which landed in a trench where he was with two other Officers. Two of the three were killed instantly and the other was blown out of the trench'.

Thomas was born at Gillingham, Kent, his father, Herbert, being an auctioneer's assistant and his mother, Amelia, a housewife, looking after Thomas and his sister Mildred. The family spent some years living in Shrewsbury before moving to Bognor shortly before the outbreak of war. Thomas opted to enlist into the County Regiment of his birth.

Private SD1201 Arthur Frederick FARLEY
12th Battalion, the Royal Sussex Regiment, 39th Division
Died of Wounds on 21 September 1916
Aged 20
Buried in the Doullens Communal Cemetery Extension No 1, France

Born in Bognor, one of four children of journeyman carpenter Arthur and his wife Henrietta, Arthur's childhood was spent in different villages of West Sussex, wherever his father was working. Tortington, South Harting, East Preston were some of their homes and Arthur (junior) moved to Midhurst when he started working as a journeyman baker, lodging with his employer's family. At this time he met Angelina West from Stedham and they were married in 1913.

Enlisting at Bognor at the outbreak of war into the Royal Sussex Regiment, Arthur died from wounds received whilst working in the trenches, at the 35th Casualty Clearing Station, in September 1916.

In a letter to Angelina, the Chaplain wrote:

'He passed away peacefully, I visited him twice a day and as the end drew near I saw him oftener. It will be of comfort to you to know that he passed away trusting in the Saviour and with the Peace of God in his heart. He was as brave in bearing pain as he was under shellfire. He made the greatest sacrifice a man could make and the cause for which he thus gave his life was worthy of it. Thus he did his part in preventing a calamity greater than words can express, from sweeping over our homes and destroying the noblest and best in civilisation. Now you are called on your part in this great conflict, by the great sorrow and bereavement that has come to you. I earnestly pray that God may give you His comfort and His strength to bear the sad burden. Will you please accept my sincerest sympathy in you great sorrow'.

Quarter Master Sergeant SD3260 Herbert Edwin Thomas WALTERS
6 Wishfield Terrace, Chichester Road, Bognor
13th Battalion, the Royal Sussex Regiment, 39th Division
Died of Wounds on 30 September 1916
Aged 28
Buried in the Cabaret Rouge British Cemetery, France

Born in Pagham, Herbert Walters was wounded on the Rue de Bois on 30 June 1916 and initially reported as missing. The son of Ephraim and Sarah Walters, he married Emily and had a young son, also Herbert. He had worked for Messrs Newell, the builders of London Road as a bricklayer's labourer prior to enlisting and went to the Front on 5 March 1916.

'Private Herbert Walters, of the Royal Sussex Regiment, who was recently reported as missing, is now reported to have died whilst a prisoner of war in Germany on 30 September 1916. He was the husband of Emily Walters, of 6 Wishfield Terrace, Chichester Road, Bognor'.

He was another soldier whose death came as a result of being wounded on 'the Day that Sussex Died' *(see June 1916)*.

Lance-Corporal G1522 Albert George JANMAN
Aldwick Farm Cottage, Pagham
7th Battalion, the Royal West Kent Regiment, 18th Division
Killed in Action on 5 October 1916
Aged 29
Commemorated on the Thiepval Memorial, France

Albert was one of twelve children of farm worker Thomas and his wife Mary. He was born in Pagham, the family living at Aldwick Farm Cottage and later in Barrack Lane. On leaving school Albert also took employment on the farm as a carter's boy. He enlisted at Tonbridge into the Royal West Kent Regiment which was raised on 5 September 1914. Following training at Colchester and Salisbury Plain the Battalion proceeded to France on 27 July 1915, operating in the Fleselles area. In 1916 they were in action on the Somme, taking part in the Battle of Albert. On 1 October 1916 Albert was reported missing and subsequently it was learnt he had received severe wounds from which he had died on 5 October. On that day he had taken part in an attack on the Stuff Redoubt, a formidable German field fortification north of Thiepval and although the Redoubt was briefly taken, it proved impossible to hold. Albert's wrist watch was sent home to his mother a few weeks later.

Lance-Corporal G984 Edgar William PAICE
24 Grove Road, Chichester
7th Battalion, the Royal Sussex Regiment, 12th Division
Killed in Action on 5 October 1916
Aged 34
Commemorated on the Thiepval Memorial, France

A Chichester man whose name also appears on their War Memorial, Edgar lived with his parents, Thomas and Emily Paice. He enlisted in the City into the Royal Sussex Regiment.

On 1 October the 7th Battalion were back on the Somme front line, after a month away in a quieter area. Conditions under foot were terrible, due to heavy rains and shell fire, leaving the ground churned up with deep heavy mud, described as being a 'moonscape'. Progress was virtually impossible and on 5 October 1916, Private Edgar Paice was killed in action.

Private 43419 Albert HACKETT
52 Essex Road, Bognor
17th Battalion, the Manchester Regiment, 30th Division
Killed in Action on 12 October 1916
Aged 32
Commemorated on the Thiepval Memorial, Belgium

The eldest of seven children born to George, a railway worker and his wife, Ellen Hackett, Albert was born in Horley, Surrey. Albert's father was originally from Chichester, the family eventually returning to settle in Bognor. Albert was one of five brothers who fought for their Country. On leaving school Albert was employed as a porter at Bognor railway station, before becoming a bricklayer's labourer. He enlisted at Bognor and was killed in action on the Somme.

Company Quartermaster Sergeant 2785 Bernard Samuel WARDLEY
The Steyne, Bognor
1/6th Battalion, the Royal Warwickshire Regiment, 48th Division
Killed in Action on 14 October 1916
Aged 36
Buried in the Hebutene Military Cemetery, France

A commercial traveller, who followed his father earning his living selling stationery, Bernard, who was born in Cheshire, had moved to Bognor where he met and married his wife, Ethel. Bernard joined the Colours at the outbreak of war, enlisting in the Royal Warwickshire Regiment and within eighteen months had risen to the rank of Sergeant, becoming Company Quartermaster. He was killed in action on the Somme; the *Bognor Observer* commented:

'Another Bognor name has to be added to those who made the supreme sacrifice. He was killed by a shell bursting in the building in which he happened to be at the time'.

His Company Commander wrote:

'The whole Battalion and 'D' Company in particular mourn the loss of a bright, cheery, genial comrade, who has put in consistent good work and won the sympathy and appreciation of all those for whom and under whom he worked'.

For some reason Sergeant Wardley's name has been omitted from the Bognor War Memorial.

Private 29503 Arthur Percy BALE
Milford House, the Steyne, Bognor
2nd Battalion, the Hampshire Regiment, 29th Division
Killed in Action on 16 October 1916
Aged 20
Commemorated on the Thiepval Memorial France

Arthur Bale was the only son of music hall artiste Frank and, like his two sisters, was born at Paddington. The family moved to Bognor in the early 1900s, living at 6 Norfolk Street. It was not long before Arthur followed his father onto the stage where he was known as 'Little Tygo', the child juggler. For many seasons he entertained residents and visitors alike with his father, Frank Bale, who was now known as 'the Bognor Clown'. Arthur enlisted at Southampton in February 1916, following the Regiment's return from Gallipolli and Egypt. His Regiment was sent to the Western Front in March 1916 and fought on the Somme, where Arthur lost his life.

'He was always a great credit to the Regiment and carried out his duties satisfactorily', stated the letter his parents received later that month. This was small comfort for the loss of a talented 20 year old son who had been at the Front for only ten weeks.

THE ATTACK ON STUFF TRENCH

October 1916 found the 11th, 12th and 13th Battalions of the Royal Sussex Regiment in the front line and subjected to heavy shelling. An attack was planned for 21 October on Stuff Trench, a line held by the Germans, on a ridge of open ground. The attack commenced just after midnight when the Sussex went 'over the top' behind an artillery barrage which crept forward ahead of them. Although the assault was successfully over fairly quickly, casualties were heavy on both sides and many men were missing.

Private G16028 Thomas Walter GEALL
1 Atholl Villas, Sheepwash Lane, Bognor
13th Battalion, the Royal Sussex Regiment, 39th Division
Killed in Action on 21 October 1916
Aged 18
Commemorated on the Thiepval Memorial, Pas de Calais, France

One of the missing men was Private Thomas Geall, the son of brick maker and contractor Henry Geall and his wife, Elizabeth. For nearly six months they waited for confirmation of the fate of their youngest son. It had been a traumatic time for them, not knowing whether Thomas had been captured or killed. Henry had enlisted the assistance of the Red Cross in their attempts to trace his whereabouts and eventually they received the news they had been dreading - that 18 year old Thomas, who before the war had been a promising player with the Woolwich Arsenal Football Club and who enlisted at Southwark, had been 'killed instantly, on the Somme, whilst sitting on some steps leading to a German dugout'.

The *Bognor Observer* reported the news thus:

'After a period of six months Mr Henry Geall, of Bersted Brickfields, has received a Certificate from the War Office, stating that his son has been killed in action. Mr Geall would like to thank all his kind friends for their sympathy and the Red Cross Society for the trouble they took to make enquiries during his six months of suspense'.

Private L11063 Ernest Alfred JONES
75 Sugden Road, Worthing
11th Battalion, the Royal Sussex Regiment, 39th Division
Killed in Action on 21 October 1916
Aged 20
Commemorated on the Thiepval Memorial, France

Private Ernest Jones was born in Worthing, where he lived with his sister. He enlisted in Chichester but his Bognor connection has not been established, although his name appears on the Bognor War Memorial. On 21 October the Sussex went 'over the top' to attack Stuff Trench, of which they took possession, but at a cost of many lives. For the next few days much time was spent recovering the wounded and burying the dead. Private Ernest Jones was one of four local men to lose their lives in the attack.

Private SD2724 William Russell KEATES
Chalcraft Village Street, North Bersted, Bognor
11th Battalion, the Royal Sussex Regiment, 39th Division
Killed in Action on 21 October 1916
Aged 22
Commemorated on the Thiepval Memorial

Private William Keates also lost his life in the attack on Stuff Trench. William was born at Bersted, the son of farm labourer William and his wife, Rachel. Formerly an employee of Mr Smart, a farmer of Pagham, William enlisted at Chichester and had been at the Front since March 1916.

Private G15954 Alfred Charles NORRIS
28 Nyetimber, Pagham
13th Battalion, the Royal Sussex Regiment, 39th Division
Killed in Action on 21 October 1916
Aged 40
Commemorated on the Thiepval Cemetery, Somme, France

Another local soldier to die in the Stuff Trench attack was Private Alfred Norris. Born at Pagham, the son of a widowed father, Alfred had two brothers and a sister. A single man, Alfred was an agricultural labourer before enlisting at Chichester and was considerably older than his comrades. It is thought that he died in the same incident as William Keates *(above)*.

THE ATTACK ON ZENITH TRENCH

In a further attempt to 'push the line forward' the 2nd Scottish Rifles and 2nd Middlesex Regiment attacked another enemy trench nearby on 23 October. For two days these trenches had been bombarded by British guns 'of all calibre' and from Zero Hour the German lines were covered by a creeping barrage.

The two Battalions 'advanced with great steadiness', inflicting heavy losses on the enemy in a 'stiff hand to hand fight'. Within a couple of hours they had achieved their objectives and repulsed two counter-attacks.

'The brilliant manner in which 2nd Middlesex had carried out the task allotted to them drew praise from the Brigadier'.

The Battle of Zenith Trench lasted less than three hours, during which time the Middlesex lost six Officers and sixty two other ranks; in addition many more were missing and wounded.

Private F3090 Harold F BAKER
2nd Battalion, the Middlesex Regiment, 8th Division
Killed in Action on 23 October 1916
Aged 20
Commemorated on the Thiepval Memorial, France

The son of cabman Charles and his wife Mary Anne Baker, Harold, the seventh of eight children, was born in John Street, Bognor in 1896. By 1914 Harold had become firstly an ironmonger's assistant, before taking up a milkman's round. He enlisted at Chichester.

Private Harold Baker was killed in action that afternoon.

'Another name has been added to the lengthening list of those Bognor men who have given their lives to the war', lamented the *Bognor Observer*. 'This is Private Harold Baker, whose home is in Bedford Street. Young Baker joined the Middlesex Regiment and was drafted to the Expeditionary Force in France, but he fell fighting with his Battalion a few days since'.

WESTERN FRONT

Company Sergeant Major 7264 William R NEW
1st Battalion, the Hampshire Regiment, 4th Division
Killed in Action on 24 October 1916
Aged 29
Commemorated on the Thiepval Memorial, France

William had been in the Army for 12 years and was 'time expired'. When war broke out he re-enlisted and had been in France since 22 August 1914. Granted leave in June 1916 William returned, arriving just as the Somme Offensive was launched.

Company Sergeant Major New was killed in action on 24 October 1916.

'He met a heroic death while in the act of rescuing a brother Sergeant under fire in the Battles of the Somme. He was home on leave in June and had married last November'.

A letter from his Commanding Officer appeared in the paper a few weeks later:

'He was one who may be called one of the very best. He was a personal friend of mine as we had gone through some very rough times together. I can assure you it was his cheerfulness that kept me going. His death has struck me very hard as I am going back to France after being injured and was looking forward to his being my Sergeant Major. He was absolutely fearless, nobody knows that better than I do, he would always have given his life to save somebody. When I get back to France I will make it my business to see his grave and have it made up properly with a good cross as my token to his great gallantry and zeal which he has displayed throughout this war'.

Private G40162 Sidney John BOOKER
2 Brookfield Terrace, Highfield Road, South Bersted, Bognor
1st Battalion, the Middlesex Regiment, 33rd Division
Killed in Action on 28 October 1916
Aged 19
Commemorated on the Thiepval Memorial, France

The son of the South Bersted Sub Postmaster, Sidney Booker was a Sergeant in the Church Lads Brigade. On leaving school he joined the Bognor Gas, Light and Coke Company clerical staff in Argyle Road. Living with his parents, Staff Sergeant (Royal Defence Corps) and Mrs Arthur Booker, Sidney enlisted at Brighton on 20 October 1915 into the Sussex Yeomanry before transferring into the Middlesex Regiment and was sent to the Front early in 1916.

Private Sidney Booker survived the Battle of Zenith Trench on 23 October in which his friend, Private Harold Baker, had been killed *(see Roll of Honour, October 1916)* and for the next five days the remains of his Battalion 'consolidated the position gained under heavy shell fire'. A few hours before the Battalion was to be withdrawn from the line, 'tired and worn out', Private Sidney Booker was killed 'instantaneously' by a shell and buried at the spot he died, just one year after he enlisted.

Private G16401 William Walter BAILEY
2 Gordon Terrace, Felpham, Bognor
13th Battalion, the Royal Sussex Regiment, 39th Division
Killed in Action on 3 November 1916
Aged 41
Commemorated on the Thiepval Memorial, France

Born at Tangmere, the son of Ephraim, a general labourer and widower, William and his father were lodging throughout the 1890s with William's sister and family at 3 Canada Villas, Station Road, Bognor. For fourteen years William Bailey worked for the Bognor Urban Council before enlisting. Then aged 41, he answered the call, leaving Alice, his wife and their four children at home, never to return.

Heavy rains in October had turned the battleground into a quagmire, as the fighting in the Somme began to subside. This allowed some much needed rest and the chance to bury the fallen. On 3 November 1916, Private Walter Bailey fell 'whilst out on a working party'.

Lance-Corporal STK285 Geoffrey Alfred WILSON
West Haven, Annandale Avenue, Bognor
10th Battalion, the Royal Fusiliers, 12th Division
Killed in Action on 18 November 1916
Aged 36
Commemorated on the Thiepval Memorial, France

and

Corporal STK286 Hubert Willoughby WILSON
West Haven, Annandale Avenue, Bognor
10th Battalion, the Royal Fusiliers, 12th Division
Died of Wounds on 18 November 1916
Aged 28
Commemorated on the Thiepval Memorial, France

'A terrible blow has befallen Mr and Mrs Wilson of West Haven, Annandale Avenue, who in one day's fighting have lost two fine sons', wrote the *West Sussex Gazette*. 'Both were magnificent types of manhood, being well over six feet high, who farmed at Westergate. They both joined the Royal Fusiliers on the same day in August 1914 and had been in many big engagements with the Regiment, the elder brother had been several times wounded'.

'Both fell about the same time at different parts of the Front', wrote the Battalion Chaplain. 'Neither knew about the other's death. The oldest one, already wounded for the fourth time, in the face, was on his way to the dressing station, when a sniper hit him and he was killed instantly. The younger one had been injured in the head and died at the aid post to which he had been taken. He had been slightly wounded before'.

Tributes came in from their comrades:

'These young men are typical of the troops England has been sending forth on the crusade against the tyranny that has created hell upon earth in so many lands in Europe', wrote one.

'The brothers Wilson were hardworking, clean living gentlemen, whose deaths are worthy of their cause. Geoffrey was a thoughtful and religious student and the tender love of his brother and comrade in arms, Hubert, strengthened him in all he has undergone', wrote another.

'A third brother, Private Metcalf Wilson is serving as a motor driver in the Ammunition Corps and both of their sisters are nursing at Graylingwell and the war work of the rest of the family makes a fine record', concluded the *West Sussex Gazette.*

Private G14190 Robert James BEGG
Lyora, Gordon Avenue, Bognor
7th Battalion, the Royal West Surrey Regiment, 18th Division
Died of Wounds on 1 December 1916
Aged 26
Buried in St Sever Cemetery Extension, Seine-Maritime, France.

If Mrs Annie Begg had heard the words of the Recruiting Officer at a meeting in Bognor in 1915, when he stated, 'if a soldier is shot at six in the morning, he will be in bed in England at six in the evening', she would, no doubt, have been very angry.

Her husband, Robert, was shot in the left leg on the morning of 18 November 1916 and lay in the mud on the battlefield for two days and nights before being found.

The son of gardener Robert and his wife Annie, Robert (junior) was born in Frimley, Surrey, where he spent his childhood. He had moved to Bognor by 1911 and was living as a boarder with the Towse family at 2 Baden Villas, Merchant Street and was employed by Messrs Bickleys, the ironmongers of West Street, before marrying Annie. He enlisted into his home County Regiment, the Royal West Surreys, which had been raised at Guildford in September 1914 and he was wounded on the last day of the Battle of Ancre. Following his eventual rescue, Robert was taken to the base hospital at Rouen, where he died of his wounds. The following letter was received by his widow from the Matron a few days later:

'I am very grieved to tell you that your dear husband died early this morning. He had an attack of haemorrhage and was taken to the operating theatre and obliged to have his leg amputated, he died some few hours after it. He will be buried with full Military Honours. The cemetery is quite well kept and the graves well looked after. I am indeed sorry for you in this dreadful sorrow and you will be glad to know that we all did our very best for him'.

Private G6349 Harry James LAMBERT
3 Wiversfield Terrace, North Bersted, Bognor
2nd Battalion, the Royal Sussex Regiment, 1st Division
Died of Wounds on 9 December 1916
Aged 29
Buried in the Dernancourt Communal Cemetery Extension, France

'Yet another Bersted man has been noted on the Roll of Honour of those who have made the supreme sacrifice', wrote the *Bognor Observer* in December 1916.

Harry Lambert, who lived with his wife, Charlotte and three young children, had been employed at the Felpham Sewage Works before the war and had been a member of the Royal Sussex Reserve. Eventually he served with the 2nd Battalion and died of wounds on 9 December 1916, a day when both sides' artillery were in action.

Charlotte received two letters from the base hospital where he had been taken. The first was from the Chaplain:

'I much regret to inform you of rather bad news. Your husband was rather severely wounded this morning, through the bursting of a shell on the roof of the dugout where he and some others were at the time. He was sent down at once to a Casualty Clearing Station. We hope he will do well. It will be some time before he will be able to leave hospital. May you find the heavenly father very near you in your time of anxiety'.

Later on a Nursing Sister wrote:

'I very much regret having to tell you that your husband was admitted to hospital last night with very severe wounds in both hands and feet. Everything possible was done for him, but in spite of all, he passed peacefully away today at noon. Just before he died he asked me to write to you to tell you he was alright and would soon be in England. This will be a terrible blow to you, but I am sure you will be given health and strength to bear up bravely'.

Second Lieutenant Leslie Palmer HUMPHREYS
Address Unknown
1st Battalion the Honourable Artillery Company (Infantry), 63rd Division
Died of Wounds received on 13 December 1916
Aged 28
Buried in the Etaples Military Cemetery, France

Leslie Humphreys was the son of property surveyor, William and his wife, Emma and grew up in London. On leaving school Leslie commenced a banking career in the City. What his connection with Bognor was has not been established, but his name appears on the Bognor War Memorial. Second Lieutenant Leslie Humphreys died of wounds at the base hospital at Etaples.

Private G10673 Herbert George DIBLEY
Westergate Street, Aldingbourne, Sussex
1st Battalion, the West Surrey Regiment, 33rd Division
Died of Wounds on 21 December 1916
Aged 26
Buried in the St Sever Cemetery, Seine-Maritime, France.

Herbert Dibley had been born in Westergate, one of six children of George, a labourer on a mushroom farm and his wife, Charlotte. He was the brother of Wilfred *(see Roll of Honour, September 1917)* and enlisted in Bognor into the West Surrey Regiment, having married Winifred and set up home there. It is likely that Herbert was a regular soldier, the 1st Battalion having been in France since 1914 lost many men.

MESOPOTAMIA

Whilst the Somme battles were raging in Europe, the situation in Mesopotamia was appalling. You will recall that in the autumn of 1915 the British Forces had reached and held the town of Kut to the south of Baghdad and were expecting to march on the capital in due course. The situation then changed rapidly. In the Battle of Ctesiphon fought in November, Turkish troops, despite heavy casualties, withstood further British and Indian advances, killing or wounding around half of them. The survivors then retreated to Kut, where they were besieged for one hundred and forty days. Several attempts to relieve the Garrison were beaten back, whilst living conditions in Kut became intolerable. Apart from the illnesses that abounded, the condition of the men was severely weakened by a lack of food, as stocks dwindled. At the end of 1915 the Commanding Officer, Major General Charles Townsend, issued a *communiqué* outlining their situation in which he said:

'I have ample food for eighty four days and that is not counting the three thousand animals which can be eaten'.

A desperate attempt to re-supply Kut via the River Tigress using a paddle steamer failed. The Turks closed in with 'numerous and severe' assaults, but were 'repulsed with such heavy losses that no serious attempts to storm the town were made for the remainder of the siege'. Starvation was the real enemy and after 'a most gallant and tenacious defence of one hundred and forty seven days' the Garrison was forced to surrender.

During the last weeks of the siege, men engaged in trench-digging were so weak that after ten minutes work they had to rest awhile; men on sentry duty would drop down and those carrying loads would rest every few hundred yards. Others took every opportunity to lie down. Illnesses also took their toll, many men succumbing to diarrhoea, as their bodies had lost all powers to fight it off.

Inevitably the Garrison surrendered, but captivity did not relieve their plight. The Turks' treatment of their prisoners of war was appalling. Forced marches in searing heat, constant beatings, small and poor rations, their boots and clothing stolen by Turkish soldiers, leaving them only a blanket and a quilt to live and sleep in. The Officers were separated from the men for the marches, one surviving Officer describing the event after the war said:

'We tingled with anger and shame at seeing a sad little column of British troops who had marched from Kut, driven by a wild crowd of Kurdish horsemen, who brandished sticks and what looked like whips. The eyes of our men stared from their white faces as they dragged one foot in front of the other and those with the rearguard came in for blows from cudgels and sticks. Some had been thrashed to death, some killed and some left to be tortured by the Arabs. Men were dying of cholera and dysentery and often fell out from sheer weakness. Enteritis, a form of cholera, attacked the whole Garrison after Kut fell; a man turned green and foamed at the mouth, his eyes became sightless and the most terrible moans conceivable came from his inner being. One saw British soldiers dying of enteritis with green ooze issuing from their lips, their mouths fixed open, in and out of which flies walked. They died one and all with terrible suddenness'.

Gunner 71157 Richard POWELL
Rose Cottage, Ivy Lane, South Bersted, Bognor
82nd Battery, the Royal Artillery
Died in Captivity on 5 September 1916
Aged 23
Buried in the Baghdad North Gate Cemetery, Iraq

Richard Powell was one of three brothers, the sons of Frank and Mary Powell, of South Bersted, who all lost their lives in the war *(see Walter Powell, Roll of Honour, March 1918 and William Powell, Roll of Honour, September 1918).*

'Mrs Powell of Rose Cottage whose husband and three sons are serving, heard this week that her son Richard, who was a gunner in the Royal Field Artillery and was among the prisoners taken at Kut, died on 5 September last. She last heard from him over twelve months ago'.

Corporal 8368 Albert Edward POWELL
2 Homestead Cottages, Ivy Lane, South Bersted, Bognor
1st Battalion the Oxfordshire and Buckinghamshire Light Infantry,
6th Indian Division
Died in Captivity on 1 November 1916
Aged 30
Buried in the Baghdad North Gate Cemetery, Iraq

The son of George and Emma Powell of 2 Homestead Cottages, Ivy Lane, Albert, a regular soldier, was stationed in India at the outbreak of the war. From there he wrote to the *Bognor Observer*, who published the letter in May 1915:

'I think the people of Bognor would like to know that the old country is represented not only in the main theatre of war, but in the minor struggles which are taking place in our great Empire. I have had your paper regularly in the seven years during my travels in Burma and India and I find it an invaluable link with the old home and the friends I left behind. My mother who resides at the Homestead, South Bersted is a widow with four sons all of whom are serving with two in the Army *(see Frank Powell, Roll of Honour, August 1917)* and two in the Navy'.

Having spent seven years in India, the Regiment moved to Mesopotamia to carry on the war against Turkey on their territory. Albert sent a letter to his mother describing his first contact with the Turkish forces:

'I am in one of the hottest positions it is possible to think of. We engaged the enemy outpost for the first time at dawn and were within the range of their camp before they were awake. As soon as they became aware of our presence they opened fire and we had a funny feeling for a time the bullets were flying all around us. The artillery came up behind us and opened fire on their camp. For over an hour we lay there expecting to get a shell in our midst, but luckily for us the enemy could not get the correct range. It gives one a fright, the sound of a big gun and having to wait to hear the shell coming slower and slower and as soon as they pass over our heads we sit up and see the result of it. Their first shell to land in the trench did not explode or it would have done terrible damage. After we had been in the place for an hour we got the order to advance, it was hard to realise we were facing death. We had not gone many yards when the first man fell with a bullet in the leg and then we began to see the seriousness of it all. We came across a stream twenty five yards wide and of course no-one knew how deep and our men were doubtful about crossing it. As we halted, the enemy who had been hiding in trenches poured a terrific fire into us from all ways. The bullets dropped into the water like hailstones. We knew that to stand there was to covet death and there was no means of escape. I wanted to get across the stream and no-one would try it so I had to lead the way. I plunged in and the water came up to my waist. It was just lovely almost like ice. You can guess what it was like, struggling through the water with the bullets flying all about. It seems a marvel that all our men were not cut up. We had a marvellous escape. The only thing that saved us was a naval boat, which blew up their trenches with Lyddite shells. The effect of that was simply awful, I saw about thirty men come out of the trench and a shell burst in front of them, when the dust had cleared away there was no-one to be seen. They had all gone. I had a very narrow escape'.

Having survived the siege Albert died in captivity. Of the three hundred and thirty men taken prisoner, only ninety survived until the end of the war.

DIED AT HOME

Seaman Paul GRISEWOOD
The Den, Bognor
Public Schools Battalion, Royal Naval Reserve
Died of Illness on 3 August 1916
Aged 28

Paul Grisewood was the third son of Lieutenant Colonel Harman Grisewood of the Den, Bognor, to be killed (see Captain George Grisewood, Roll of Honour, March 1916 and

Lieutenant Francis Grisewood, Roll of Honour, June 1916). Born in Bognor, he was educated at Beaumont College, Windsor and the Oratory School, Edgbaston, Birmingham and enlisted in November 1914. He was taken ill and died of Plithesis at Birchington 'brought on by the hardships of active service' on 3 August 1916. Paul was married to Margaret in 1908.

THE LOSS OF HM SUBMARINE *E16*

Leading Seaman J4675 William Henry BULBECK
HM Submarine *E16* Royal Navy
Lost at Sea on 22 August 1916
Aged 22
Commemorated on the Royal Naval Memorial, Southsea, Hampshire

Mystery surrounds the disappearance of HM Submarine *E16,* on which Seaman Bulbeck was serving. One of the largest submarines to serve during the Great War, *E16* had been built by Vickers, in Barrow-in-Furness and was launched in May 1915. She left her base at Blyth, in Northumbria on 22 August 1916, 'to find and destroy German ships' and was last sighted by HM Submarine *E38* some thirty five miles east of Yarmouth. *E38* later observed a group of German warships heading the same way and 'splashes' in the water, indicating that perhaps *E16* was being either depth charged, torpedoed or mined. No trace of *E16* was ever found; lost with all hands, including Leading Seaman William Bulbeck, whose family may have lived at the Prince of Wales Inn, Upper Bognor Road, Bognor.

Born in September 1893 in Petersfield, Hampshire, the son of farm manager George and his wife, William grew up in Chobham, married Winifred and lived in Rochester close to his naval base of Chatham.

THE LOSS OF HMS *GENISTA*

HMS *Genista*, was a new ship launched in February 1916 and she was torpedoed and sunk by the German submarine *U57* in the North Sea on 23 October the same year. HMS *Genista* sank 'very quickly' and of the crew only twelve ratings survived.

Chief Petty Officer Stoker 300013 Walter Louis MOORE
HMS *Genista* Royal Navy
Lost at Sea on 23 October 1916
Aged 34
Commemorated on the Portsmouth Naval Memorial, Southsea, Hampshire

Chief Petty Officer Walter Moore was the eldest son of house painter Walter (senior) and his wife, Fanny and was born in Bognor, before his family moved to Hove. His father died whilst Walter was still a child. Walter (junior) married his wife Florence Emily and lived for a while in Bristol. Having enlisted into the Royal Navy, Walter had previously served aboard HMS *Arabis*, a minesweeping sloop.

THE LOSS OF HM SUBMARINE *E30*

HM Submarine *E30* was fairly new, having been launched in June 1915. She was first reported missing in the North Sea on 22 November 1916, before it was established that she had been mined off the Suffolk coast and lost with all thirty hands.

Leading Stoker 305430 Thomas William WELLFARE
7 Gravitts Lane, Bognor
HM Submarine *E30* Royal Navy
Lost at Sea on 22 November 1916
Aged 32
Commemorated on the Portsmouth Naval Memorial, Southsea, Hampshire

Submariner Thomas Wellfare was the son of Mr & Mrs W J Wellfare and the husband of Charlotte Welfare of Kentish Town, London and was a regular sailor.

1917

DIED AT HOME

Lance-Corporal G1090 William F CREIGHTON
Anvil Cottage, Chichester Road, Bognor
Royal Sussex Regiment (Medal Rolls)
Died after Discharge
Aged 36
Location Unknown

The son of bricklayer and labourer Oswald Creighton, William was one of six children (four brothers and two sisters). He served in the Royal Sussex Regiment and passed away after being discharged, the circumstances of which are unknown. He had married Emma Etherington during the summer of 1917.

WESTERN FRONT

Private 9258 William Henry TIPPER
Orleans House, Highfield Road
1st Battalion, the Hampshire Regiment, 4th Division
Killed in Action on 22 January 1917
Aged 21
Buried in the Peronne Communal Cemetery Extension

William Tipper was born in Fratton, Portsmouth and spent part of his childhood living with his grandparents, retired postman Charles and his wife Fanny, a charwoman. On leaving school, William became an auctioneer's clerk employed by Messrs Whitehead and Whitehead.

He enlisted into the Hampshire Regiment before the war, moving to France on 23 August 1914. Wounded in May 1915, three chums from Bognor, including William Tipper, wrote that they had all met up in France in hospital:

'After a long time we had the luck to meet each other at the Base Hospital having all been wounded, but Tipper never had the luck to get home. So we thought we would like our mates at Bognor to know that we are all three together in the same company somewhere in France'.

He came home on leave for Christmas 1916 for what was to prove to be his last visit:

'Private Tipper of the Hampshire Regiment has again returned to his home on leave, he has been on active service throughout the war having joined the Army about five years ago'.

Returning to the Front in January, Private Tipper was killed in action a few days later.

DIED AT SEA

Stoker Petty Officer George POTTER
14 Essex Road, Bognor
HMS *Liverpool* Royal Navy
Died of Illness on 15 February 1917
Aged 29
Buried in the Bari War Cemetery, Italy

The husband of Mary May and the father of six year old Frederick, George was a regular sailor serving on the Bristol Class Light Cruiser HMS *Liverpool*, as part of the Grand Fleet. In February 1917 HMS *Liverpool* was attached to the Adriatic Squadron and based at Brindisi, Italy, at the entrance to the Adriatic. It was here that George was taken ill and died. No further details have emerged.

Private GS1218 Arthur Albert WHITE
26 Essex Road, Bognor
2nd Battalion, the Royal Sussex Regiment, 1st Division
Died of Wounds on 28 February 1917
Aged 25
Buried in the Bersted Roman Catholic Cemetery, Bognor

Arthur White, the son of Thomas and Minnie White, a reservist called up at the outbreak of war, landed in France on 13 August 1914. He was invalided home in March 1915, suffering from severe frostbite, following a long winter in the waterlogged trenches around Bethune 'doing duty in the fighting line'. A further spell of sick leave occurred in April 1916, when Arthur was suffering from chronic arthritis.

Returning to the Front, he wrote home to thank the manager of the Kursaal Skating Rink, on the seafront at Bognor, for sending cigarettes and tobacco:

'I was one of the boys who used to frequent the rink a lot when I was home two months ago, but I have returned to the Front again and hope I shall have the luck to return to Bognor to have a few more enjoyable evenings'.

His hope never materialised: having survived the Somme he was invalided home with peritonitis, passing away in Brighton Hospital.
'A military funeral was accorded Private Arthur Albert White on Tuesday. This young soldier had seen considerable service and it was fitting that he should be laid to rest with military honours'.

Private Arthur White is buried in the Roman Catholic Cemetery, Hawthorn Road, Bognor.

WESTERN FRONT

Private G19917 Charles William GRIFFIN
16 Nyetimber, Pagham, Bognor
2nd Battalion, the Royal Sussex Regiment, 1st Division
Died of Wounds on 14 March 1917
Aged 19
Buried in the Bray Military Cemetery, France

Charles was the eldest son of farm worker Charles and his wife Fanny and had been born in North Mundham; he had one younger brother. On leaving school he probably worked on the land before enlisting at Eastbourne.

In March 1917 his Battalion were in reserve during a quieter time, engaged in road repairs, cleaning and training. The weather was snowy at times and they were under sporadic shell fire. The exact circumstances of Charles Griffin's wounds are not known but it is very likely that they were caused by a German shell.

THE LOSS OF HMS *PARAGON*

One of twenty Acasta class destroyers, HMS *Paragon* was launched in 1913, joining the Grand Fleet in August 1914. In March 1917, in company with HMS *Lellwellyn* she was attacked by eight German destroyers off Dover. Hit first by a torpedo, she was then raked with gunfire and broke in half, sinking in under eight minutes. Some of her own depth charges also exploded killing many of those who had survived the original attack. Her compliment of seventy five were all lost in the attack.

First Class Petty Officer Stoker K450 Robert SMITH
Hawthorn Cottage, North Bersted, Bognor
HMS *Paragon* Royal Navy
Lost at Sea on 17 March 1917
Aged 26
Commemorated on the Portsmouth Naval Memorial, Southsea, Hampshire

'Mrs L Bailey, of Hawthorn Cottage, North Bersted has sustained a second bereavement through the war in the loss of a son, First Class Petty Officer Stoker R Smith, who has lost his life at sea. Deceased was 26 years old and leaves a widow and two children, with whom general sympathy will be felt. The news comes as a great shock to the mother who has been bed ridden for some time'.

Robert was serving aboard the destroyer HMS *Paragon*, once part of the Grand Fleet, now based on the Humber, but which had been moved first to Portsmouth and then Devonport. On 17 March 1917 she was one of five British destroyers torpedoed and sunk in the Straits of Dover, with a heavy loss of life.

(It is possible that Mrs Bailey's first bereavement was Able Seaman 'Bobs' Smith, whose name appears on the Bognor War Memorial, but no other information has come to hand).

DIED AT HOME

Private 3120 Thomas Edward Horace GILBERT
Penzance Villa, Highfield Road, Bognor
27th Battalion, the Middlesex Regiment
Died at Home on 24 March 1917
Aged 20
Buried in Bognor Town Cemetery, West Sussex

Thomas Gilbert was born in South Bersted, one of eight children and the eldest son of Ernest, a bricklayer and his wife Emily. He died at the family home 'having been cared for by his parents and his two sisters, Emily and Lillian'; he also had three brothers. A bricklayer's apprentice before the war, Thomas spent the early months of 1917 in the line at the Kemmel sector. Whether he succumbed to a wound or illness is not known. He was, however, one of a very few who were able to see their loved ones before they died.

'Mr and Mrs Gilbert would like to thank all kind friends for their kind sympathy and flowers sent during their recent sad bereavement'.

THE FIRST BATTLE OF GAZA

The first Battle of Gaza was an attempt to dislodge the Turkish forces from the series of ridges they held between Gaza and Beersheba, thereby opening the way to Palestine. Although numerically superior, the task was a difficult one, the British attack being launched on 26 March, advancing under the protection of a dense sea fog. The attack was led by the cavalry with the infantry following, advancing across difficult terrain. A misunderstanding at Command level led the British to withdraw the cavalry under the impression that the infantry attack had failed. In fact, a British victory was on the cards; even the German commander of the Turkish forces thought the day had been lost. The British attack resumed the following day, by which time the Turks had reinforced their positions and the Battle ended in a costly stalemate. Some four thousand British soldiers were wounded or killed in action.

Four local men were killed in the First Battle, all serving with the 1/4th Battalion the Royal Sussex Regiment. Having left Gallipolli in December 1915 they spent some time in Egypt before moving to Palestine in early 1917.

Private TF200421 Gilbert BEER
Clyde Villa, Clyde Road, Felpham
1/4th Battalion, the Royal Sussex Regiment, 53rd Division
Killed in Action on 26 March 1917
Aged 18
Commemorated on the Jerusalem Memorial, Israel

Gilbert Beer, the youngest son of general labourer Francis and Clare Beer of Felpham, was born and grew up in Felpham. He enlisted at Horsham. News reached Felpham in June 1917 that he was 'reported missing'; subsequent enquiries established that he had been 'killed in action' at the first Battle of Gaza, on 26 March 1917, three months earlier.

Private TF200569 Reginald Charles DELL
The Cottage, Aldwick Place, Bognor
1/4th Battalion the Royal Sussex Regiment, 53rd Division
Killed in Action on 26 March 1917
Aged 20
Commemorated on the Jerusalem Memorial, Israel

Reginald Dell, one of nine children of Charles, a gardener and Matilda, was born in Godstone, Surrey, the family subsequently moving to Aldwick. On leaving school he was employed as a baker's errand lad. He enlisted at Horsham and lost his life in the First Battle of Gaza.

Private TF200325 Percival Reginald NOVELL
12 Gainsborough Road, Bognor
1/4 Battalion, the Royal Sussex Regiment, 53rd Division
Killed in Action on 26 March 1917
Aged 21
Commemorated on the Jerusalem Memorial, Palestine

Percival Novell was born in North Mundham, a son of traction engine driver Richard and his wife May. On leaving school Percival was employed as a cabinet maker's apprentice, before enlisting at Bognor.

Private TF200259 Albert RISHMAN
2 White Horse Cottages, Bognor
1/4 Battalion, the Royal Sussex Regiment, 53rd Division
Killed in Action on 27 March 1917
Aged 23
Commemorated on the Jerusalem Memorial, Palestine

The son of Frank, a bricklayer and his wife Emily, Albert was born in Norwood, Surrey. His father passed away whilst Albert was a child, his mother and brother moving to Bognor. On leaving school Albert took employment as an assistant in a drapers shop, before enlisting at Bognor. Albert lost his life on the third day of the battle.

THE SECOND BATTLE OF GAZA

This was the second British attempt to force their way through the Turkish lines, thus opening the way to Palestine and ultimately Jerusalem. However, during the intervening three weeks, Gaza had been strongly reinforced and garrisoned.

The Battle commenced on 17 April 1917, with numerically stronger British forces supported by eight tanks, twenty five aircraft, a French destroyer and two British monitors. Two days later the 53rd Division, including 1/4th Royal Sussex Regiment, joined the Battle at 0730 hrs. The attack was a total failure, costing 6444 British casualties: the Turkish losses were much lower.

Private TF200650 Harry Charles BENHAM
21 Ockley Road, Bognor
1/4 Battalion, the Royal Sussex Regiment, 53rd Division
Killed in Action on 19 April 1917
Aged 21
Buried in the Gaza War Cemetery, Palestine

An ex-Sergeant of the Church Lads Brigade, Harry was the son of George Benham, who ran an upholstering business at 20 Wood Street, Bognor. Harry was in business as a painter and decorator before enlisting into the Royal Sussex Regiment. Whilst fighting at Gallipolli he contracted a severe bout of dysentery and was invalided home. Having recovered, he rejoined his Regiment in Egypt, only to lose his life in the Second Gaza battle.

Private Harry Charles NEWMAN
Killed in Action in April 1917

The second son of George Newman, Harry was 'one of the first to go' when the call came in 1914, leaving his father to manage their business alone. Whilst in Gallipolli he survived a serious bout of dysentery and was killed in action in April 1917. No other information has come to hand.

Lieutenant Jack Ronald Lewis MACKENZIE
1st Battalion, the Seaforth Highlanders, 7th Indian Division
Killed in Action on 21 April 1917
Aged 20
Commemorated on the Basra Memorial, Iraq

Lieutenant Jack Mackenzie is named on the Bognor War Memorial, although it has not been possible to establish a Bognor connection. He was born in Shropshire and educated at the Felstead School where he was a boarder. His father was Colonel D Mackenzie of Gluck and appears to have been stationed in Bermuda for some years and it was to that address that his son's medals were forwarded after his death.

The 1st Battalion the Seaforth Highlanders were stationed in India at the outbreak of war, being hastily recalled to the Western Front, subsequently moving to Mesopotamia in December 1915.

DIED AT HOME

Able Seaman PO226270 William John MARNER
Waterworks Cottage, South Bersted
HMS *Victory* Royal Navy
Died at Home on 15 April 1917
Aged 29
Buried in the Bognor Town Cemetery, Sussex

William Marner was the second son of farm worker Charles and his wife, Elizabeth. He had a fairly nomadic childhood, the family moving frequently with Charles' employment, from Hampshire to Madehurst, Aldingbourne, Eartham, Sidlesham, Pagham and North Bersted.

Able Seaman William Marner was serving in the Shore Establishment at Portsmouth, HMS *Victory*, which was the Depot. He became ill and was sent home where he subsequently passed away.

WESTERN FRONT

The Battle of Arras was a British offensive alongside Canadian, New Zealanders and Australian troops, on the German defences near the French city of Arras. Planned in conjunction with a massive French offensive some eighty kilometres to the south, it was thought that the British would draw German troops away from the French attack and thus to take the German-held high ground. It was a determined British offensive to break the German lines near the French city of Arras. Once broken, it was felt that the numerically inferior German army would be easier to deal with in 'a war of movement' in the open ground behind their lines. If successful the Allies aim was to end the war within 48 hours.

In heavy snow the first phase of the offensive began with battles being fought at the Scarpe; the Canadians captured Vimy Ridge and Bullecourt. This phase ended on 14 April. The second phase saw more fighting on the Scarpe, Bullecourt and Arleux. The Offensive officially ended on 16 June and although significant advances had been made, a breakthrough had not been achieved and this sector reverted to the entrenched stalemate.

Sergeant G931 Alfred William BEALE MM
Gordon Lodge, Bognor
7th Battalion, the Royal Sussex Regiment, 12th Division
Killed in Action on 9 April 1917
Aged 24
Commemorated on the Arras Memorial, Pas de Calais, France

'Sergeant AW Beale who was mentioned in Sir Douglas Haigh's last despatches *(October 1916)* has now been awarded the Military Medal. He is the son of Mr Alfred Beale of Bognor. Sergeant Beale enlisted soon after the outbreak of war into the Royal Sussex Regiment. He soon received promotion and it was as an Acting Sergeant in charge of a Company at the taking of the Hohenzollern Redoubt in February, that he gained his third stripe and was recommended for the above honours. He is in England now recovering from wounds received near Ovilliers during the great advance in July *(1916)'*.

That report was from the *Bognor Observer* in 1916. Sergeant Beale recovered from his wounds and soon rejoined his unit.

On that first day the Royal Sussex Regiment engaged the Germans, supported by 11th Middlesex Regiment and 8th/10th Gordon Highlanders. The Sussex were set to attack on a two hundred and fifty yard frontage, to capture two German trenches. The Battalion's War Diaries take up the story:

'At 0530 hrs the tremendous barrage began and the advance started. In the darkness and smoke it was extremely difficult to find our way and the ground bore no resemblance to the neat trenches over which we had practised so carefully. We met with very little opposition from a dazed enemy and gained all our objectives up to time. The barrage was to pause in front of our objectives for some time to allow our reserves to come up and it was at this period the majority of our casualties were sustained, for enemy riflemen and machine gunners, just out of range of the barrage, were very active and hit many men who were engaged in reorganisation and consolidation'.

Sergeant Alfred Beale lost his life that day. No further information has come to hand for Sergeant Beale, who was born in Bournemouth and enlisted in Horsham, but whose close family lived in Bognor.

Private 814816 David Thomas RICKIE (REIKIE on War Memorial)
Princess Patricia's Canadian Light Infantry (Eastern Ontario Regiment)
Killed in Action on 9 April 1917
Aged 22
Commemorated on the Vimy Ridge Memorial

David Rickie was the second of three brothers, the sons of Mr Thomas Rickie of London Road, who were fighting in France. He was serving with Princess Patricia's Canadian Light Infantry (East Ontario Regiment), 3rd Canadian Division. David lost his life at the Battle of Vimy Ridge on 9 April 1917.

'Bognor has this week lost another lad in David Rickie', wrote the *Bognor Observer*.

'An Officer writes highly of him in a letter to his bereaved father, who will receive the sympathy of the town. A laurel wreath has been placed on the War Shrine in the Parish Church'.

(His Regiment was raised in Canada at the beginning of the war, initially financed and equipped by the millionaire Mr Hamilton Gault at his own cost.

Trooper 1645 William James LEWIS
Kingsley, Longford Road, Bognor
The Household Battalion, 4th Cavalry Division
Killed in Action on 11 April 1917
Aged 31
Buried in the Mindel Trench British Cemetery, St Laurant Blanche, France

Before the war William had been a tailor, working for Mr Gale in York Road and, prior to enlisting, he 'did good work' for the Red Cross for many months, doing duty as a night orderly at Graylingwell War Memorial Hospital.

In the autumn of 1915 he married Clara Bowman and shortly afterwards enlisted into the Household Battalion. After training William arrived in France on 9 November 1916 and was attached to 10th Brigade of the 4th Division, an experienced formation of the regular army that had been in France since August 1914. The Battle of Arras saw the Division heavily engaged for the first time.

The West Sussex Gazette reported his death thus:

'News has come in a sympathetic letter to his widow of the death in action in France of Trooper W J Lewis. At the time of his death he had been attached to a machine gun section and was killed instantaneously by shrapnel fire while on a carrying job. Several others of the same party were wounded by the same shell and one of the Officers died that same evening. He was killed whilst dressing the wounds of one of his comrades and was found lying by the man he was helping'.

Private 75488 William Vernon ABRAHAM
6 St Margaret's Terrace, Longford Road, Bognor
Royal Army Medical Corps
Killed in Action on 22 April 1917
Age 30
Buried in Philosophe British Cemetery, Mazingarbe, Pas de Calais, France

It was forbidden for advancing troops to stop and care for wounded comrades. All men carried with them an emergency field dressing with which to dress their own wounds if possible and then wait until stretcher bearers arrived. Each Company had four stretcher bearers allocated to them and in good conditions two men could carry a wounded soldier, but after heavy rain it took four or more, dragging their feet out of the mud and trying not to increase the pain of the wounded man by rocking the stretcher. Once rescued, the wounded soldier would be taken to the reserve trenches where a first aid post would be set up. From there, having been cleaned up and bandaged, the injured man would be taken to the Casualty Clearing Station where operations took place.

Stretcher bearing was a dangerous, hard and heart rending job, often carried out under fire. Stretcher bearers were special people; one such was William Vernon Abraham.

Born in South Bersted in 1887, William was affectionately known as 'Joey'. He had an elder brother, Walter and two younger sisters, Eleanor and Georgina. On leaving South Bersted School, William became an apprentice printer with Webster and Webb, High Street, Bognor, a firm who were still employing him when he enlisted at Aldershot. A prominent member of the St John's Church choir, William served with 16th Field Ambulance, Royal Medical Corps as a stretcher bearer. Initially he served in Salonika and was afterwards sent to France in 1916.

Private Abraham's unit was sent up the line in the New Year. He was killed in action on 22 April 1917, whilst rescuing some wounded Serbian men and bringing them to the relative safety of a trench for treatment. Within seconds a shell 'dropped into the trench', instantly killing Private Abraham and three other men, with two others wounded.

The *Bognor Observer* reported:

'Another Bognor man, Private Abraham, of the Royal Army Medical Corps, the son of Mr and Mrs Abraham, of 6 St Margaret's Terrace, Longford Road, has been killed in action. He was thirty years of age and was formerly a member of the Parish Church choir, the Bognor Yeomanry and the Church Lads Brigade. The deceased was well known and very much liked in the town and the news of his death has occasioned much regret. He was killed by a shell whilst engaged in bringing in some wounded men, his death being instantaneous. In a letter to his parents, his Commanding Officer described Private Abraham as being a splendid soldier and a good worker, who died nobly, doing his duty for his Country'.

Private Harry BARROW
8 Chapel Street, Bognor
1st Battalion, the City of London Regiment, the Royal Fusiliers
Killed in Action on 26 April 1917
Aged 29

William Barrow was a general labourer, born and bought up in Petersfield, Hampshire, who married Caroline, a Bognor girl, the couple settling in her town with their three children.

On leaving school, Harry, their oldest son, moved to London, where he was employed as a porter in a large retail business. From there he enlisted into the London Regiment.
In May 1917 the *Bognor Observer* carried the following report:

'News has been received by Mrs Caroline Barrow, that her son, Private Harry Barrow, of the London Regiment, was killed in action on 26 April 1917. He was invalided home with enteric from the Dardanelles, but recovered and had been back in France some five months'.

Lance-Corporal G44058 Albert Henry MUNDAY
18 Essex Road, Bognor
16th Battalion, the Middlesex Regiment, 2nd Division
Killed in Action on 28 April 1917
Aged 37
Commemorated on the Arras Memorial

The son of Henry Munday, a bricklayer and his wife Francis, Albert had a brother and two sisters. Formerly employed by Mrs Croxton Johnson, of Paradise, Aldwick, Albert enlisted into the Middlesex Regiment in the autumn of 1915.

April 1917 found his Regiment near Oppy Wood, which it was tasked to capture, along with the village. Here the Regiment was pitched 'against some of the finest fighting troops then in the German army'. In reality, Oppy Wood was a scorched and shell blasted mass of tree stumps, whilst the villages of Oppy and Arleux were in ruins.

'The Battalion marched from Roclincourt on the evening of the 27th and formed up in its battle formation opposite Oppy Wood and the village of Oppy. The forming up was carried out without a hitch and in perfect silence, in spite of the steady shelling of the front areas. At 0425hrs our barrage came down and at 0433hrs the leading wave entered the enemy's front line trench. Serious heavy fighting took place and a strong German counter attack on the British flanks saw them re-occupy the wood. In this Battle, the 17th Middlesex Regiment 'lost eleven Officers and four hundred and fifty one men, killed, wounded or missing, but again the Die-Hard spirit was demonstrated in the stubborn resistance against superior numbers of the enemy and in the grim manner in which both Officers and men fought to the very last'.

During this battle Lance Corporal Munday was 'shot by a sniper and killed instantly'.

Private PEACOCK
17th Battalion, the Middlesex Regiment,
Killed in Action on 28 April 1917
Age Unknown

This soldier's name does not appear on the Bognor War Memorial, although for many years prior to enlisting Private Peacock was employed by the butchers, Messrs Burtons and Sons. A member of the Middlesex Regiment, Private Peacock was killed in action on 28 April 1917, during a day of 'heroic, hard fighting, but of heavy losses, an intense struggle'.

Private Peacock left a young widow to mourn for him.

Private GS177 William GEORGE
3 Ithica Terrace, Felpham, Bognor
7th Battalion, the Royal Sussex Regiment, 12th Division
Killed in Action on 3 May 1917
Aged 34
Commemorated on the Arras Memorial, Pas de Calais, France

William was born in Southwick, Sussex, the son of a Royal Navy pensioner, Thomas and his wife, Emily. The family moved to Southampton, where at the age of 17 William was working as a milkman. Having met and married his wife, Elizabeth, they lived in Bognor, where William was now a bricklayer's labourer. He was also a Special Reservist, who enlisted at Chichester into the Royal Sussex Regiment. On 3 May, William was killed in action at Arras, alongside some forty of his comrades, whilst attacking and capturing two German trenches known as Bayonet and Scabbard.

Lance Corporal 3046 William Henry RICHARDSON
Waterloo Cottages, Felpham, Bognor
7th Battalion, the Royal Sussex Regiment,
Killed in Action on 3 May 1917
Aged 44

William Richardson's name does not appear on the Bognor or Felpham War Memorials, although he was born in Bognor and lived in Felpham. His details are scanty and have been developed from a short sentence in the *Bognor Observer* reporting his death. He married his wife, Esther, with whom he had three sons and a daughter. Prior to enlisting in 1914 he worked as a bricklayer's labourer. He was killed in action fighting alongside William George (above).

Private G37548 Charles BACON
7 Essex Road, Bognor
2nd Battalion, the Royal Fusiliers, 29th Division
Died of Wounds on 13 May 1917
Age 28
Buried in Duisans British Cemetery, Etrun, Pas de Calais, France

Charles was born in Camberwell 1889, the son of greengrocer, Thomas and his wife Ellen, a laundress. Later, when Charles was a gardener, he was living with his grandparents, retired agricultural labourer William and Harriet Bacon. He married

Elizabeth Bartholomew in 1913. Charles Bacon enlisted at Chichester into the Royal Fusiliers and went to the Front in March 1916. He died of wounds on 13 May 1917.

Rifleman A201223 Horace Raymond BROWN
4 Franklin Terrace, Highfield Road, Bognor
16th Battalion, the King's Royal Rifle Corps, 33rd Division
Killed in Action on 20 May 1917
Aged 19
Commemorated on the Arras Memorial, Pas de Calais, France

A member of the South Bersted Church Choir and a Sergeant in the Church Lads Brigade, Horace was born in Bognor in 1898 and lived his early days at South Bersted. He became a gardener on leaving school, working for both Mr Jacobs' nursery in Argyle Road and later for Mr Whiffin at Barn Rocks, Aldwick. Horace enlisted at Worthing, joining the Kings Royal Rifles in June 1916. This Battalion had been formed in September 1914 at Denham, Buckinghamshire, by Field Marshall Lord Grenfell, the commandant of the Church Lads Brigade, from previous and current members of that organisation. After training in England, the Battalion landed in France on 17 November 1915. Rifleman Horace Brown was killed instantly on 20 May 1917, when a shell landed in the trench in which he and his comrades were: they were buried at that spot.

Horace was the last surviving son of his widowed mother Charlotte who, by some twist of fate, received notification of his death a year to the day that she had previously been notified of the death of her other son, Private Sidney Brown *(See Roll of Honour, July 1916)*.

DIED AT HOME

Private TR10 27534 Thomas Humphrey BISHOP
Eden Vale, Highfield Road, Bognor
31st Training Reserve Battalion
Died at Home on 22 April 1917
Aged 18
Buried in the Bognor Town Cemetery, West Sussex

Thomas was born in Finchley, Middlesex, where his father, Sidney was a wine shipper. His mother, Hilda was assisted in looking after Thomas and his two elder brothers by a nurse, a cook and a housemaid. His father may have died whilst Thomas was a child, because by 1911 his mother had remarried to the dairy farmer, George Cowley, who kept his herd on land adjacent to Highfield Road, Bognor. Thomas, having enlisted at Chichester into the 31st Training Division, died at home; no other details have emerged.

Private 33169 S Henry Gordon PRINCE
3 Evergreens, South Bersted, Bognor
1st Battalion, the Northamptonshire Regiment (Labour Company)
Died at Home on 26 April 1917
Aged 40
Buried in the Shorncliffe Military Cemetery, Kent, England

Henry Prince's father was a fly man, plying around Brighton, although both he and his wife, Charlotte were born in Chichester. Henry, their oldest son was born in Brighton, as were his brother and sister. Charlotte was widowed and by 1911 was living at South Bersted with Henry, who was employed as a builder. Henry, who enlisted at Chichester, died in England on 26 April 1917; the circumstances of his death are not known.

WESTERN FRONT

The Battle of Messines Ridge was one of the most successful British attacks of the war which took place from 7 June to 14 June 1917, designed to force the Germans to move reserves to Flanders, thus relieving the pressure on the French army at both the Arras and Aisne fronts and to capture the German defences on the top of the ridge. The attack commenced with the detonation of nineteen British mines which smashed open the German front line defences. This was followed by a creeping artillery barrage, behind which British infantry and tanks could advance. The attack was over in a short time, a complete success. Both 7th and 9th Battalions of the Royal Sussex Regiment were involved. Sadly, the planners had not made any arrangements for further onward movement, so a great opportunity to progress was missed. Instead, there followed a six week lull before the next stage, the Third Battle of Ypres commenced, by which time the Germans had recovered and were well prepared. Two local men were killed in action, one during the Battle and the other in the days that followed.

Private G17624 Ridley Gordon RICHARDSON
30 West Street, Bognor
9th Battalion, the Royal Sussex Regiment, 24th Division
Killed in Action on 11 June 1917
Aged 20
Commemorated on the Menin Gate Memorial, Ypres, Belgium

A former employee of Charles Knowles Ltd of Station Road, the Bersted Coal Company and Reynolds House Furnishers, Ridley lived with his parents and was one of four brothers serving. He enlisted in Bognor into the Royal Sussex Regiment in 1916.

'Mr and Mrs Richardson of West Street have heard that their son has been killed in action in France. One of his three brothers, Percy, actually saw him killed'.

Richardson's, the bakers and confectioners in West Street, was a popular shop in the years leading up to the outbreak of war. John and Charlotte Richardson had four sons serving, two of them in the 9th Battalion, the Royal Sussex Regiment.

Lance Corporal SD823 John MARSHALL
The Sack, Lidsey, Bognor
9th Battalion, the Royal Sussex Regiment, 24th Division
Killed in Action on 20 June 1917
Aged 21
Commemorated on the Menin Gate Memorial, Ypres, Belgium

Like his father before him, John Marshall was a horseman on the farm at Lidsey. The family had previously lived at North Mundham, John having been born at Bosham. John's mother died when he was very young, leaving his father to bring up five children. When war was declared John enlisted in Lowthers Lambs and had previously been wounded in October 1916. He was killed in the aftermath of the Messines Battle.

THE LOSS OF HMS *VANGUARD*

Just before midnight on Monday 9 July 1917, HMS *Vanguard* anchored at Scapa Flow, exploded in a ball of fire, following a detonation in one of her magazines. The cause of the explosion has never been fully explained, theories ranging from a spontaneous detonation of unstable cordite, a fire, or even sabotage. A trawler close by at the time was said to have been 'smothered in blood and pieces of human flesh', shortly afterwards 'picking up half the body of a marine'. Of the crew of over eight hundred, only one hundred and eighty seven bodies were recovered from the sea, just two men surviving the disaster.

Stoker First Class K21078 William Augustine Stanfield CASS
2 Somerset Terrace, Lyon Street, Bognor
HMS *Vanguard*, Royal Navy
Lost at Sea on 9 July 1917
Aged 22
Commemorated on the Chatham Royal Naval Memorial, Kent, England

'A Bognor family has been plunged into sorrow by the terrible explosion on board HMS *Vanguard*, lost when the ship blew up in Scapa Flow on 9 July 1917'.

William Cass had worked for Mr Hart, the draper, at his West Street shop for four years, before enlisting in the Royal Navy and joining HMS *Vanguard*, which had fought in the Battle of Jutland and was now anchored at Scapa Flow. Some of the crew were given the chance of well earned leave. Stoker First Class William Cass had a week's leave due to him, but delayed visiting his parents, William and Alice, giving his place to a shipmate, also from Bognor, a Chief Petty Officer Stoker Powell. Stoker First Class William Cass lost his life with hundreds of his shipmates.

'The loss was all the greater as he was the eldest son and main support of his mother, his father being a chronic invalid, unable even to participate in domestic affairs', wrote the *Bognor Observer'*. 'Aged 22, he was a fine specimen of a "tar" and had many friends in Bognor. General sympathy is felt for the parents and family in the loss of a devoted son. It is remarkable that young Cass had postponed his leave until this week, to complete some handiwork for presents to friends and had exchanged the leave week with a shipmate, CPO Stoker Powell, also from Bognor. Another remarkable fact is that the deceased had left HMS *Bulwark* shortly before that ship was blown up and he had also gone through the Battle of Jutland without a scratch'.

Chief Petty Officer Stoker Powell wrote to the *Bognor Observer* the following week in tribute:

'I was extremely lucky to have been on leave and have lost one of the best pals I have ever had'.

In terms of lives lost, estimated at eight hundred and three, the explosion on HMS *Vanguard* remains the most catastrophic disaster in the history of the Royal Navy.

EGYPT

Signaller Albert Gerry WAY
25 Essex Road, Bognor
The Sussex Yeomanry
Killed in Action on 11 July 1917
Aged 27

The son of George Way, an Army pensioner, Signaller Way, 'a well known Bognor resident', was serving with the Special Signal Unit, made up of all Bognor men in Gallipolli, when he wrote the following to a wounded comrade, Signaller W Underdown, recovering in hospital in Brighton:

'All the boys are serene and seem quite happy although they have arrived at one of the most god forsaken holes you could ever come across. We have to rough it a bit here, no feather beds and no sixty hours leave. We are issued with rum, cigarettes, lime juice and now I hear we are going to get an issue of the ships cocoa, so you see we don't want for much. The biscuits we are given, Army rock, come in as a second course. We get one and powder it up with a hammer or clean stone then mix it with a little milk and water then make it into little patties and fry them in some fat, then close our eyes and eat them with some jam. At present it is raining and of course that has put the blooming lid on it.

'Here we are, your old pals Lucas, Killick, Wood, Gapp and Co Ltd including yours truly having a sing song and our pals on the other side joining in the harmony with their high toned musical shells (shrapnel shells)'.

In another letter to Signaller Underdown, Lance Corporal Way writes cheerfully from somewhere in Turkey:

'The food is plentiful and we are in a place where we can shift it. I am on a nice little station out here with Charlie Gapp and Sid Lucas and a nice little crowd we are. We draw our own rations and do our own cooking. Yesterday we had some steak and onions and rice and currents for seconds and of course we have a cup of tea with every meal. One can always add a little extra at the canteen as we always have a good supply of money. We are well stocked up with tobacco and everybody is taking to a pipe'.

In 1917 saw Signaller Way serving with the 74th Yeomanry Division in Egypt and it was during this period that he lost his life in circumstances unknown.

WESTERN FRONT

Gunner 102259 Edward E ASHCROFT
Hill View, London Road, Bognor
234 Siege Battery, the Royal Garrison Artillery
Died of Wounds on 17 July 1917
Aged 30
Buried in Brandhoek Military Cemetery, Belgium

Edward was born in the Cambridgeshire village of Croxton, where his father Thomas was the local blacksmith, a skill Edward took up after leaving school, before working for the Mitcham Gas Company as a meter inspector. In 1910 he married his wife, Fanny, who was a schoolteacher at Croydon and nearly twice his age. At some stage they moved to Felpham and then to Bognor, before he enlisted into the Royal Garrison Artillery at Chichester in 1916.

'Official news has been received by Mrs E Ashcroft that her husband, Gunner E Ashcroft, died of wounds on 17 July 1917, aged 30. He joined the Colours just a year ago and went to France last January. He leaves a widow and one child'.

DIED AT HOME

Chief Boatswain Matthew ALLEN
7 Canada Grove, Bognor
HMS *Vivid* Royal Navy
Died at Home on 18 July 1917
Aged 53
Buried in the Ford Park Cemetery, Plymouth

Born in Portfield, Chichester, Matthew Allen was the son of Thomas, a French polisher and Sarah, who worked in a laundry. Matthew enlisted in the Royal Navy as a fourteen year old boy, rising to the rank of Boy 1st Class two years later. By 1901 he had married and held the rank of Signal Boatswain and was serving aboard HMS *Ophir* in the Mediterranean. At some stage leading up to the war he and his wife moved first to Hunston and then Bognor. His death occurred at Plymouth. Chief Boatswain Matthew Allen's name does not appear on the Bognor War Memorial.

WESTERN FRONT

Private Henry (Hubert) John SQUIRES
17 Ockley Road, Bognor
8th Battalion, the East Kent Regiment, 24th Division
Killed in Action on 27 July 1917
Age 28
Commemorated on the Menin Gate Memorial, Ypres, Belgium

Henry Squires was born in Aldingbourne, the family moving to Bognor, where his father was employed by the Urban District Council. One of seven children, Henry became a domestic gardener before enlisting in Tonbridge, Kent, in 1915. He had seen two years service, including fighting in the Dardenelles, from where he was invalided home with enteric. Having recovered, he rejoined his Regiment in France and had been there some five mont hs when he was killed in action. He was one of several brothers serving and left a widow and two young children. On the day he was killed, a photograph of the deceased fell from the wall at his home and the frame and glass were smashed.

Lance-Corporal G6739 Reginald TWIBILL
Elm Villa, Longford Road, Bognor
7th Battalion, the Royal Sussex Regiment, 12th Division
Killed in Action on 28 July 1917
Aged 20
Commemorated on the Arras Memorial

Reginald Twiball, the son of Mrs Eliza Letitia Waight, was born in South Bersted and before enlisting had been employed by St Michaels School. He was serving with the Royal Sussex Regiment and had been wounded twice in 1916. In July 1917 'whilst he was with several others on a wiring party, he was shot through the heart by a sniper and died instantaneously'.

His Platoon Sergeant wrote to his mother:

'Your son was well liked by all those in his Company, especially in his Platoon and was always so merry and so willing and did not fear anything'.

PASSCHENDAELE

Unlike the first and second Battles of Ypres which were prompted by German attacks, the third was spearheaded by the British. One objective was the destruction of Germany's submarine bases on the Belgium coast and the attack was launched against the mistaken British belief that the German Army was on the brink of collapse and could not withstand a major Allied assault. Nine British and six French Divisions launched the attack preceded by a 3000 gun barrage and initial progress was made, albeit at a high cost in lives. As August progressed, heavy rains and thick mud slowed down the Allies. Some limited gains were made in September, but the heaviest fighting occurred in October around the village of Passchendaele, the village eventually being captured by British and Canadian troops on 6 November.

The Third Battle of Ypres, or Passchendaele as it is often referred, was one of the most costly of the war. Although 'claimed' as an Allied victory they suffered more casualties than the Germans!

Lowthers Lambs were in the thick of the Battle, leading the attack, losing three men on the first day, in appalling wet weather.

Lance-Corporal SD780 William George COURT
The Bungalow, Barnham, Bognor
11th Battalion, the Royal Sussex Regiment, 39th Division
Killed in Action on 31 July 1917
Aged 25
Commemorated on the Menin Gate Memorial, Ypres, Belgium

Born in Aldingbourne, William, a carter in a nursery, lived with his parents, Harry, an agricultural engine driver and his wife Harriet. William was their eldest son and had two sisters and a younger brother. He enlisted into the Royal Sussex Regiment at Bognor and was killed in action at St Julien, Ypres, within a few hours of the commencement of hostilities.

Private G8133 Alfred Benjamin SQUIRES
Flint Cottage, near Robin Hood, Shripney, Bognor
13th Battalion, the Royal Sussex Regiment, 39th Division
Killed in Action at Ypres on 31 July 1917
Aged 31
Buried in the Buffs Road Cemetery, Ypres, Belgium

The son of Mrs A Squires, Alfred was born in Felpham and before enlisting in Bognor he worked as a carter on the farm at Shripney, for Mr Hogben. He was married to Ellen, who came from Bournemouth and they had three young children.

Alfred joined the Royal Sussex Regiment and moved to France in March 1916, going into the line in the Ypres sector in December of that year. On 31 July 1917 Alfred was killed in action.

Private SD849 Henry Bunn STERK
11 Waterloo Square, Bognor
11th Battalion, the Royal Sussex Regiment, 39th Division
Killed in Action on 31 July 1917
Aged 25
Commemorated on the Menin Gate Memorial, Ypres, Belgium

Formerly employed by Messrs Leverett and Frye, who had shops in the High Street, Henry, the son of Albert and Rachael, enlisted at Bognor into the Royal Sussex Regiment, deploying to France on 5 March 1916. There then followed a period on the Somme Front where, on one occasion, they spent thirty five continuous days in the trenches without relief. Henry Sterk was killed in action at Ypres on 31 July 1917.

Writing to his parents, his Captain described Henry 'as a very capable and fine Lewis gunner, who always went about his work cheerfully and did his duty very satisfactorily'.

Lance-Corporal G8325 Cyril George SPARSHOTT
Compton House, Golf Links Avenue, Felpham, Bognor
8th (Pioneer) Regiment, the Royal Sussex Regiment, 18th Division
Died of Wounds on 6 August 1917
Aged 29
Buried in the Calais (Southern) Cemetery, France

A local Felpham lad, Cyril was the eldest son of Joseph, a beer retailer and Eliza Sparshott. Before enlisting into the Royal Sussex Regiment, Cyril was employed as a carpenter by Mr Bicknell of Felpham and was a regular player in the Felpham football team.

When the battle commenced the 8th Battalion were engaged repairing tracks used by the Allied tanks. They soon came under intensive enemy fire which became so heavy that by mid morning all repair work had to cease. However, by this time several Pioneers had been killed either by the bullets or the heavier gas shells that were landing around them. Others were wounded and had to be evacuated, including Lance Corporal Sparshott, who died of his wounds received, at the Base Hospital in Calais a week later.

Private William James TADD
1 Phipps Cottages, Bognor
The East Surrey Regiment
Believed Killed in Action on 9 August 1917
Aged 32

'Mrs Boyling has received news that her second son Private William Tadd of the East Surrey Regiment who had been reported missing since 9 August 1917 is now believed to have been killed on that date. He volunteered when the war broke out but was rejected then. He passed in the Derby groups later and joined up on 10 June 1916 and was sent to France in September of that year. He was wounded in the Battle of Arras on Easter Monday 1917 and sent to the 2nd Canadian General Hospital, Le Treport and had been back in the line five weeks when he was reported missing. He leaves a widow, Susan and one child. He will be remembered by many as the errand boy for the late Miss Loweth, milliner, of 67 High Street, with who he remained for four years, after which he went to Lancing College as page boy, rising to butler. He was there close on nine years and then through the recommendation of the college secretary, was given the post of book seller at Westminster Abbey, where he remained until joining up. His younger brother has been in France since 1914'.

That report in the *Bognor Observer* was followed early in 1918 by the following letter written by the Reverend Westlake, the Custodian of Westminster Abbey, to his mother:

'It is with the greatest of regret that I hear that the War Office now believes your son was killed on or about 9 August last year. I knew him of course from his boyhood onwards and had the very highest respect for his character. His final appointment as bookstall attendant at the Abbey was one not only of responsibility but of considerable trust and he performed all his duties with ability and integrity. I hardly like to speak of our loss in comparison with yourself, but it is none the less very real and I know you would like to hear how much he was esteemed here. To me personally, after my long association with him, his loss is more than that of a trusted employee; it is the loss of a friend'.

Private 20896 James Henry CARTER
6 Albert Road, Bognor
11th Battalion, the Royal Fusiliers, 18th Division
Killed in Action on 10 August 1917
Aged 23
Commemorated on the Menin Gate Memorial, Belgium

James was the son of James and Sarah Elizabeth Carter, who ran a lodging house at Leicester House, Clarence Road, before moving to a twelve roomed property at 6 Albert Road, Bognor. On leaving school James became an apprentice printer and bookbinder. He enlisted into the 11th Battalion, the Royal Fusiliers, who were formed in Hounslow in September 1914 and went to France in July 1915.

Private SD1204 Frank John POWELL
Queens Gate, North Bersted, Bognor
9th Battalion, the Royal Sussex Regiment, 24th Division
Died of Wounds on 13 August 1917
Age 30
Buried in the Huts Cemetery, Dickebusch, Belgium

Frank lived with his wife, Nellie, at 1 Outerwick Cottages, Felpham, after their marriage in 1910 and by 1917 they had two children and had moved to Queens Gate, North Bersted. Before enlisting into the 9th Battalion, the Royal Sussex Regiment, Frank was employed by Mr F J Neale as a farm labourer. His Battalion moved to France in August 1915 after intensive training in England. Frank was then wounded twice and had recovered. However, he was not so lucky the third time.

On 3 August, the 9th Battalion, who had been in close support of the fighting, were moved and took over part of the front line. The weather was bad and the ground described as a 'vast morass', with men sinking knee deep and sometimes thigh deep in mud. German bombing attacks occurred but were beaten off and casualties were light. Sadly, one of them was Frank Powell, who died of wounds received during one of the attacks. His parents John and Emily Powell of Manor Cottages, Felpham receiving the following notification from his Company Commander:

'It is with deep regret that I have to report that your son died of wounds. He will be missed by all the Company as he showed good qualities, doing his work well and cheerfully, always willing to help others. I don't think he suffered as he was wounded in the back, which seems to have destroyed all feelings. I have met his brother and we had a long chat. I'm afraid I cannot offer any adequate consolation in your loss. We shall always hold his memory dear for the help and sacrifice he made to protect all that we value on this earth. His private effects and the site of his grave will be sent to you'.

Private G15947 Thomas MEDHURST
3 Essex Road, Bognor
13th Battalion, the Royal Sussex Regiment, 39th Division
Died of Wounds on 15 August 1917
Aged 20
Buried in the Wimereux Communal Cemetery, France

Thomas and Kate Medhurst were at one time Bognor fishmongers and lived at 3 Essex Road. They brought up nine children, two of whom, Frank *(see Roll of Honour, October 1917)* and Thomas, lost their lives in the war, within a couple of months of each other, by which time Kate herself had been widowed.

Thomas died of wounds on 15 August 1917, whilst serving with the 13th Battalion Royal Sussex Regiment:

'After having been severely wounded in the neck, jaw and spine, the youngest son of Kate Medhurst, a widow, of 3 Essex Road, has died in hospital. He had been in France about eighteen months and prior to enlisting two years ago was employed at Shripney Farm, by Mr Munday.

'At the time of his death he was engaged at night with around one hundred comrades preparing a mule track to be used to bring their rations and water to the front line. During this task they were under German shell and gas attack, from which Private Medhurst received his wounds'.

Private 491089 William Gordon CHEAL
Wick, Littlehampton
Machine Gun Corps (Infantry)
Died of Wounds on 16 August 1917
Aged 32
Buried in the Potijze Chateau Lawn Cemetery, Belgium

William was born in Wick, Littlehampton, the son of Edith, a domestic servant. When he was a young child they lived with Edith's parents. In 1905 he married his wife Rose. The couple lived temporarily at Bognor with their three children, during which time he joined the Royal Sussex Regiment, before transferring to the Machine Gun Corps in July 1916, with whom he lost his life.

Second Lieutenant Walter Houlden THIRWELL
Bradley, Annandale Avenue, Bognor
The East Surrey Regiment
Killed in Action on 16 August 1917
Aged 32
Buried in the Canada Farm Cemetery, Belgium

Walter Thirwell left his home and parents, Carl and Martha, at Bradley, Annandale Avenue, to live and work in the East Indies where he managed a rubber plantation; he was their eldest son. This was a different scene to the rest of his family, who at that time were well known in horse racing circles, his uncle, Richard Marsh, being a famous trainer of the day, who had won many trophies.

Returning to England Walter enlisted into the East Surrey Regiment, where he was commissioned and moved to France in February 1917. He was then attached to 176th Company Machine Gun Corps and was killed in action, his parents being notified by telegram as reported in the *Bognor Observer*:

'A telegram from the War Office on Tuesday, 21 August, conveyed to Mr and Mrs Thirwell of Annandale Avenue, the sad news of the death in action on 16 August of their eldest son, Second Lieutenant Walter Houlden Thirwell, of the East Surrey Regiment. At the outbreak of war he was managing a large rubber plantation in the East Indies. He was a capital rider and won many trophies. A brother of the deceased, Lieutenant Dennis Thirlwell, won a Military Cross in the Battle of the Somme'.

Lance Corporal 26238 Thomas SHELLEY
Manor Place, Bognor
3rd Battalion, Grenadier Guards, the Guards Division
Killed in Action on 19 September 1917
Aged 29
Commemorated on the Tyne Cot Memorial, Belgium

Lance Corporal Thomas Shelley enlisted into Grenadier Guards at Bognor. Married with two children, he was killed in action on 19 September 1917, the *Bognor Observer* reporting thus:

'Among the latest to make the supreme sacrifice for King and Country is Private Tom Shelley of the Grenadier Guards, whose home was in Manor Place, Bognor. He enlisted about 18 months ago and his wife was notified last week of his death in action in France'.

His Commanding Officer wrote:

'Please accept my sincere sympathy in your loss. Private T Shelley was killed by a shell on 19 September. He was with the other stretcher bearer, Fergusson, in a small shelter and a shell pitched on the top and must have killed them both simultaneously. I think they were probably asleep and their faces were quite calm and their eyes shut. They were buried that afternoon by the Chaplain and Platoon Sergeant, two men and myself were present. We could not have any more men there as it was not safe to expose them. Crosses have been placed on their graves. Private Shelley's body was not much disfigured. All his effects were collected including his tunic buttons which I thought you might be glad to have and they will be forwarded later. He did exceedingly well in the trenches about 6 weeks ago and showed great courage and resource in treating the wounded and carrying them back to safety. After this he was made a stretcher bearer and his strength and cheerfulness would have been of the utmost use to us all. The whole Platoon would wish to join me in the deepest sympathy for your terrible loss'.

Private SD820 William James MITCHELL
Laburnam Cottage, North Bersted, Bognor
11th Battalion, the Royal Sussex Regiment, 39th Division
Killed in Action on 18 September 1917
Aged 19
Buried in La Clytte Military Cemetery, Belgium

William Mitchell had formerly been employed in the butchery department of Mr Tregear's shop in Aldwick Road and had enlisted in 1914. He had been in France for almost two years, having never come home on leave during that time.

His Platoon Sergeant, in a letter to his parents, stated:

'I feel it my painful duty to write and tell you that your son William has made the great sacrifice and given his life for King and Country. The sad event happened last evening about 6 o'clock, just as we were waiting to move off after relief. He was standing with a group of other fellows just outside the Battalion Headquarters, when a large howitzer pitched right amongst them with disastrous results. I had been speaking to Will not half a minute before and from the position I left him as compared with the shell hole I am certain that he must have been killed instantaneously and could not possibly have suffered any pain. A party of his colleagues have gone up today to fetch his body and bring it down to the Military Cemetery for burial by our own Chaplain. His death has come as a very severe blow to us all as I'm sure it must have to you. As a Battalion runner he had been under my control for several months now and I must say that I never wished to meet a better comrade or a more trustworthy helper. He always did his duty cheerfully and well and his loss will be felt by us for many a long day. His personal effects will be collected and sent to you through the usual channels'.

One of his comrades, obviously distressed by losing his chum, also wrote:

'I expect by now you have heard the news of poor Will and him being one of my dearest friends, I wished to send my greatest sympathy to you in your great loss. I have always found him to be a good living and God fearing young man and feel I have lost one of my best friends'.

Private G995 James HEATHER
24 Essex Road, Bognor
12th Battalion, the Royal Sussex Regiment, 39th Division
Killed in Action on 20 September 1917
Aged 21
Commemorated on the Tyne Cot Memorial, Belgium

Aged just 21 years old when he was killed in action at Ypres on 20 September 1917, Private Heather had already suffered three bad wounds and had been gassed once. James was born in a farm cottage close to Stopham Bridge, near Pulborough, one of thirteen children born to Henry and Margaret Heather, who moved to Bognor. Before enlisting at Chichester, James was living and working as a farm labourer at Shripney. For almost two weeks he was believed to be missing, before it was confirmed that he had been killed in action, possibly by a gas shell.

Private 461 Sidney Taylor HOTSTON
12th Battalion, the East Surrey Regiment, 41st Division
Killed in Action on 20 September 1917
Aged 26
Buried in the Ferme Olivier Cemetery, France

Hailing from Yapton, Sussex, Sydney was the son of Harry, a groom and his wife Martha, of Bilsham Lane. A resident of Bognor, Sidney enlisted at Kingston on Thames into the East Surrey Regiment and was reported as wounded in January 1917. Having recovered he rejoined his Regiment, which fought with distinction at Ypres, where he was killed in action.

Private G21692 William Douglas RUSTELL (RUSTHALL on the War Memorial)
10th Battalion, the Royal West Surrey Regiment, 41st Division
Killed in Action on 22 September 1917
Aged 22
Commemorated on the Tyne Cot Memorial, Belgium

Formerly a member of the Sussex Yeomanry, William Rustell, was born in Horsham, his family moving to Bordon, Hampshire.   William re-enlisted at Brighton into the Royal West Surrey Regiment and lost his life near Ypres. His Bognor connection has not been established and his name is incorrect on the town's War Memorial

Private 40875 Wilfred DIBLEY
Westergate Street, West Side, Aldingbourne
1/1 Battalion, the Hertfordshire Regiment, 39th Division
Killed in Action on 22 September 1917
Aged 19
Commemorated on the Tyne Cot Cemetery, Belgium

The brother of Herbert *(see Roll of Honour, December 1916),* Wilfred originally enlisted into the Northamptonshire Regiment, transferring to 1st Battalion Hertfordshire Regiment and was killed in action on 22 September 1917, aged 19. A few weeks later the *Bognor Observer* published the following letter from one of his comrades:

'Can you put me in touch with the parents of Private Dibley, of the Hertfordshire Regiment, who was killed in action on 22 September last? I was with him when he was hit and could probably acquaint his parents with the circumstances of his death. He told me he lived in Bognor'.

His parents lived in Westergate where his father, George, worked on a mushroom farm.

Corporal SD/809 Harry IDE
11th Battalion, the Royal Sussex Regiment, 39th Division
Killed in Action on 24 September 1917
Aged 35
Commemorated on the Menin Gate Memorial Ypres, Belgium

The son of Mr and Mrs Ide, of 17 Gainsborough Road, Bognor, he was 'well known' in football circles in the town. On leaving school Harry worked as a labourer, marrying his wife Frances, in 1903. They then lived in Newhaven with their four young children, enlisting at Bognor early in the war.

Harry Ide had enlisted at Bognor into the Royal Sussex Regiment, serving with 39th Division and was killed in action at Ypres on 24 September 1917.   On that day his

Battalion was holding the line south of the Menin Road and Harry along with over thirty of his comrades were killed during a German attack.

'News has been received that Harry Ide has been killed in action. Popularly known as "Bluffer", he was one of five sons of William Ide, a fisherman, of Chapel Street. He enlisted when recruits were appealed for into Lowthers Lambs and had been on active service in France since March 1916, having been through most of the big battles since that period'.

Lance Corporal SD1282 Frederick CASSE
12th Battalion, the Royal Sussex Regiment, 39th Division
Killed in Action on 25 September 1917
Aged 26
Buried in the Ypres Reservoir Cemetery, Belgium

The son of Mr and Mrs Casse of Henry Street, Bognor, Frederick was born in Kingston on Thames. He enlisted into the Royal Sussex Regiment and was killed in action the day after Harry Ide on 25 September 1917. On that day Lowthers Lambs launched their own attack on the German lines and took all their objectives, but at a high price, with nearly fifty men, including Frederick, losing their lives.

Second Lieutenant Reginald George William GILLHAM
Railway Station, Station Road, Bognor
13th Battalion the Royal Sussex Regiment, 39th Division
Killed in Action on 26 September 1917
Aged 22
Commemorated on the Tyne Cot Memorial, Belgium

Reginald Gillham was the only son of the Bognor Station Master and before the war worked as the clerk at Angmering Railway Station. A member of the Sussex Yeomanry, he trained at Canterbury, before serving in the Dardenelles, attached to the Headquarters Signalling Section. Trooper Gillham was evacuated from the Dardanelles to a hospital in Cairo in February 1916, with a foot wound which had become poisoned. He was 'gazetted' to Second Lieutenant into the Royal Sussex Regiment in August 1917, for 'conspicuous bravery' whilst in Egypt.

Second Lieutenant Gillham was 'killed instantly by an explosive bullet', the fourth Bognorian in three days to lose his life. His Commanding Officer, Lieutenant Colonel

Robinson, stated in a letter to Frederick's family that 'the young man gave promise of becoming a fine Officer'.

Corporal SD815 Thomas Frederick LEARY
7 Retort Cottages, South Bersted, Bognor
11th Battalion, the Royal Sussex Regiment, 39th Division
Killed in Action on 29 September 1917
Age 21
Commemorated on the Tyne Cot Memorial, Belgium

Thomas Leary, the son of George, a carpenter and Edith, a monthly nurse, was born in Felpham and was the brother of Percy *(see Roll of Honour, September 1918)*. Aged only seventeen when he enlisted, he had been in France for one year and eight months. In 1916 he had been wounded, but recovered to rejoin his Regiment and had just celebrated his 21st birthday.

His Commanding Officer at the time, Lieutenant DH Hanson, who was a former teacher at the Lancastrian School in Chichester, wrote to his mother:

'It is with the deepest regret and sympathy that I write to inform you of the sad death of your son, Corporal *(Private on War Memorial)* Thomas Frederick, who was killed in action in the heavy fighting of 29 September, following the Battle of Pozieres in the Mailly Maillet and Auchenvillers neighbourhood. It may comfort you to know that his death was instantaneous, as he was killed by a fragment of a shell striking him in the head. He was buried by one of his comrades, Corporal Baker. Your son was a great favourite of us all and I feel his loss as being personal. My home being at Chichester, we were often able to have little chats over the places we both knew. He was an excellent soldier, who died as he lived, bravely and fearlessly. Allow me to assure you of the sincere sympathy of all the Officers, NCO's and men of A Company, which is extended to you, in this, your sad bereavement. My great hope is that God, in His mercy, will comfort you in this hour of trial'.

Lance-Corporal M2 078425 Frank Henry BUTTERS
Mechanical Transport 153rd Ammunition Column, Royal Army Service Corps
Died of Wounds on 30 September 1917
Age Unknown
Buried in the Locre Hospice Cemetery, Belgium

Frank Butters is another soldier whose connections with Bognor and its War Memorial are not known. His Army record of death states he was living in Dorking, Surrey, when he enlisted in London. A Frank Butters was born in Lavant, Chichester in 1877 who may have been the above, but nothing has come to light to substantiate that.

Private 73274 Frank BEER
Clyde Villa, Clyde Road, Felpham, Bognor
123rd Company, the Labour Corps
Died of Wounds on 4 October 1917
Aged 22
Buried in the Bedford House Cemetery, Enclosure No 2, Belgium

Hailing from Felpham, Frank Beer *(related to Hugh Beer, see Roll of Honour, 17 August 1916)* enlisted at Byfleet, Surrey into the Royal West Surrey Regiment, before transferring to 123rd Labour Corps. He died of wounds received on 4 October 1917.

Corporal 70680 Frederick James (John?) BROOKS
White Cottage, Bedford Street, Bognor
15th Brigade the Royal Field Artillery
Killed in Action on 8 October 1917
Aged 25
Buried in the Hooge Crater Cemetery, Belgium

Before enlisting into the Royal Field Artillery, Frederick Brooks was employed as an assistant by Leverett and Fry, greengrocers at their High Street premises and lived with his widowed mother. He enlisted into the Royal Field Artillery and went to the Front in September 1914. Having received a gift parcel from a Mrs Hampton of Bognor in May 1915, he wrote thanking her:

'I have just received your parcel and I must thank you for the pleasant surprise it afforded me. How deeply I appreciate your kindness to me, I cannot express this in words. You seem to know just what I am in need of, for the soap and towel were at once used. Needles and buttons are always handy and the toffees I have no need to say were at once attended to by my colleagues and myself and we are all looking forward to a nice cup of cocoa later on. But the last word in my thanks must be for the cigarettes. They are of the greatest comfort to us and they help to pass the time away which otherwise would be very monotonous.

'To say that there has been terrible fighting out here is indeed putting it mildly, for I am sure that if the public at large could only see what is going on here at times they would be heartbroken, what with the dead horses and our poor infantry suffering terribly under this most agonising gas business. I myself have only had a slight meeting with it and I felt bad for hours after. I must also state here that our artillery men are magnificent and I think that the British soldier is a man to be proud of.

'On the morning of 26th I was on duty and at 0245 hrs when this gas began coming over and it lasted four to five hours. Thank goodness we have been issued with respirators and every guard is taken against being overcome by it. It is terrible in its designs, for it causes the most awful agony in the stomach if it gets a proper hold of one'.

In another letter later that year, he described a German attack on a British Hospital:

'On the further side of Ypres there was an emergency hospital. One morning very heavy shells started coming over and were seen to be gradually falling near the hospital and eventually we could see that the cowardly curs were shelling it, which happened to have a good number of inmates. Two shells crashed through the roof killing many on the spot and as four of us were only a short distance away we went at once to the assistance of our unfortunate comrades. Five lay dead outside the door, two being blown into a ditch. On going inside we went to the cellar and there found some RAMC *(Royal Army Medical Corps)* men with their Captain trying to remove some very serious cases. The Captain and I tried to remove one who had a smashed leg, but the poor man shrieked with agony. A shell at this moment struck the further end of the hospital and the doctor said we shall have to be cruel to be kind, so we made a sort of hammock with a blanket and after a time got him to the reserve trenches. We went back again three or four times, while of course those who had use of their legs ran out on the arrival of the first shell and it was heart rending to see them running in all directions. Several were re-wounded by the shrapnel, which the dogs send after their heavy shells, to catch the fleeing men'.

The son of Benjamin and Sarah Brooks, of White Cottage, Bedford Street, Bognor, Frederick was killed in action near Ypres on 8 October 1917, aged 25. Mrs Brooks received a final letter from the Front, this time from his Commanding Officer:

'I am afraid that apparently a mail to you must have been lost because I have already written to you regarding the sad loss of your son, explaining how popular he was with both the Officers and men of this battery and that he will be greatly missed, good men such as he now being very rare. I may say that he was killed instantaneously. We were experiencing very heavy shelling on our position and your son was at that moment in a telephone dug out, when a shell burst just at the entrance and it was the back burst from this that caused his death. Please accept the very deepest sympathy in your sad loss. I can assure you that the Army feels the loss of such men as your son very much'.

Private 17905 Thomas GROUT
North View, Chichester Road, Bognor
3rd Battalion Coldstream Guards, the Guards Division
Killed in Action on 9 October 1917
Aged 23
Commemorated on the Tyne Cot Memorial, Belgium

Thomas Grout, the younger brother of Frank, was born in North Bersted, the youngest of eleven children born to bricklayer Egbert and his wife Susan, who was a laundress. On leaving school Thomas became a brick maker before enlisting at Chichester into 3rd Battalion, the Coldstream Guards. He married Lily Clinch in 1916 and set up home at North View, Chichester Road, Bognor, sadly not for long.

'Mrs Grout has been notified officially of the death of her husband. They were only married on 1 October 1916 and he went out to the Front a week later, having been there ever since'.

Driver 64563 Henry George SHARP
21 Essex Road, Bognor
The Royal Field Artillery
Killed in Action on 9 October 1917
Age Unknown
Buried in the Perth Cemetery (China Wall), Belgium.

The son of George Sharp, a brick maker's carter and his wife Elizabeth, Henry lived with his parents and two brothers and two sisters. A driver with 49th Battery Royal Field Artillery, Henry enlisted at Portsmouth and was killed in action at Ypres on 9 October 1917.

Private G40252 Frank MEDHURST
3 Essex Road, Bognor
2nd Battalion, the Royal West Surrey Regiment, 33rd Division
Killed in Action on 26 October 1917
Age 25
Commemorated on the Tyne Cot Memorial, Belgium

Prior to the war Frank Medhurst was a carter working for Bognor Urban District Council. He had been bought up with his nine brothers *(including Thomas, see Roll of Honour,15 August 1917)* and sisters, their parents being fishmongers, Thomas and Kate.

Two months after the death of Thomas, another buff OHMS envelope landed on Kate's doormat, informing her that Frank had also been killed in action. He had enlisted at Bognor into the Royal Sussex Regiment, but at the time of his death was serving with 2nd Battalion the Royal West Surrey Regiment.

Kate's three other serving sons, Private Charles Medhurst, serving with the Royal Fusiliers, Private Frederick Medhurst, serving with the Royal Garrison Artillery and Private George Medhurst, serving with the Royal Sussex Regiment; all survived the conflict.

Private 67342 Charles JOHNSON
10 Canada Grove, Bognor
9th Battalion, the Royal Sussex Regiment,
Killed in Action on 28 October 1917
Age Believed to have been 24
Buried in the Hargicourt British Cemetery, Aisne

No details were immediately found of this man, other than his name appearing on the Bognor War Memorial and tracing him was difficult. However, research has pointed to Charles Johnson, the son of gardener George and his wife Alice, who at one time lived at 3 Argyle Terrace and who enlisted at Brighton into the Royal Sussex Regiment. He is believed to have been the steward at the Bognor Golf Club before enlisting. During October there were quiet times. However, sporadic skirmishes occurred, during which Charles Johnson lost his life.

Rifleman 374520 Thomas Harold Trewin HOLE
4 Chichester Road, Bognor
2/8th Battalion, the London Regiment (the Post Office Rifles), 60th London Division
Killed in Action on 30 October 1917
Aged 19
Commemorated on the Tyne Cot Memorial, Belgium

The son of George and Harriett Hole, Thomas was born in Torquay, Devon, where his father and elder brother worked as grocers. The family moved to London where George became a timekeeper at a chocolate manufactory, before moving again to Bognor at some time before the outbreak of war.

Thomas enlisted at Kensington into the Post Office Rifles. He was initially reported as wounded and missing, but after a week or two of uncertainty it was confirmed that he had been killed in action at Ypres.

Lieutenant Victor Auge STONE
Canadian Infantry
Killed in Action on 10 November 1917
Aged 39

Born in Amberley, Victor was the second son of Thomas and Rebecca Stone and the younger brother of RSM Bernard Stone *(see Roll of Honour 1918)*. On leaving school Victor became a Rate Collectors Clerk before emigrating to Canada and was one of Canada's first sons to answer the call of the mother country, returning to England in 1914. It is likely that he had had some previous military service before emigrating. Having been badly gassed at Ypres, he was returned to England and offered a staff position in Hastings, which he refused and having obtained a commission, was soon back in the thick of the fighting.

Lieutenant Victor Stone was killed in action in France on 10 November 1917. The *Bognor Observer* stated that both brothers were 'very well known at Bognor and Amberley where they had lived for many years and where their father Mr T Stone was the schoolmaster'.

Second Lieutenant Robert Cuthbert STOWELL
Loretto, the Esplanade, Bognor
1st Battalion, the Kings Own Royal Lancaster Regiment, 4th Division
Killed in Action on 20 November 1917
Aged 29
Buried in the Monchy British Cemetery, Monchy-le-Preux, France

The eldest son of Mr and Mrs A J Stowell, Robert was born in Wimbledon. His father had a successful career in banking, becoming the Chief Inspector of the London and County and Westminster Bank: Robert, set out on a career at their Bognor Branch in the High Street, his younger brother Wilfred *(see Roll of Honour 1918)* following a similar path.

On the outbreak of war Robert was commissioned with the Kings Own Royal Lancaster Regiment and was killed in action near Cambrai on 10 November 1917.

THE THIRD BATTLE OF GAZA

Private TF200568 Christopher NEWPORT
The Anchorage, Park Road, Bognor
1/4 Battalion, the Royal Sussex Regiment, 53rd Division
Killed in Action on 4 November 1917
Aged 20
Buried in the Beersheba War Cemetery, Palestine

'Mr and Mrs Newport of The Anchorage, 3 Park Road, have heard that their son Private Newport has been killed in action in Palestine'.

Christopher Newport had been born in Ireland, where his father was serving in the Royal Navy. On retirement the family had settled in Bognor. It was from here that Christopher left the family home, his two sisters, Dorothy and Mary and his younger brother Eric, to enlist in the Royal Sussex Regiment at Horsham.

Having survived the ordeals of Gallipolli, the Battalion were moved to Egypt and then to Palestine, where Christopher fought in the first two Battles of Gaza. The British Commander was withdrawn, to be replaced by General Sir Edmund Allenby. After re-organising the troops under his command and ensuring adequate water supplies were available in forward positions, the Third Battle of Gaza was launched on 31 October 1917, when the British Infantry attacked Beersheba. Backed up by the Desert Mounted Corps, Beersheba was finally taken following a Cavalry charge by the Australian 4th Light Horse Brigade against the Turkish positions. Operations against Gaza commenced on 2 November with a night attack along the coast. The British advanced two miles and held their positions until a further assault commenced on 6 November. Private Christopher Newport lost his life during a Turkish counter attack. His name does not appear on the Bognor War Memorial.

WESTERN FRONT

Trooper Basil Godfrey HUMPHREYS
Cottesmore, Gordon Avenue, Bognor
1st King Edwards Horse
Killed in Action on 20 November 1917
Aged Unknown
Commemorated on the Cambrai Memorial

The Humphreys family, William Barclay and Emma Maria had five sons, all of whom were serving. Basil was born in Canada and enlisted into the King Edward's Horse, a regiment of the Special Reserve. On 20 November 1917 the 1st King Edwards Horse were taking part in the Battle of Cambrai; their objective was to advance towards Graincourt les Havrincourt and secure the main Bapaume Road, beside the Canal du Nord. The 2/5th Duke of Wellingtons Battalion reached Graincourt, covered by the Kind Edwards Horse on their right. With Graincourt secured, the King Edwards Horse were ordered towards Anneux, but found that the wire was uncut and many, including Trooper Humphreys, fell victim of very heavy machine gun fire. His was the third loss his family had sustained *(see Roll of Honour, Second Lieutenant GF Humphreys, August 1916 and Second Lieutenant Leslie Humphreys, December 1916).*

Private G17962 George Edward LITTLECHILD
3 Victoria Cottages, South Bersted, Bognor
7th Battalion, the Royal Sussex Regiment, 12th Division
Killed in Action on 30 November 1917
Aged 30
Commemorated on the Cambrai Memorial

George Littlechild, a builder, was the son of Edwin, a baker, bread man and confectioner and his wife Eliza, who was a caretaker. On leaving school George became an errand boy, before taking up building, lodging and working for a while in Worthing. He enlisted into the Royal Sussex Regiment when war broke out. All his five brothers were also serving and one, gunner Frederick Littlechild, was killed in the Battle of Ypres *(see Roll of Honour, May 1915).*

Private Edward Littlechild had been wounded early on in his service life, but had returned to the Front. In November 1917, following intensive training with tanks, a move was made to Gonnelieu, to form up for the Battle of Cambrai. The Battalion was involved in the capture of the Hindenburg outpost and main line near La Vaquerie. On 30 November a heavy counter-attack occurred and it was on that day George Littlechild lost his life.

His Platoon Officer wrote to his parents:

'I am indeed sorry to have to tell you of the death of your son, although I expect you have been informed by the War Office, but I thought you would like to hear how he met his death.

'Unfortunately I was not in the Cambrai myself, but I have the details from one of his comrades in the Platoon. From the day when the Company went over the top on the 20th to the day he was killed on the 30th he played a man's part all through. He went through all the hardest fighting, he fought splendidly and was a splendid example to comrades by his unfailing cheerfulness and then on the 30th he was killed by a shell, while on duty in the trench. His death was instantaneous and was due to concussion'.

Gunner 101220 John Edward MILES
Barn Rocks Cottage, Aldwick, Bognor
225 Siege Battery, the Royal Garrison Artillery
Killed in Action on 1 December 1917
Aged 37
Buried in the Rocquigny-Equancourt Road British Cemetery, Manancourt,
The Somme, France

John Miles was born in Sherborne, Hampshire, the son of a bricklayer's apprentice, at some stage moving to Aldwick, where he settled with his wife, Annie. A domestic gardener, he enlisted into the Royal Garrison Artillery on 15 June 1916 and was killed in action eighteen months later.

THE LOSS OF HMS *MARY ROSE*

On 15 October 1917, the destroyers HMS *Mary Rose* and her sister ship HMS *Strongbow* left Lerwick to escort an eastbound convoy to Norway. The destroyers separated at midday, HMS *Strongbow* staying with the eastbound convey and HMS *Mary Rose* going ahead to meet a westbound convoy leaving Norway the following day.

Two days later HMS *Mary Rose* met up with HMS *Strongbow* and both escorted the westbound merchant convoy consisting of two British, one Belgian and the rest of the ships from neutral Scandinavia. HMS *Mary Rose* was steaming some miles ahead of the convoy when her crew heard gunfire. Immediately she turned back to assist.

In the meantime two German mine laying cruisers, the *Brummer* and the *Bremse*, had made a surprise attack on the convoy. HMS *Strongbow* had spotted the two warships which, in the high seas and poor visibility, she mistook for British, as they had been deliberately rigged to give that impression. The Germans opened fire, hitting and jamming *Strongbow*'s radio. The fire from the two heavyweights was devastating; HMS

Strongbow was no match for them, the Captain ordering that the ship be abandoned and every man for himself.

By the time HMS *Mary Rose* had reached the scene the German cruisers had sunk nine merchantmen. Against all odds, HMS *Mary Rose* took up the fight and approached the German cruisers at high speed to get close enough for a torpedo attack, at the same time firing at them. Both the German ships then got her range, opened fire together and sunk her in a few minutes. HMS *Mary Rose* went down, guns blazing. The Germans then shelled her lifeboats and rafts. Only ten men survived, making it back to the Norwegian coast, where they were rescued by some lighthouse keepers.

Seaman J51186 Alfred HOLDEN
The Cottage, nr Pagham Church, Pagham, Bognor
HMS *Mary Rose* Royal Navy
Aged 32
Lost at Sea on 17 October 1917
Body Recovered and Buried in the Fredrikstad Military Cemetery, Norway.

Seaman Alfred Holden lost his life on HMS *Mary Rose*. Born in Wick, Littlehampton, Alfred was one of eight sons of Mr and Mrs John Holden of the Cottage, near Pagham Church serving and the only one not to return.

WESTERN FRONT

Trooper William E BAKER
Longford Road, Bognor
The Sussex Yeomanry
Killed in Action on 2 December 1917
Aged 31

The Bognor War Memorial contains the name W E Baker and no further information. It is possible that he was the following, reported wounded earlier in the war:

'Mrs Baker of Longford Road, has received news that her son has been wounded in France and is now in hospital in Newcastle. Before enlisting he was in the employ of Messrs Leverett and Frye's Fish Depot. One of his brothers has been killed in action and two others are still serving'.

DIED AT HOME

Lieutenant Reginald Simon Macnamara CREAGH
14th Battalion, the Rifle Brigade
Died at Home on 5 December 1917
Aged 32
Buried in the Kensal Green (St Marys) Roman Catholic Cemetery, London

Born in Steyning, Sussex, what the Bognor connection is for Lieutenant Creagh, who was the son of Major Simon and Mrs Creagh of Hove, is not known. He was married to Zoe Rich in 1912 and they lived at Langdale Road, Hove.

Reginald served with 14th Battalion, the Rifle Brigade and died at home on 5 December 1917 and was buried in London. He is commemorated on both the Hove Library and Bognor War Memorials.

THE LOSS OF HM TRAWLER *APLEY*

Able Seaman 17847 Ernest Alfred CONSTANT
St Anne's, Crescent Road, Bognor
HM Trawler *Apley* Royal Navy
Lost at Sea on 6 December 1917
Aged 41
Commemorated on the Portsmouth Naval Memorial, Southsea, Hampshire

One of Bognor's well known fishermen, Ernest Constant, a very capable sailor and a respected member of the Bognor fishing community, lost his life whilst serving as a deck hand on the minesweeper HMS *Apley* on 6 December 1917.

Ernest was born in Selsey, the son of Thomas Constant, a fisherman and spent part of his childhood living in Fish Lane. The family moved to Bognor where, for a few years, his father became the innkeeper at the Fountain Inn, in Bognor High Street, by which time Ernest had become a fisherman. He married Louisa Parfitt and they moved to Crescent Road, where their son, also Ernest, was born in 1911. Ernest (senior) enlisted into the Royal Naval Reserve in August 1917.

'The deceased was home on leave only a week or two ago. He had spent his life as a fisherman, even from early boyhood and when only 11 years old achieved a record for one so young by taking, single handed, one of the largest sailing ships known locally, from the Owers Lightship to Selsey. He has left a widow and a child about six years old', reported the *Bognor Observer*.

The Bognor Fishermen's Association sent a comforting letter to Ernest's widow, expressing their sorrow that Ernest had fallen at the post of duty for his Country's sake. A collection was subsequently taken at their annual meeting 'which realized a goodly sum'.

In January 1918 the following was placed in the *Bognor Observer*:

'Mrs Constant of St Annes, Crescent Road, the widow of the late Mr Ernest Constant, the well known Bognor fisherman, begs gratefully to thank the Bognor fishermen and other kind friends for their assistance and for contributing towards a fund for her benefit, which she greatly appreciates and which will be of material help to her at the present time. It will be remembered that Mr Constant lost his life at sea whilst engaged in a minesweeper, through the ship coming into contact with a mine and being blown up. Mr Constant was at his post as lookout at the time and his end was very sudden. His death is felt keenly by his many friends amongst the Bognor anglers'.

MESOPOTAMIA

After the fall of Kut a new commander, Major General Stanley Maude, took over command of the British Army in Mesopotamia and a change of tactic saw the defeat of the Turks in a series of battles throughout 1917. These culminated in the Battle of Tikrit fought on 5 November. Overall conditions, however, were still appalling for the Officers and men, extreme temperatures, flies, mosquitoes and other vermin making life intolerable, with, apart from those killed in action, many dying of sickness. Medical arrangements were really bad, with men suffering from wounds having to wait on boats for up to two weeks before reaching a hospital.

Sergeant 47535 William LAGGETT
South Bersted, Bognor
14th Kings Hussars, Indian Cavalry Division, Mesopotamia
Died of Wounds on 6 December 1917
Aged 31
Commemorated on the Basra Memorial, Iraq

William Leggett was the son of general labourer, Maurice and his wife, Fanny, the family living in the early 1890s in Henry Street, Bognor.

The 14th Kings Hussars were serving in India when the war broke out, moving to Mesopotamia in November 1915. They fought in the Battle of Tikrit in November 1917 and that is probably when William received the wounds that took his life a month later.

ITALY

In 1917 British troops were sent to Italy, moving directly from Flanders and France, to stop her forces collapsing in the face of German attacks, which had been boosted by soldiers released from the Russian Front. Sometimes referred to as the Forgotten Front, British troops were to stay there until the Armistice and many hundreds lost their lives in the battles that took place, including one man from Bognor.

Gunner 184118 Henry George BROWN
1 Somerset Terrace, Lyon Street, Bognor
247 Siege Battery, the Royal Garrison Artillery (Italy)
Died of Wounds on 21 December 1917
Aged 42
Buried in the Giavera British Cemetery, Arcade, Italy

Henry Brown had worked for the Southern Dairies Limited in Aldwick Road, Bognor, enlisting at Chichester into the Royal Garrison Artillery and serving on the Western Front for three years before moving to Italy. He was born near Godstone, Surrey, where his father, Thomas, worked as a stockman. After marrying Elizabeth, the couple lived in Brighton, where their three daughters were born, subsequently moving to Bognor by 1909 when William, their son, was born.

Elizabeth, received two letters informing her that Henry had died of wounds. The first was from a Chaplain:

'It is with deep regret that I have to inform you of the death of your husband yesterday afternoon. He was severely wounded in the abdomen by an enemy shell and immediately bought to the Field Hospital. A Baptist doctor attended to him and told me of his condition. Nothing, alas, was of use to save his life and I stayed with him until he passed away. He was just able to tell me about yourself and the children and to give me your address. I told him I would write to you and send his love to you all and he understood and wished me to do so. We prayed together, commending him and you all to the care of God. I conducted his funeral today and his body now lies with those other gallant soldiers in a British Cemetery, behind the Front Line. A cross has been erected over his grave and the Cemetery will always be cared for. Your husband's small personal belongings will be sent to you in due course by the Army. This will be terrible news to you I am sure, God alone can comfort and sustain you, may He do so and guide the future of yourself and the children. May you find hope and consolation in the thought that this is not the end, there is the great reunion of loved ones in the hereafter. With my personal sympathy,

Yours very truly,

(signed) Reverend T H Burnett

Wesleyan Chaplain'.

A further letter was received from his Battalion Sergeant-Major:

'I offer you the sincerest sympathy of every Officer, NCO and man of the battery. He was such a splendid soldier, always cheerful and a more willing worker it is impossible to find, for no matter how miserable the conditions, he was always one of the first to turnout, always setting a fine example to many men (junior) in age. As for myself I will miss him very much, for like me, he was a Sussex man. We were the only two in the Battery and our talks about our county were many, more especially about Bognor, as I have relatives there. I can assure you there is great consolation in having a chum from the same county as yourself, as it helps to pass away many a weary hour.

(signed) C Harrop, Sergeant-Major,

Siege Battery, British Expeditionary Force, Italy'.

PALESTINE

Private G8913 Frank Henry WHITE
Elbridge Cottages, Chichester Road, North Bersted
16th Battalion, the Royal Sussex Regiment, 74th Division
Killed in Action on 29 December 1917
Aged 26
Buried in the Jerusalem War Cemetery, Palestine

Frank White was born in North Bersted and lived in Elbridge, between Bognor and Chichester. He was the eldest child of Frank, who was an agricultural labourer employed by Butterlees Farm, North Bersted and Catherine, nee Wingate, who was possibly related to the Wingate Dairy family. Her father, retired farm bailiff, William Wingate, also lived with them.   On leaving school, Frank became a domestic gardener, by which time his father was the farm foreman. Another son and three daughters completed the family.

Frank enlisted into 16th Battalion, the Royal Sussex Regiment.   In March 1917 he was stationed at East Tilbury, Essex and wrote home:

'Just a few lines hoping you are quite well at home. I hope to be home in the next three or four weeks, that is if nothing fresh crops up, which is more than likely here. I expect you saw by the papers we have had another visit by the Zeppelins last night. I was up in charge of the guard, but we did not see one at all, the searchlights were flashing about all night. I had a couple of recruits on with me that had not been on guard before. Eight of them were inoculated the other day and they were fainting and falling all over the place. I am up on the machine guns again now, several of our machine gunners have gone away, there are only five of us and two Corporals left here now and this morning they wired from Cliffe to know if we could spare any for there. I will close now, with love to all, Frank'.

Frank went to Egypt later that year and was killed in action on 29 December.   The notification of his death did not appear in the *Bognor Observer* until June 1918, which must have been an anxious time for his family

WESTERN FRONT

Second Lieutenant John Lawrence MATTHEWS
Aldwick House, Aldwick, Bognor
7th Battalion, the Royal Sussex Regiment
Died of Wounds on 29 December 1917
Aged 20
Buried in the Bur Aire Communal Cemetery, Pas de Calais, France

The son of Mr and Mrs Henry Matthews, John was educated at Hollyrood School in Victoria Drive, Bognor and joined the Inns of Court Officer Training Corps immediately after matriculation at London in 1915. He obtained a commission in the Special Reserve of the Royal Sussex Regiment, but an accident at drill brought about knee trouble and caused him to be invalided out in September 1916.

Later on, the young Officer succeeded in convincing a medical board that he was fit for service.   The notice of his relinquishing his commission was cancelled and he was gazetted Lieutenant in 1916, taking part in the fighting around Arras and near Cambrai.

He was then attached to a Signal Company of the Royal Engineers and being badly injured on 29 December 1917, he died later that day in the Casualty Clearing Centre.

THE LOSS OF HMS *ARAGON* AND HMS *ATTACK*.....

In the company of the destroyer HMS *Attack*, the *Aragon*, a liner requisitioned from the Royal Mail Steam Packet Company, was completing the last stage of her journey to Egypt, having spent Christmas at Malta and was within sight of the port of Alexandria, which the ships were unable to enter immediately. The *Aragon* was carrying all the Christmas mail for the troops stationed in Egypt, comprising some 2500 mailbags, as well as 160 nursing sisters, 2200 troops and the crew of 340, totalling 2700 souls in all. Having followed HMS *Attack* towards the port entrance and then having to turn back to sea, she was attacked by the lurking German submarine, *UC34*, which fired off a torpedo, scoring a devastating hit. Immediately the *Aragon* was abandoned, priority being given to the nursing sisters, who all got clear before she started to list heavily to starboard and sink from the stern. For the next fifteen minutes or so the crew managed to get more boats away, although several had become jammed. Ropes were attached to HMS *Attack* and these became a means of escape. With the ship sinking fast, the order was given - 'every man for himself'. The troops 'clung on to each other cheering and singing until they reached the water level and then broke up into struggling masses'. The *Aragon* then rapidly sank astern and disappeared. HMS *Attack* picked up hundreds of men; 'some were wounded and bleeding, others stripped of clothes, many laid out and dying'. The nursing sisters were doing sterling work on the destroyer, when there was 'a terrific explosion'. The middle of the destroyer had been smashed by another torpedo and men were 'blown into the air'. She sank rapidly. By now, trawlers from the port had raced to pick up as many survivors as they could; 'these boats did wonderful work', but the loss of life was great.

The *Aragon* was attacked at 1100 hrs on Sunday, 30 December 1917 and sank within twenty minutes. HMS *Attack* was sunk five to seven minutes later 'in the act of rescuing survivors' and sank almost immediately.

....AND A ROYAL FLYING CORPS MAN

Air Mechanic Second Class 85472 William JONES
2 Argyle Road, Bognor
Royal Flying Corps
Lost at Sea on Hospital Ship HMS *Aragon* on 30 December 1917
Aged 34
Commemorated on the Chatby Memorial, Alexandria, Egypt

Airman Second Class Jones, of the Royal Flying Corps, was a carpenter by trade and lived with his wife Elizabeth. He had previously worked for Messrs. Reynolds of Bognor and was one of 610 who lost their lives that Sunday morning. He was the eldest son of John, a bespoke tailor and his wife Ann and had been posted to the Middle East, travelling on HMS *Aragon*.

1918

DIED AT HOME

Private 29471 Herbert Arthur REDMAN
2 New Street, St John's Terrace, Bognor
The Kings Royal Rifle Corps, transferred to the Labour Corps
Died at Home on 5 January 1918
Aged 20
Buried in Bognor Town Cemetery, West Sussex

Herbert was the son of James Harvey Redman, a builder, carpenter and house decorator and his wife, Charlotte, who died whilst Herbert was a young boy. On leaving school Herbert joined his father and elder brother in the family business, before enlisting into the Kings Royal Rifle Corps. The circumstances of Private Redman's death are unknown, as he died at his home. He had been transferred to the Labour Corps who did vital work, repairing roads smashed up because of war damage, thus keeping supply lines open. No further information has come to hand.

Private 33171 Thomas BROCKHURST
Spire Cottage, Chalcraft Lane, North Bersted, Bognor
106th Company, the Labour Corps
Died of Wounds at Home on 10 January 1918
Aged 31
Buried in the Bognor Town Cemetery, Bognor

A former Royal Fusilier, Thomas was the husband of Kate Amy Brockhurst. Upon leaving the Royal Fusiliers, he was employed maintaining the Bognor Croquet Grounds in Victoria Gardens and re-enlisted as part of the Derby Groups on 29 May 1916, sailing for France less than a month later. On 14 September 1917 he received serious gunshot wounds to his face and also suffered a fractured spine. He was transferred back to

Blighty for treatment in No 2 New Zealand General Hospital, where he lay seriously ill until his death on 10 January 1918.

'The funeral took place on 15 January 1918, at the Cemetery, Bognor, of Private Thomas Brockhurst, who died of wounds received in France on 2 September last year. The coffin which was covered with the Union Jack and bore the inscription 'Reg. No 63286 Private Thomas Brockhurst, No 106 Labour Company, died 10 January 1918, aged 31 years'. The mourners were his wife and little daughter, mother and sister and other members of the family. There were many beautiful floral tributes, amongst them being those from his wife and daughter and including one from the sisters, nurses and boys in Ward 5, No 2 New Zealand Hospital, Walton-on-Thames'.

THE LOSS OF HMS *OPAL* and HMS *NARBOROUGH*

HMS *Opal,* an M Class destroyer was launched at Sunderland in 1915. She fought at the Battle of Jutland, after which she was engaged in minesweeping, convoy protection and anti-submarine patrols in the North Sea. On the night of 12 January 1918, accompanied by her sister ship HMS *Narborough* and the light cruiser HMS *Boadicea*, she set out to hunt German auxiliary warships suspected of laying mines off the Scottish coast. The weather when they left port was 'favourable', but started to deteriorate in the late afternoon, to such a degree that the both *Opal* and *Narborough* were ordered back to port by the *Boadicea*. Very soon heavy snow set in and both ships were sailing 'blind', but continuing to send regular reports indicating their course and intention to return. On shore the fog horns were sounding their warnings, but their signals were intermittent and ceased altogether because of the cold. In what turned out to be her last message *Opal* signalled 'blinding snow', followed by an unintelligible message, then nothing. She had hit the rocks and run aground. *Narborough* passed close by her a minute or so later and suffered the same fate; both ships were broken up by the impact, heavy seas and high winds. All the crew aboard the *Narborough* were lost. On HMS *Opal* only one man survived.

The appalling weather prevented any ships leaving port until daybreak to conduct a search, the wrecks being discovered at 0930 hrs by HMS *Caster*. The one survivor was found sheltering in a small cave immediately above both wrecks. In his evidence given later at the Court of Enquiry, he described how HMS *Opal* hit the rocks heavily 'about three times' and then slid into deep water, losing her mast and funnels which were carried away in the darkness. HMS *Narborough* suffered the same fate a minute or two later. The wrecks were abandoned and broken up by the sea over the next few weeks, taking most of the dead of both crews with them. A handful of graves are situated in the local Lyness Cemetery.

Engineer Lieutenant Commander Thomas Henry Fielder DAMPIER-CHILD
Avilion, North Bersted, Bognor
HMS *Opal* Royal Navy
Lost at Sea on 12 January 1918
Aged 37
Commemorated on the Portsmouth Naval Memorial, Southsea, Hampshire

'News has been received by the relatives, of the death by drowning of Engineering Lieutenant Commander Dampier-Child, he leaves a widow and three little daughters'.

Born at Sandown on the Isle of Wight, Thomas, an engineering student at the Royal Naval College, Devonport, became a career officer and a graduate of the Royal Naval College, Greenwich, where he remained for a year. His first appointment was on HMS *Albion*, which for two years was at the China Station. In 1905 he was appointed to HMS *Grafton*, a guard ship in Portsmouth. In 1907 he married Isabel, the youngest daughter of the late Reverend Alfred Child of Chertsey, Surrey. After his marriage he took a course in gunnery at HMS *Vernon* and was re-appointed in 1908 to the China Station, this time on HMS *Monmouth*. His next appointment was to the Dreadnought Class, HMS *Temeraire*, a battleship of over 18000 tons, followed by a short tour on a torpedo boat destroyer. In May 1915 he went to Sunderland to superintend the building of the ship to which he was commissioned, HMS *Opal*, which was launched in 1915 and on which he lost his life in the violent storm off the Scottish Coast on 12 January 1918.

WESTERN FRONT

Signaller 7348 Frank Herbert LEMMON
The Drapers Shop, 1 High Street, Bognor
11th Australian Infantry Battalion, 1st Australian Division
Killed in Action on 21 January 1918
Aged 35
Buried in the Messines Ridge British Cemetery, Belgium

One of five sons of Frank and Sarah Lemmon, Frank had emigrated to Australia and enlisted into the Australian Army at the outbreak of war and was killed in action on 21

January 1918. He was the brother of Private William Lemmon *(see Roll of Honour 1916)*.

'Much sympathy will be felt in Bognor for Mr and Mrs F Lemmon, who have unofficially heard of the death of their second son, Signaller Frank H Lemmon, of the Australian Forces. It will be remembered that some time ago another son who came over with the Canadian Expeditionary Force was killed in action', reported the *Bognor Observer.*

THE LOSS OF THE SS *HUNTSMAN*

The SS *Huntsman* was a passenger/cargo vessel built in 1904 and owned by the Charente Steamship Company of Liverpool. Brought into war service, she was en route from Liverpool to Calcutta, when she was attacked 180 miles west of Fastnet and sunk by the German submarine U50 *(The Charente Steamship Company lost 27 of their fleet of 70 ships in the war).*

Second Officer George MURRAY
Ealing Villa, Linden Road, Bognor
SS *Huntsman*, Mercantile Marine
Lost at Sea on 28 February 1918
Aged 22
Commemorated on the Tower Hill Memorial, London

The only son of George and Anne Murray, 'Boy' George was born in Chorlton, Lancashire, serving in the Merchant Marine as the Second Officer, on the SS *Huntsman* and was one of two crew members to lose their lives in the attack.

PALESTINE

Private TF315217 Henry John (James on War Memorial) DINHAM
5 Strathmore Gardens, William Street, Bognor
16th Battalion, the Royal Sussex Regiment, 74th Division
Killed in Action on 10 March 1918
Aged 32
Buried in the Jerusalem War Cemetery, Israel

Henry Dinham lived with his wife, Alice and their young child. For some years he had worked at Messrs. Buckle and Clithero, the grocers, of 21 High Street. He was born at

Regents Park, Middlesex and enlisted in 1916 into the Royal Sussex Regiment, the 16th Battalion of which was formed from the dismounted Sussex Yeomanry troops in Egypt. He had been in the East for some thirteen months and his Battalion were preparing to be sent to the European Western Front, when he was killed in action. He left effects to the value of £885 to Alice.

THE MARCH RETREAT

The March Retreat was the Germans' last throw of the dice. Their numbers were boosted by Russia's withdrawal from the war, releasing nearly fifty Divisions of German soldiers who could now be deployed on the Western Front. They also knew that with the entry of the United States into the war, with their overwhelming numbers of men and materials, their only chance of victory was to defeat the Allies before the Americans arrived. Thus in March the Germans embarked on the offensive which made the deepest advances of the war by either side. Their strategy was to aim the main thrust of their attack at the British Army and when they were defeated it was hoped that the French would seek an Armistice. The offensive was fast moving, lead by storm troopers, who, not carrying enough food or ammunition to sustain themselves, eventually stretched their supply lines to breaking point. This, coupled with a lack of clear objectives once the attack had started and heavy German casualties, saw the offensive grind to a halt. By the end of April it became clear that the danger of a complete German breakthrough had passed, although the fighting continued. They had suffered heavy casualties and had used many of their reserves.

Rifleman S15900 Albert George CHAFFER
Strathmore Villa, Bognor
11th Battalion, the Rifle Brigade, 37th Division
Killed in Action on 20 March 1918
Aged 26
Commemorated on the Thiepval Memorial, Pas de Calais, France

Albert, born in 1892, was the second son of bricklayer Henry Chaffer and his wife Elizabeth. Henry had passed away by start of the war. Albert, one of four sons, all of whom served, enlisted into the Rifle Brigade and had been in France for three years, during which time he had been both wounded and had suffered badly from trench fever. Mrs Chaffer had received notification that Albert had been reported missing 'from about 22 March 1918'. This was followed two weeks later by the sad news that he had been killed in action.

Able Seaman Z5510 Thomas HOMER
Drake Battalion, the Royal Naval Volunteer Reserve
Killed in Action on 21 March 1918
Age 22
Commemorated on the Arras Memorial, Pas de Calais, France

Born in Portfield, Chichester, Thomas was a son of Noah, a farm worker and his wife Ann. He was married and at the time of his death the couple were living in Gateshead. Thomas enlisted into the Drake Battalion on 10 January 1916 and went to the Front in March of that year. He was invalided back to the United Kingdom in May 1916 and re-enlisted into the Drake Battalion on 19 February 1918. A month later he was killed in action. He was the brother of Charles Homer *(see Roll of Honour, October 1918).*

Major Henry Archer Hope JOHNSTONE
Fairmead, Risley, Derbyshire
152 Brigade, the Royal Field Artillery
Killed in Action on 21 March 1918
Aged 28
Buried in the Wancourt British Cemetery, France

Born in Nottingham, the son of a solicitor, Henry Johnstone was probably a career soldier. He does not appear to have married, his effects valued at £932 being left to his mother, Ada, who was by then a widow. No connection with Bognor been established, although his name appears on the Bognor War Memorial. At the time of his death he was a Captain with the acting rank of Major. He had been wounded early in the conflict in 1914.

Second Lieutenant Ernest Henry SKINNER
1/1st Battalion, the Cambridgeshire Regiment, 39th Division
Killed in Action between 21/31 March 1918
Age Unknown
Commemorated on the Pozieres Memorial

Ernest Skinner is another soldier whose name appears on the Bognor War Memorial but for whom no other Bognor connection has been found. He enlisted into 1st Battalion, the Cambridgeshire Regiment, serving in 24th Division. At some time between 21 March and 31 March Henry was killed in action, whilst taking part in the March Retreat.

Second Lieutenant Wilfred STOWELL
2nd Battalion, the Leinster Regiment, 16th Division
Killed in Action in March 1918
Aged 27
Commemorated on the Pozieres Memorial

The second son of Mr and Mrs A J Stowell, of Loretto, the Esplanade and the husband of Agnes, Wilfred worked at the London County and Westminster Bank in Bognor before enlisting. He served with 2nd Battalion, the Leinster Regiment and was killed in action within four months of his brother Robert *(see Roll of Honour, November 1917)*

'We regret to announce the death of Second Lieutenant Wilfred Stowell who was formerly with the London County and Westminster Bank at Chichester, Redhill and Littlehampton. A short time ago his brother was also killed in action', reported the *Bognor Observer.*

Sergeant M1 08848 Frank COSENS
Ye Olde Cottage, Glamis Street, Bognor
Royal Army Service Corps attached to the 5th London Field Ambulance, the Royal Army Medical Corps
Died of Wounds on 22 March 1918
Aged 37
Buried in Rocquigny-Equancourt Road British Cemetery, Manoncourt, France

Born in Walberton, near Arundel, Sussex, the youngest son of farm manager Albert and Elizabeth Cosens, Frank had already served in the Royal Horse Artillery, signing on in 1901 and buying himself out in 1904. He then took employment as a tram conductor in Wandsworth and married Lydia Toop, of Church Farm, Aldingbourne in 1910. The family moved back to Sussex, where Frank became a motor van driver which was ideal for him re-enlisting into the Royal Army Service Corps in October 1914. From there he was attached to 5th London Field Ambulance, Royal Army Medical Corps and died of wounds in March 1918.

Private G28403 Walter POWELL
Rose Cottage, South Bersted, Bognor
8th Battalion, the Queens Royal West Kent Regiment, 24th Division
Killed in Action on 22 March 1918
Aged 19
Commemorated on the Pozieres Memorial

Walter was the brother of Richard *(see Roll of Honour, September 1916)* and William *(see Roll of Honour, September 1918)*. His father, Frank, was an Army Reservist and therefore sometimes away from home during Walter's childhood. On leaving school Walter became an errand boy, before enlisting into the Queens Royal West Kent Regiment and was killed in action on 22 March 1918 at Vandencourt, near Vermand, during the March Retreat.

'News has been received by Mr and Mrs Powell of Rose Cottage, South Bersted, that their youngest son, Private Walter Powell of the Royal West Kents, was killed in action in France on 22 March', reported the *Bognor Observer.*

Private G7369 George STRUDWICK
Decoy Farm Cottages, Tangmere, Sussex
8th Battalion, the Royal West Kent Regiment, 24th Division
Killed in Action on 22 March 1918
Aged 26
Commemorated on the Pozieres Memorial

George was born in Littlehampton, the son of Henry, a journeyman bricklayer and his wife, Caroline. The family moved to Tangmere, where George was employed as a milkman at Decoy Farm, whether that was before or after he previously served with the Royal Sussex Regiment is not known. With the outbreak of war George re-enlisted at Chichester, this time into the Royal West Kent Regiment, serving in France and Flanders. He lost his life during the March Retreat.

Private SD4006 William BOWLEY
2 Limmer Cottages, Aldingbourne, Sussex
13th Battalion, the Royal Sussex Regiment, 39th Division
Killed in Action on 23 March 1918
Aged 23
Commemorated on the Pozieres Memorial, France

Born in Aldingbourne, William was the son of Charles, a carter on a farm and Mary Bowley. On leaving school, William was employed as a telegraph messenger at Aldingbourne Post Office, before enlisting at Chichester into the Royal Sussex Regiment.

The Royal Sussex Regiment lost heavily during the German advances and the 13th Battalion were very depleted by the middle of March. On 23 March they were detailed to make a stand east of Peronne, but this proved to be impossible, so a withdrawal through the town became the only solution. This was completed but the bridges were successfully held, until the Royal Engineers were able to blow them up. The day, however, cost the Battalion the lives of one Officer and twenty two men, including Private William Bowley.

Sergeant 17866 James HOCKING
110th Brigade, the Royal Field Artillery
Killed in Action on 24 March 1918
Aged 25
Commemorated on the Arras Memorial

James was one of ten children born in Portsmouth to William, a sailor in the Boat Service and his wife Johannah. On leaving school James became a bar boy before enlisting at Chichester into the Royal Field Artillery. He was killed in action in the March Retreat.

Lance-Corporal 16948 Reginald George WHEATLAND
3 St Catherine's Terrace, Felpham, Bognor
25th Company, the Machine Gun Corps (Infantry)
Killed in Action on 24 March 1918
Aged 27
Commemorated on the Arras Memorial

Reginald Wheatland was the grandson of Mary Wheatland, famous in Bognor as the bathing machine owner who taught many a person to swim and received the Royal Humane Society's medal for saving over thirty souls from drowning.

The son of George and Caroline Wheatland, Reginald married his wife Margaret and set up home at Broadwater, Worthing. A career soldier, he had seen thirteen years' service with the Royal Artillery, the Royal Berkshire Regiment and latterly the Machine Gun Corps. He had fought in some of the most important engagements of the war. On two previous occasions he had been wounded and recovered. Wounded for a third time, Sister Robertson from the Corps Operating Station broke the news to the family:

'I am sorry to tell you that Lance-Corporal Wheatland has been wounded and is at present in hospital. He is badly wounded in the head and it is difficult to say to what extent his brain is injured. He is quite conscious at present, but is not suffering any pain. Everything that is possible is being done for him and we can only hope for the best. I will write to you again as soon as I can and tell you how he is getting on and trust to give you better news'.

Two weeks later he had been transferred to a London hospital where his mother was able to visit him and he was reported as 'progressing favourably'.

Despite the seriousness of his injuries, Reginald recovered, rejoining his unit, only to be killed in action during the March Retreat.

Lieutenant Harold George GRICE
Colebrooke House, the Esplanade, Bognor
4th Battalion, the Royal Scots (Queens Edinburgh Rifles), 52nd Division
Died of Wounds on 27 March 1918
Aged 27
Buried in the St Sever Cemetery, Seine-Maritime, France.

A onetime official with the London and County Bank at Chichester and Arundel, Harold Grice, the son of William and Ada Grice, enlisted into the Royal Scots Edinburgh Rifles, but was 'medically unfit and marked down for active service'. Instead he was stationed in Bermuda for a year, where he made 'many friends', being an extremely popular Officer and good at all sports 'especially association football'. However, he yearned for active service and after 'many medicals' the Board granted his request and he was attached to 2/4th Battalion, the East Yorkshire Regiment and sent to the Western Front early in 1918. After a few weeks he was 'dangerously wounded' and sent to the base hospital at Rouen, where he died.

A report of his death appeared in the *Bermuda Colonist* of 1 May 1918:

'It is with deep regret that we have to record the death in action in France of Lieutenant Harold G Grice, of the Royal Scots, who will be remembered as an attached Officer of the 2/4th Battalion, the East Yorkshire Regiment and who was stationed in the Colony for a little over twelve months. The sad news was contained in a letter received from his father in the last mail. There were few details, all that is really known is that Lieutenant Grice, who left Bermuda with a draft of the East Yorkshire Regiment last December, was sent to a Battalion of the Royal Scots on his arrival in England and went to the Western Front sometime in February. Only a few weeks later he was badly wounded and died of his wounds in the last week of March in a Base Hospital in Rouen. The late Officer came from Bognor, England. In the early days of the war he joined the Inns of Court Cadet

Battalion and on passing out was posted to the 4th Royal Scots. He was in a bad state of health at this time and on more than one occasion broke down in training, the result being he was eventually classed as unfit for general service. A month before the East Yorkshires sailed for Bermuda he was posted to that Battalion and a year of soldering in these islands gave him back the health he had lost. Towards the end of last year he expressed a strong desire to be sent home for active service, but his medical record was against him. He was again marked unfit, but so insistent was he that the Medical Board told him that if he could prove that he was strong enough he would be put in the top category. Lieutenant Grice was then stationed at St Georges and one of the tests was that he should march from there to Prospect wearing full marching order. As an evidence of his keenness it may be mentioned that he went into immediate training and one early morning in November he accomplished the task without difficulty. He was extremely popular with the Officers and men of the East Yorkshire Regiment and had a host of friends all over. He was good at all sports, especially association football. His death will be mourned by all who knew him'.

Rifleman 44828 Arthur Edwin MONEY
Manor Farm, North Bersted, Bognor
15th Battalion, the Royal Irish Rifles, 36th Division
Died of Wounds on 27 March 1918
Aged 20
Buried in the Hautmont Communal Cemetery, France

The son of Mr and Mrs Money, who ran the Central Farm Dairy in Station Road, Bognor, Arthur enlisted at Chichester into the Royal Sussex Regiment, before joining the Royal Irish Rifles. Originally reported as missing, on 27 March 1918 his parents were informed by the International Red Cross Agency in Geneva that he had been wounded in action on that day and had died later in Haumont Hospital, near Maubeuge 'of a shot skull'. He had only returned to the Front a week before following home leave.

Corporal 47328 Hugh NORRELL
Royal Oak Cottage, East Lavant
108th Siege Battery, the Royal Garrison Artillery
Killed in Action on 5 April 1918
Aged 26
Buried in the Hedauville Communal Cemetery Extension, France

Hailing from East Lavant, the son of William, a stationary engine driver and his wife Eliza, Hugh was their third child and eldest son, there being a younger son and three daughters. On leaving school, Hugh became a bricklayers apprentice, before enlisting at Lewes into the Royal Garrison Artillery, losing his life in the Spring Offensive.

DIED AT HOME

Gunner 83251 William E HALL
Laurel Cottage, Ivy Lane, South Bersted, Bognor
217th Siege Battery, Royal Garrison Artillery
Died of Wounds on 9 April 1918
Aged 21
Buried in the Aire Communal Cemetery, France

The youngest son of general labourer and builder, Kempton and his wife Ellen, William was born in Lavant, Sussex and lived at Midhurst for a while before enlisting in Bognor. In August 1917 he was reported as wounded and in hospital in France. He never recovered from his wounds, passing away some eight months later.

MARCH RETREAT

Lance Corporal 17240 Frederick Thomas WALTERS MM
2nd Battalion, the Worcestershire Regiment, 33rd Division
Killed in Action on 10 April 1918
Aged 23
Commemorated on the Ploegstreert Memorial, Belgium

Although this soldier's name appears on the War Memorial, no connection with Bognor has been established. He was born in Worcestershire, where his parents continued to live and enlisted at Evesham. At some stage during the conflict Frederick received the Military Medal. On the original Bognor Council hand written lists prepared when the War Memorial was being erected, his name has been inserted between two others almost as an afterthought. No further information is available.

Private PW3184 Frank WELCH
19 Bute Street, Brighton
Possibly 18th (Pioneer Battalion), the Middlesex Regiment, 33rd Division
Killed in Action on 13 April 1918
Aged 34
Commemorated on the Ploegsteert Memorial, Belgium

Frank Welch was born in Brighton and enlisted at Chichester. He married Florence, a Brighton lass and the couple set up home in that town, where Frank worked as a milk carrier. He enlisted at Chichester.

The Battle of Bailleul took place between 13 & 15 April 1918, as the German Offensive rolled on. The 18th Middlesex were ordered to hold the hills to the south-east of Bailleul; they were informed that a British counter attack was to be expected and that if it failed then the British would fall back to a fresh position. The fighting was hard and 'meanwhile the 18th Battalion had joined the battle, Pioneers, Cyclists and every available man from schools and reinforcement Companies were rushed into action'.

The Pioneers were split up and attached to various other units 'in a continually changing situation and by the end of the day the gallant Pioneers had lost fifteen men killed and forty wounded'.

It is not known how Private Frank Welch lost his life, or to which unit he had been attached, in the confusing situation that prevailed.

Sergeant 16512 George TITHERLY (listed on War Memorial as Tytherley)
33rd Battalion, the Machine Gun Corps
Died of Wounds on 18 April 1918
Aged 34
Buried in the Mendingham Military Cemetery, Poperinghe, Belgium

Born in Chelsea and enlisting in Fulham, George Titherley originally joined the Middlesex Regiment before transferring into 33rd Battalion Machine Gun Corps. Wounded, he died of his injuries on 18 April 1918.

PRISONER OF WAR

Private 42656 Alfred George HUMPHREY
Denmark Terrace, Glamis Street, Bognor
10th Battalion, the Lincolnshire Regiment,
Died in Captivity in Germany on 20 April 1918
Aged 19
Buried in the Niederzwerhen Cemetery, Germany

Mr and Mrs Humphrey heard in April 1918 through the Red Cross Society in Switzerland that their son, Private Alfred Humphrey of the Lincolnshire Regiment, had 'died of wounds whilst in captivity'.

Private Alfred Humphrey was one of five brothers all serving and had been posted missing on 9 April 1918. The International Red Cross, or Comite Internationale de la Croix-Rouge, had managed to establish through their Agencie Internationale des Prisonniers de Guerre, that Private Humphrey had 'died of blood poisoning and wounds of the lower jaw at Ohrdruf'.

'We are enclosing a copy of the identification of the death of Private Alfred George Humphrey. We think you will be glad to have the few details contained therein and to know that your son was buried reverently and that his resting place is marked. Should further details come to hand we will let you know'.

Before enlisting at Chichester, Alfred had worked for Mrs Piper at the China and Glass warehouse in London Road, Bognor.

Private 73489 Robert Alan BENNETT
20 Ockley Road, Bognor
15th Battalion, the Nottinghamshire & Derbyshire Regiment, 35th Division
Killed in Action on 22 April 1918
Age 19
Buried in the Martinsart British Cemetery, Somme, France

Robert was the youngest son of chimney sweep Frederick Andrew Bennett and his wife Alice. Born in Bognor, Robert enlisted at Chichester into the Sherwood Foresters in 1917, losing his life the following year. The *Bognor Observer* reported:

'Mr and Mrs Bennett, who have three sons serving, have just heard that their youngest, Robert, has laid down his life for his Country. He was just nineteen and had enlisted into the Sherwood Foresters when he became eighteen, after working with his father as a chimney sweep'.

A letter from the Battalion Chaplain arrived a few days later:

'Unless you have already heard, I fear I have bad news for you regarding your son. Our Battalion was in action on Monday and your son was among those killed outright. The task given to the men was an exceedingly difficult and arduous one and it was magnificent to note the splendid way in which the men responded to the appeal made to them. Your son was among the bravest and we deplore his loss. May God comfort and bless you in your sorrow'.

A fortnight before his death he was reunited with one of his two brothers whom he met just going into the trenches and who since that day had been wounded. His other brother was home on leave at the time of Robert's death.

Corporal SD1784 Horace F VERION
South View, North Bersted
11th Battalion, the Royal Sussex Regiment, 39th Division
Killed in Action on 22 April 1918
Aged 32
Buried in the Roisel Communal Cemetery Extension

The eldest son of laundry owner Sophia Verion and the brother of George, *(see Roll of Honour, March 1916)* Horace was born in Angmering and worked as a carter prior to enlisting at Chichester.

April 1918 saw his Battalion counter attacking in the face of enemy artillery and aircraft, which were very 'active'. In this attack, shrouded by mist, Corporal Horace Verion lost his life.

Sergeant TF205341 Edwin Leslie FLEXMAN
Mill Cottage, Felpham, Bognor
7th Battalion, the Royal West Kent Regiment, 18th Division
Killed in Action on 24 April 1918
Aged 28
Buried in the Crucifix Corner Cemetery, Villers, Bretonneux, France

The eldest son of builder William James Flexman and his wife Matilda, Edwin was born in Hammersmith, London, where his parents brought up their five children. The family appear to have moved to Felpham sometime after 1911, by which time Edwin was serving in the Kent Yeomanry, after which he enlisted into the Royal West Kent Regiment. Edwin was married to Mary and latterly had lived in Richmond, Surrey.

Regimental Sergeant Major TF200023 Bernard Alfred STONE DCM
14 Norman Terrace, Longford Road, Bognor
13th Battalion, the Royal Sussex Regiment, 39th Division
Killed in Action on 26 April 1918
Age 32
Commemorated on the Tyne Cot Memorial, Belgium

The eldest son of Thomas, the Amberley schoolmaster and Rebecca Stone, Bernard was born in Amberley. His younger brother was Lieutenant Victor Stone *(see Roll of Honour 1917)* who emigrated to Canada and returned to serve with the Canadian Forces. By the time Bernard left school to work as a butcher's assistant his mother had been widowed. Bernard then took employment as a plumber and gas fitter, moving to Bognor, having married his wife Grace, with whom he had a young son. He also spent some time in the Territorial Army before enlisting with the Royal Sussex Regiment. At the outbreak of war, Sergeant (as he then was) Stone 'did excellent service in organising the training of the 2/4th and 3/4th Battalions of the Royal Sussex Regiment'. He was then posted to 13th Battalion in France and promoted from Company to Regimental Sergeant Major. He was gazetted for the DCM in March 1918, although it seems that his wife did not receive this news for some time.

In early June 1918, Captain Gill wrote to Mrs Stone, informing her that RSM Stone had been missing in action for a couple of months. A follow up letter a week later from the Battalion Adjutant bought mixed news:

'I hope you have now had some good news from your husband by this time. No one regrets more than me the inability to give news to the relatives of those who are missing. I can only express my sympathy, which must seem so little in your anxiety. You will be pleased to know that your husband has won the DCM for Gallantry and Devotion to Duty and no one deserves it more than he. One feels honoured to work with such a man and I, as Adjutant, feel the loss of one of the best Sergeant-Majors I have known'.

At that time Mrs Stone was still without further news of her husband. Eventually the news she dreaded arrived, that Bernard had been killed in action on 26 April 1918. The 13th Battalion had taken very heavy losses in the bitter fighting to try to stem the German Offensive. The Battalion had been practically wiped out. In April the survivors were put into the line close to Kemmel, where 'what remained of the Battalion was destroyed and the 13th as a Battalion took no further part in the war, the personnel being absorbed into other units'.

Mrs Stone received official notification of Bernard's Distinguished Conduct Medal at the end of June, along with the DCM ribbon he had worn. The citation stated the award was given for:

'Conspicuous Gallantry and good leadership at Bray-sur-Somme on 26 March 1918 and during subsequent actions. This NCO acted as Platoon Commander in No 1 Battery in Colonel Hunt's force and displayed marked ability and coolness throughout the operation, in handling his Platoon at Bray-sur-Somme, when his Company was ordered to support a unit in the line. He advanced with his Platoon under very heavy shell fire and only withdrew when ordered to do so by his Company Commander. His tenacity in holding the line with his Platoon in the face of very heavy shell fire, when other troops had withdrawn, undoubtedly delayed the advance of the enemy at a very critical period and enabled our troops to effect an orderly retirement. His good leadership throughout inspired the confidence of his men and was of the greatest assistance to his Company Commander. His cheerfulness and courage under most trying conditions were an example to and the admiration of all ranks. We sincerely hope that news may arrive of his personal safety, even though he may be a prisoner in Germany'.

Private 45718 Sidney Herbert SIMMONDS
43 Nelson Street, Brighton
90th Field Company, the Royal Engineers
Died of Wounds on 12 May 1918
Aged 27
Buried in the Boulogne Eastern Cemetery, France

Sidney Simmonds' Bognor connection has not been established, although his name is on the Bognor War Memorial. He is also listed on the Brighton War Memorial, Sidney having been born in nearby Portslade. His father, Alfred was a carpenter, whilst Sidney, on leaving school, became a gas fitter. A Sapper, Sidney enlisted at Brighton into the Royal Engineers and died of wounds at Boulogne.

Private SD1180 William John EADE MM
St John's, Link Avenue, Felpham
7th (Service) Battalion, the Royal Sussex Regiment, 12th Division
Killed in Action on 20 May 1918
Age 38
Buried at Mailly Wood Cemetery, Mailly Maillet, Somme, France

The son of jobbing gardener John Eade and his wife Mary Anne, William was born on 24 September 1879. Educated in the Roman Catholic School, he became a builder before enlisting at Chichester into the Royal Sussex Regiment on 9 December 1914. He served with the Expeditionary Force in France and Flanders from March 1916. On 17 July 1917 he was wounded at Poperinghe and invalided home, returning to France on 9 November. He was killed in action at Mailly Maillet, northwest of Albert on 20 May 1918 during a relatively quiet time, the German offensive having been halted. His Battalion were holding the line but were subject to spasmodic enemy shelling.

The *Bognor Observer* wrote:

'Mrs Jane Eade has just received information that her husband Private William Eade MM, was killed in action on 20 May 1918 by the explosion of a shell. His death was instantaneous. He was one of five brothers serving, four in the Army and one in the Navy. He was previously wounded in July 1917 and returned to France in November, being awarded the Military Medal, for services on the field in the Battle of Fleurbaix on 8 March 1918'.

William was the husband of Mrs Jane Selina Eade whom he married in September 1905 and had a daughter, Mary Magdelene Eade who was born on 11 August 1914, just weeks before he enlisted.

In a letter of condolence, his Company Sergeant Major wrote:

'He will be greatly missed, as he was a thorough soldier and a man and was liked by everybody whom he came in contact with. He will be a very great loss to me as he was my batman and was a brave man as an orderly'.

Gunner 235556 Arthur Henry SNOOK
Victoria Cottage, Sea Road, Felpham
86th Brigade, the Royal Field Artillery
Died of Wounds on 23 May 1918
Aged 28
Buried in the Crouy British Cemetery, Crouy on Somme

The son of market gardener and cabman Henry Snook and his wife Emma, Arthur was the younger brother of Byron *(see Roll of Honour, December 1915)*. A gardener before the war, he lived for a while in Chichester, before enlisting at Bognor into the Royal Field Artillery.

Rifleman 46495 Harry Arthur MORLEY
The Hollies, North Bersted
3rd Battalion, the Rifle Brigade, 24th Division
Died of Wounds on 26 May 1918
Aged 19
Buried in the Pernes British Cemetery, France

Born and bred in North Bersted, the eldest son of George and Emma Morley of The Hollies, Harry had worked at Wingates Bakery, Aldwick Road, before enlisting at Chichester into the Rifle Brigade. He died of wounds on 26 May 1918.

'Mr and Mrs Morley have received news from the Chaplain of the 1st Canadian Hospital that their eldest son was seriously wounded on May 24th and passed away on Sunday. He was just over 19 years old', wrote the *Bognor Observer.*

Second Lieutenant Harold Augustus Boyd OLIVER
45 St James Square, Holland Park, Middlesex
The Irish Guards attached to the Guards Machine Gun Battalion
Killed in Action on 26 May 1918
Aged 34
Buried in the Doullens Communal Cemetery

Harold Oliver was an actor and comedian, also known as his professional name, Norman King. He was the youngest son of the Reverend and Mrs Oliver. Harold earned his living treading the boards in the Edwardian Music Halls and may well have performed in Bognor at some point. Originally with 85th Ambulance Corps, Royal Army Medical Corps, he served in Salonika before being invalided home with malaria. He was later commissioned into the Irish Guards and was attached to the Guards Machine Gun Battalion.

Lance-Corporal G980 George James HALE
7th Battalion, the Royal Sussex Regiment, 12th Division
Killed in Action on 24 June 1918
Aged 24
Buried in the Harponville Communal Cemetery Extension

An early volunteer, having enlisted at Chichester in August 1914 into the Royal Sussex Regiment, George Hale, a son of a farm labourer, James and his wife Ellen, was born in Pagham and lived in Nyetimber. He survived until nearly the end of the war, despite being wounded in 1917. His death occurred whilst his Battalion were returning to the Front Line, following a period of rest, training and the integration of new drafts of men. At Harponville they came under enemy machine gun fire which was probably when Lance Corporal Hale lost his life.

Lieutenant (Carl) Charles Herbert HARTMANN
Tythings, Craigwell, Aldwick
5th Battalion, the Royal West Kent Regiment, 12th Division
Killed in Action on 2 July 1918
Aged 31
Buried in the Bouzincourt Ridge Cemetery, Albert

Of German descent, Carl's father Augustus immigrated to England in the 1870s where he became a successful merchant. Retiring early, a couple of years before the war broke out the family had a holiday home built at Pagham. Carl Hartmann had his name changed to Charles and enlisted in Blackheath, London (where his parents lived) into the Queens Own Royal West Kent Regiment.

Charles lost his life during a strong German counter attack to retake ground that the Royal West Kent's had captured over the previous two days. Three windows in the north transept of St. Thomas A'Becket Church at Pagham were dedicated to his memory.

Gunner Andrew BAILEY
Wick Lane Cottage, Wick Lane, Felpham
1st West Riding Brigade, the Royal Garrison Artillery
Died of Wounds on 26 July 1918
Aged 37
Buried in Houchin British Cemetery, Pas de Calais, France

Born in Felpham in 1881, Andrew was the son of George Bailey, an agricultural labourer, who by 1901 was a widower. George had two sons, Alfred being five years older than Andrew and the family lived at Corner Cottage, Felpham, at the turn of the century. Andrew enlisted at Bognor and served into the Royal Garrison Artillery. Part of the Territorial Force, the Brigade had three separate batteries, each with its own ammunition column, and were equipped with 15 pounder guns. The 1st West Riding Brigade went to France in 1915, where three years later, Gunner Bailey was injured and died of his wounds.

Private T200281 Frank Kenneth JONES
1/4th Battalion, the Royal Sussex Regiment
Killed in Action on 29 July 1918
Age 20
Buried in the Raperie British Cemetery, Villemontoire, France

Frank Jones was born at Cheam, Surrey, the eldest son of Frank, a woodman and his wife Lillie. They had five other children - four boys and a girl. The family moved to East Grinstead in Sussex, where Frank (senior) worked as a labourer on Horse Shoe Farm.

Private Frank Jones enlisted at Hurstpierpoint into the Royal Sussex Regiment. On 29 July his Battalion were ordered to attack and advance towards Grand Rozoy. The day got off to a bad start when their French guide lost his way causing a significant delay. However, by the end of the afternoon they were within three hundred yards of Grand Rozoy and had suffered only light casualties. It was then that they encountered heavy machine gun fire from a wood and with the lack of artillery support, bayonet charged the enemy. It was at some stage in that attack that Private Frank Jones lost his life.

THE TIDE TURNS

With the German advances halted, the Allies launched a series of counter attacks. The Americans were now in France in large numbers with British reinforcements from the campaigns now completed in Palestine and Italy, as well as fresh troops previously held back at home. Battles took place at Amiens and on the Somme, followed by an advance to the Hindenburg Line. Here, further engagements took place - the Meuse-Argonne Offensive, the Battle of the St Quentin Canal, the Fifth Battle of Ypres, the Battle of Cambrai and the Battle of the Sambre Canal. Other battles took place involving the French, Americans, Australians and other Allies.

Rifleman 48752 Herbert C HAMMOND
37 Steyne Street, Bognor
2/10th Battalion, the London Regiment, 60th Division
Killed in Action on 9 August 1918
Aged 18
Commemorated on the Vis en Artois Memorial, France

Herbert Hammond was born in Bognor, the second son of Herbert and Ada of 37 Steyne Street. His father came from Arundel and worked as a painter and glazier, whilst his mother, who was born in the New Forest, was a housewife. In Herbert's young days the family lived at Woburn Cottage, Wood Street, Bognor. He had been a 'well known' member of the Church Lads Brigade and since leaving school had been employed by Mr Cooper, the Chemist in West Street, for four years. Herbert enlisted in Brighton into the London Regiment in November 1917 and had been in France for only thirteen weeks when he was killed.

Private G26000 Charles LANGRISH
Russell Street, Chichester
1st Battalion, the East Kent Regiment, 6th Division
Killed in Action on 10 August 1918
Aged 36
Commemorated on the Vis en Artois Memorial, France

Born in Lavant, Charles was the son of John and Rebecca Langrish. His father was an agricultural labourer, who died when Charles was just four years old. Rebecca then became a laundress, whilst Charles, on leaving school became an agricultural labourer. In 1906 he married Annie Flora Kent, the daughter of the Fishbourne postman, setting up home in Chichester. Private Charles Langrish enlisted into the East Kent Regiment and was killed in action. He is commemorated on the Portfield War Memorial, Chichester and the Bognor War Memorial, although no Bognor connection has been established.

INFLUENZA PANDEMIC

Throughout 1918 and lasting well after the war had finished, the influenza pandemic swept the world. It is said that the war with its massive troop movements hastened and increased transmission of the lethal virus. Certainly the Government's wartime censors attempted to play down the situation, mainly to maintain morale, but many servicemen died because of it, including several local men.

Sergeant GS190 William James BRITTON
16 Essex Road, Bognor
3rd Battalion, the Royal Sussex Regiment (Home Reserve)
Died at Home on 19 March 1918
Aged 36
Buried in Bognor Town Cemetery, Bognor

William came from Portslade, one of the seven children born to gardener William (senior) and his laundress wife Annie. The family moved to Felpham, living for a while at the Triangle Laundry and later moved to 1 Crescent Cottages, Ivy Lane, South Bersted, by which time William (junior) had become a merchant seaman. Leaving the sea, he was employed by the Railway Company Engineering Department as a permanent way engineer. He married Alice and by the outbreak of war they had four children when William enlisted in the National Reserve with the Royal Sussex Regiment in August 1914. Throughout the war the 3rd Battalion were stationed at the Newhaven Garrison, training drafts for the Royal Sussex Battalions overseas.

Sergeant Britton became a victim of the pneumonia pandemic which swept the country in 1918, passing away in the General Hospital at Altringham, Cheshire and was interred in the Bognor Cemetery.

Private T386387 Richard Haynes Nelson MINTORN
Royal Army Service Corps attached to the 20th Battalion, the Royal Fusiliers
Died at Home on 28 April 1918
Aged 50
Buried in St Mary's Churchyard, Harrow, Middlesex

Described as a Bognor resident, Richard Mintorn's parents lived in Gloucestershire, although Richard had been born in Harrow and had enlisted in London. He had formerly served with the Royal Fusiliers and had re-enlisted at the outbreak of war. Little is known of his military career which must have been quite lengthy, as he was still serving in the Royal Army Service Corps, attached to the Royal Fusiliers, when he died 'at home' on 28 April 1918.

Lance-Corporal GS413 James MARCHANT
Felpham, Bognor
9th Battalion, the Royal Sussex Regiment, 24th Division
Died at Home 6 May 1918
Aged 43
Buried in St Mary's Churchyard, Felpham

Born in Fletching, Sussex, on leaving school James became a horse carter's boy. However, by 1900 he was a journeyman baker/servant for Kate Scott, who ran a baker's business in Felpham, which had been started by her father George in the 1850s. James stayed resident at Felpham, becoming a Special Reservist. At the outbreak of war he enlisted into the Royal Sussex Regiment. After training in England, the Battalion arrived in France on 1 September 1915 and were in early action at the Battle of Loos. At first it was thought that James was killed in action on 14 February 1916. However, he was badly wounded but survived, being invalided home. The *Bognor Observer* of July 1918 contains the following report:

'The deceased was a National Reservist and joined the Royal Sussex Regiment immediately after the outbreak of war. He was wounded in the elbow which practically paralysed his lower arm and hand. The circumstances of his death were very sad. After being in hospital for ten months he came to Felpham on a visit for a few days to Miss Scott, in whose services and that of Mrs Scott he had been in for twenty four years. Although he complained of a slight cold, it was not thought at all serious and he was feeling worse about 8pm on Monday night. On arriving at Miss Scott's he complained at not feeling at all well and at 10 o clock Miss Scott telephoned Dr Collins, but before the arrival of the doctor he had passed away. At the inquest death was shown to be due to pneumonia and heart trouble'.

Lance Corporal James Marchant, aged 43, was buried in Felpham Churchyard. His coffin was covered with a Union Jack lent by the Coastguards and during the service the vicar referred to him in his younger life as both a church bell ringer and sidesman.

Private G7234 Benjamin SAIGEMAN
9th Battalion, the Royal Sussex Regiment, 24th Division
Died of the Influenza Pandemic on 13 June 1918
Aged 36
Buried in the Premont British Cemetery, France

Benjamin Saigeman was born in Littlehampton and was the third son of Jonathan, a labourer and his wife Mary Ann and the younger brother on Jonathan *(see Roll of Honour, November 1914)*. On leaving school became a builder/labourer before enlisting at Bognor into the Royal Sussex Regiment. His death in June was due to the influenza pandemic, which hospitalized five Officers and 250 men of his Battalion. Sadly, Benjamin did not survive the illness.

Able Seaman Thomas WICHELOW
Lyme Cottage, the Steyne, Bognor
HMS *Victory* Royal Navy
Died at Home on 12 September 1918
Aged 18
Buried in the Bognor Town Cemetery, West Sussex

Thomas was one of six children born to carpenter Elijah and his wife Alice, who had had moved to Bognor from Ealing in Middlesex. They had previously lived at 7 Parramatta Terrace, Ockley Road, where they had let apartments.
In 1918 Thomas was serving at HMS *Victory* and had been sent home ill, a victim of the influenza pandemic.

Private 23600 Edmund John RUFF
The Evergreens, South Bersted, Bognor
7th Battalion, the Royal West Kent Regiment
Died at Home on 13 September 1918
Aged 22
Buried in the Bognor Town Cemetery

Edmund was the ninth of twelve children born to George, a farm labourer and his wife Caroline. On leaving school he was employed as a 'cowboy' before enlisting into the Royal West Kent Regiment. He died at home, probably of influenza.

Sergeant 37552 Frederick George PAY
Church Farm Dairy, Felpham
Royal Air Force
Died at Home of the Influenza Pandemic on 17 October 1918
Aged 29
Buried in St Mary's Churchyard, Felpham, Bognor, West Sussex

The only son of Harry and his wife Maria, Frederick was born in Felpham where he grew up with his sister Bessie. Harry went on to run the National Telephone Call Office in Felpham, whilst Frederick became an employee of the Bognor Gasworks prior to enlisting, by which time he was married to Gladys. A Sergeant in the newly formed Royal Air Force, Frederick lost his life in the influenza pandemic in St Albans Hospital on 17 October 1918.

'On Tuesday last, the 22nd inst., the funeral of Sergeant FG Pay of the RAF took place at Felpham. Sergeant Pay died of pneumonia following an attack of influenza at RAF St Albans after an illness of three or four days'.

Many floral tributes were in evidence from RAF stations at his funeral, his widow, Gladys 'being too unwell to attend'.

Air Mechanic Third Class 116666 E E THORNTON
No 12 Training Depot Royal Air Force
Died at Home on 21 October 1918
Aged 28
Buried in St Georges Churchyard, Eastergate, West Sussex

An early Royal Air Force entrant, Air Mechanic Thornton came from Amersham, Buckinghamshire, but probably had family connections in the Bognor area because this was where he died 'at home' of pneumonia. Nothing else is known of this man.

Lance-Bombardier 30754 Charles HOMER
1/1st North Midland Heavy Battery, the Royal Garrison Artillery
Died at Home on 27 October 27 1918
Age 27
Buried in St Marys Churchyard, Felpham, Bognor

A regular soldier, Charles Homer enlisted in January 1909 and was drafted to Gibraltar where he served with the Royal Garrison Artillery until the outbreak of war, returning to England in October 1914. In March 1915 he was sent with his unit to France and served there continuously until he was taken ill two weeks before he died.

Lance-Bombardier Charles Homer was one of five soldier sons of Mrs Homer of Felpham and brother of Lance-Sergeant Arthur Homer *(see Roll of Honour September 1916)* and Thomas Homer *(see Roll of Honour, March 1918)*. In October 1918 he contracted pneumonia and was repatriated to the Winter Street Hospital in Sheffield where he died on 27 October.

'Deceased was bought from Sheffield and met by Mr C Reynolds, the undertaker at Bognor Railway Station. Four soldiers carried his coffin, two of them being his old school chums'.

THE LOSS OF HMS *SCOTT*

Less than a year after entering service, HMS *Scott*, a destroyer leader, a class of ship built to be Flotilla Leaders and named after Captain Scott of Antarctic fame, was lost. Launched in October 1917 she was patrolling off the Dutch Coast when she was sunk. It is not known definitely if she hit a mine or was sunk by a torpedo fired by the German submarine *UC 17*, which was known to have been in the area at the time. Some of the crew escaped.

Able Seaman 218925 Herbert James Burt BISHOP
Nestor, Highfield Road, Bognor
HMS *Scott* Royal Navy
Lost at Sea on 15 August 1918
Aged 31
Commemorated on the Chatham Naval Memorial, Kent

According to the *Bognor Observer* in June 1916, Able Seaman Bishop had been in action in the Battle of Jutland. He later served on HMS *Scott*, joining the ship as she entered service. Able Seaman Scott was born in Hastings, but his Bognor connection has not been established.

WESTERN FRONT

Private G14457 Archibald Frederick MARSH
3 East View Cottages, Limmer Lane, Felpham
7th Battalion, the East Kent Regiment, 18th Division
Killed in Action on 22 August 1918
Age 18
Buried in the Albert Communal Cemetery Extension

The son of Mark and Anna Maria Marsh, Archibald was born in Selsey, the family of nine living at 14 Manor Road. His father, born in Appledram, was a 'foreman of navvies'. The family moved around a little - Appledram, Chichester, Littlehampton, before settling in Bognor. When he was old enough Archibald enlisted at Brighton into the East Kent Regiment and was killed in action, having been in France only a few weeks.

Rifleman 44539 Alfred George ALLEN
Nyewood Cottage, Nyewood Lane, Bognor
1st Battalion, the Kings Royal Rifle Corps, 2nd Division
Killed in Action on 23 August 1918
Aged 18
Commemorated on the Vis en Artois Memorial, France

In 1918 Mr and Mrs George Allen of Nyewood Cottage, Nyewood Lane, received notification from the War Office that their only son had been wounded. He was eighteen and had been at the Front for only a few weeks.

Alfred George Allen was the son of cabinet maker George, who had been born in Bognor and his wife Edith Allen, who was born and bought up in Sidlesham. Their first child, Dora, was five years old when Alfred was born. The family were then living at 1 Soudan Terrace, Merchant Street, Bognor, before moving to Nyewood Lane, which in those days was a dusty track in summer and a quagmire in winter. Aged only fourteen when the war broke out, on reaching his nineteenth birthday young Alfred enlisted into the Kings Royal Rifle Corps and was soon serving in France. For his parents, August 1918 was a worrying time. Having not heard from Alfred himself for some weeks, they had received an official notice from the Army Records Office at Winchester informing him that he had been wounded on 2 August, but had remained on duty. It was therefore a terrible blow to them when they received a letter dated 29 August 1918 from their son's Captain:

'I very much regret to tell you that your son was killed on 23 August in action. He was killed instantly and felt no pain. He was doing fine work at the time and showed up splendidly. The Battalion had taken nine hundred prisoners, that is no consolation to you, but that gives you an idea of the fine action in which your son played a great hand'.

The *Bognor Observer* added:

'He was only 18 years old and well known in the town. His many friends will be grieved to learn of his death, although very proud of the noble part he displayed, when facing death, in the fight for freedom'.

Rifleman 608455 Harold Etherington HAY
1/18th Battalion, the London Regiment (London Irish Rifles)
Killed in Action on 23 August 1918
Aged 24
Commemorated on the Vis en Artois Memorial, France

Harold Hay, the only son of Herbert and Emma Hay, was born in Wandsworth, where his father was the foreman in a waste paper business. The family moved to Bognor where he then became the manager of the Queens Concert Hall in Canada Grove. Harold, who had worked as a shop assistant, enlisted at Bunhill Row into the London Regiment and was killed in action.

DIED AT HOME

Air Mechanic Second Class 49873 Arthur Henry FOX
Dorset House, London Road, Bognor
Royal Air Force
Died at Home on 23 August 1918
Aged 32
Buried in St Marys Churchyard, Fairford, Gloucestershire

'The many friends in Bognor of Air Mechanic Arthur Fox have received with regret the news that he passed away at Shorncliffe Military Hospital, on Saturday week last. Not of robust physique, he succumbed, after an immediate operation for appendicitis. He had been in Bognor for several years, originally as a photographer with Mr Donald Massey. After twice being rejected for the Army, he eventually passed for the Royal Naval Air Service as a photographer and after a short training proceeded to Salonica, where he remained for two years, receiving Commendatory Reports from his Commanding Officer. As a member of the newly formed Royal Air Force, he returned in June last to take up an appointment as an Instructor to the RAF School of Photography at Hythe, Kent. The funeral took place last week', wrote the *Bognor Observer.*

WESTERN FRONT

Private 92959 William George JONES
12 East Street, Portslade
2/4th Battalion, the London Regiment (Royal Fusiliers), 58th (London) Division
Killed in Action on 24 August 1918
Aged 18
Buried in the Bronfay Farm Military Cemetery, Bray sur Somme, France

William was born in Hove, lived in Portslade and enlisted in Brighton. No connection with Bognor has been established although his name is on the Bognor War Memorial.

Rifleman R40595 Sydney George ATTRIDGE
15 Gravitts Lane, Bognor
9th Battalion, the London Regiment, (Queen Victoria's Rifles), 58th (London) Division
Killed in Action on 25 August 1918
Age 19
Commemorated on the Vis en Artois Memorial, France

Born in Portsmouth, one of twelve children, Sidney Attridge was the son of Thomas, an Irishman, who had served long enough in the Royal Navy to be in receipt of a naval pension. Thomas was twenty two years older than his wife Sarah, who was born in Weymouth. Living firstly at Southsea, the family moved to 9 Crescent Road, Bognor. Sydney was originally a cavalryman who then served with the London Regiment. Whether his change of Regiment was enforced or by choice is unknown. He was killed in action in France, where he had been for over a year, on 25 August 1918 'within a fortnight of his 20th birthday'.

Lance-Corporal 32236 Frederick CONNOR
St Clair, Ockley Road, Bognor
8th Battalion, the East Surrey Regiment, 18th Division
Killed in Action on 26 August 1918
Age 37
Buried in Quarry Cemetery, Moutauban

Frederick Connor was born in Chichester and had already served many years in the Army as a regular soldier, having previously fought in the Boer War, followed by a number of years stationed in India, before being demobbed. He settled into civilian life with his wife Flora Nellie Flossy, at her parents' house and worked as a builder for Mr Thomas Start. When war broke out Frederick again answered the call and enlisted at Chichester into East Surrey Regiment, subsequently being killed in action. The sad tidings of his death reached his wife on their eighth wedding anniversary.

Lance-Corporal Frederick George HODGES
Pagham
7th Battalion, thc Royal Sussex Regiment, 12th Division
Killed in Action on 29 August 1918
Aged 21
Commemorated on the Vis en Artois Memorial, France

Born in Angmering where his father Frederick had a grocery business in the Square, the family were comparatively well off. Frederick (senior) and his wife Clara employed three servants, two of whom worked in the shop, whilst the third was a housemaid. From Angmering the family moved to Worthing, where Frederick (senior) became a brewer's canvasser.
Young Frederick enlisted at Chichester into the Royal Sussex Regiment at the outbreak of war and was sent to France in May 1915. The 7th Battalion took part in some severe fighting, suffering heavy losses, Frederick having been injured on two occasions and then invalided home in August 1916.

'Lance Corporal Hodges has been wounded for the second time at Ovilliers and is in hospital in Liverpool. He has a fractured arm and a gunshot wound, he has been at the Front for thirteen months', said the *Bognor Observer.*

A year later he was back home suffering from frostbite:

'I am just leaving England on my fourth trip to France', he told the *Bognor Observer*, describing himself as one of the 'Bognor Boys'.

By July 1917 Frederick had fought in the Battle of the Craters and the Battle of Loos in 1915, the Battle of March in 1916 and the Somme in January 1917. He had been invalided home again in the spring of 1917 and on his return to France went straight into action, volunteering to cover the retreat of his Company with a machine gun, for which act he was recommended for the Military Medal by his Colonel. Unfortunately he was denied this Honour as the Colonel was killed shortly afterwards in another engagement, before he had chance to write up his report. Frederick was invalided back home again in early 1918, with trench foot, recovering in Woking Hospital.

'Lance-Corporal Hodges returned to France on 9 March for the fifth time following a spell of recuperation, when he was said to be 'well known' in the Lamb Inn at Pagham', wrote the *Bognor Observer.*

Lance Corporal Frederick Hodges was killed a few months later within a few days of his 22nd birthday, during a quieter period and is commemorated on the Vis en Artois Memorial.

Private G11464 Frederick J BLACKMAN
25 Nyetimber, Pagham
1/4th Battalion, the Royal Sussex Regiment, 34th Division
Died of Wounds on 2 September 1918
Aged 18
Buried in the St Sever Cemetery Extension, Seine-Maritime, France.

Frederick Blackman was the son of John, a carter on a farm and his wife Ellen, a laundress. The family had moved to Pagham from Poling. Frederick, like his two older brothers, probably followed his father into farm work, before enlisting into the Royal Sussex Regiment. He died of wounds at the Base Hospital, Rouen, on 2 September 1918, having been the victim of machine gun fire. He was the elder brother of Maurice *(see Roll of Honour, May 1915)*

Private 49307 Frank Henry MISSELBROOK
27 Nyetimber, Pagham
6th Battalion, the Northamptonshire Regiment, 18th Division
Died of Wounds on 2 September 1918
Aged 19
Buried in the Heilly Station Cemetery, Mericourt L'Abbe, France

One of two brothers who lost their lives within days of each other only two months before the end of the war, was Frank Misselbrook *(See Stephen Misselbrook, Roll of Honour, September 1918)*. The sons of Frank (senior), a farm stockman and his wife Jane, Frank (junior) died of wounds. The news came as a shock to his parents and three sisters, but more bad news for the family was to soon follow.

Private T4 142091 William POWELL
Rose Cottage, South Bersted
Railhead Supply Depot
Royal Army Service Corps
Died on 15 September 1918
Aged 29
Buried in the Terlincthun British Cemetery, Wimile

William was eldest and the third brother to lose his life in the war; firstly Richard *(see Roll of Honour, September 1916)* and then Walter *(see Roll of Honour, March 1918)*. He had enlisted at Bognor in November 1915 into the Royal Army Service Corps, serving with the Railhead Supply Department, prior to which he had been employed as a carman.

'Mr and Mrs Powell have received news that their son William has died in the Canadian Hospital, Boulogne. General sympathy is felt for the parents as he was the third son they have lost in the war'.

Private TF315324 William Henry MUNDAY
Ingeborg Villas, Cemetery Road, Bognor
16th Battalion, the Royal Sussex Regiment, 74th Division
Killed in Action on 16 September 1918
Aged 28
Buried in the Peronne Communal Cemetery Extension, France

A playing member of the Bognor Football Club, William Munday was one of eight children born to bricklayer and paper hanger Frank and his wife Fanny. On leaving school William worked for Warnetts the butchers, before enlisting at Chichester into Royal Sussex Regiment.

He was injured early in the war in October 1914 and sent home to Southampton Hospital with wounds to his arm and shoulder. After a spell of recuperation at home, he returned to the Front. On 16 September 1918 Private Munday was killed in a German air raid.

Private 279315 Charles John LEE
Annandale, Gordon Avenue, Bognor
2/2 Battalion, the London Regiment, 58th Division
Killed in Action on 18 September 1918
Aged 19
Buried in the Epehy Wood Farm Cemetery, Epehy

Born in South Bersted, Charles was the eldest son of John Lee, who was the manager of a Fish, Poultry and Fruit Depot and Harriett his wife.   Before enlisting, Charles was a Corporal in the Church Lads Brigade, where he played the 'big drum' in the band. He had previously been employed by the Bognor Gas, Light and Coke Company as a junior clerk and then as an assistant at Leverett and Fry's ironmongery shop, 51 High Street, Bognor. Charles enlisted into the London Regiment and was posted 'missing' on 18 September 1918.   It was not until after the Armistice that his parents received the following communication from the War Office:

'September 1919. We regret to record that Private Charles John Lee of the London Regiment, who was reported missing on 18 September 1918, is now concluded to be dead'.

Private Stephen MISSELBROOK
7th Battalion, the Royal Sussex Regiment, 12th Division
Killed in Action on 18 September 1918
Aged 29
Buried in the Epehy Wood Cemetery

Stephen Misselbrook, who was killed in action less than three weeks after his younger brother Frank *(see Roll of Honour, September 1918),* was serving in the Royal Sussex Regiment.   Prior to enlisting at Bognor he was employed as a waggoner.   A letter to his mother from one of his comrades was received before the official notification from the War Office. In it he says:

'That as one of the old comrades he would be greatly missed, for he was a good, cheerful and staunch chum'.

On 18 September the Royal Sussex were attacking Epehy, commencing early in the morning in darkness and heavy rain. The going was hard for both men and tanks as they struggled through the mud. As dawn broke a heavy mist clouded the way and a smoke barrage laid by the British artillery caused confusion and loss of direction. Many men unexpectedly came across a thick barbed wire barrier not shown on their maps and were lost to concentrated enemy machine gun fire. On that day Private Stephen Misselbrook lost his life. It is not known whether he was aware his younger brother Frank had been killed two weeks earlier.

Private G24775 Percy George LEARY
7 Retort Cottages, Ivy Lane, South Bersted
23rd Battalion, the Royal Fusiliers, 33rd Division
Died of Wounds on 29 September 1918
Aged 26
Buried in the Beaumetz Cross Roads Cemetery, Beaumetz les Cambrai

Percy, the son of George and Ellen Leary, was also the elder brother of Thomas *(see Roll of Honour, September 1917)* and died of wounds a year to the day after him. He had worked for nine years as a gardener at St Michaels School, Bognor, before enlisting into the Royal Fusiliers.

Lance Corporal 220720 Frederick Charles Richard STONER
Lim House, Pagham, Bognor
1st Battalion, the Princess Charlotte of Wales Royal Berkshire Regiment, 2nd Division
Killed in Action on 8 October 1918
Aged 19
Buried in the Forenville Military Cemetery, Nord, France

Originally Private Stoner served with the Hertfordshire Yeomanry, but later joined the Royal Berkshire Regiment. Frederick, the son of house decorator, Charles and Ellen Stoner, was born in South Bersted, the family then moving to Pagham.

Sapper Albert Armand BENNETT
7th Battalion, the Royal Sussex Regiment, 12th Division
22 Gravitts Lane, Bognor
Died of Illness on 17 October 1918
Aged 41
Buried in the Houchin British Cemetery, Pas de Calais, France

Albert was the son of Dandine, a widow, who was born in Switzerland but became a naturalized British subject; she ran a confectioners shop in London Road next to the Alexandra Tavern. Albert was born in Wales and like so many of his countrymen had a fine voice. Before the war he had been a regular member of the choir of St. John's, the Parish Church in London Road; he was also a Special Reservist. Albert lived with his wife Flora and four children and was a carpenter who, before enlisting at Chichester, was an employee of the builder and plumber Mr Thomas Start. Having been at the Front continually for three years and four months, Albert returned home on leave in September 1918. Returning to France, he was struck down with acute appendicitis from which he died on 17 October 1918.

Gunner 651827 Charles Reginald JONES
'B' Battery, 161 Brigade, the Royal Field Artillery
Killed in Action on 20 October 1918
Aged 20
Buried in the Busigny Communal Cemetery Extension, France

Charles was born in Derby and enlisted into the Royal Field Artillery in Chichester, although he is believed to have lived in Felpham. Serving with B Battery, 161 Brigade, he was killed in action on 20 October 1918, just three weeks before the Armistice.

Captain Kenneth Carlyle GILL MC
Strathmore, High Street, Bognor
1st Battalion, the Cambridgeshire Regiment
Attached to 22 Squadron Royal Air Force
Died of Wounds on 23 October 1918
Age 22
Buried in the Fillievres British Cemetery, France

One of eleven children born to Reverend and Mrs A T Gill, the vicar of Bognor, Kenneth was born in Brighton, educated at St John's School, Leatherhead and then studied for two years at St Catherine's College, Cambridge, intending to take Holy Orders, with a view to becoming a missionary. The outbreak of war changed his life and he enlisted into the Cambridgeshire Regiment.

In 1915 he was severely injured and repatriated to hospital in England. A lady whose son was in the same hospital wrote praising Lt Gills gallantry:

I hear from other wounded Officers that Lieutenant Gill is one of the most gallant Officers in the Army and splendidly brave, you may be proud of him, he has done many gallant deeds'.

A few months later the full story of Lieutenant Gill's gallantry became public when he was awarded the Military Cross:

'For gallant and most useful work on patrol duty, on several occasions near Ypres he went with another Officer along the line of the enemy's trenches to investigate some dead ground concealed from our trenches. On 14 May he went out and remained on the German parapet for an hour and a half gathering very valuable information. On the night of 1 June near Houplines, when reconnoitring hostile wire with another Officer, the patrol was discovered and heavily fired on. Lieutenant Gill, although severely wounded, made repeated efforts to bring in his brother Officer, who was mortally wounded and unable to move and lay within twenty yards of the German trenches'.

Lieutenant Gill spent ten months in hospital, undergoing an operation on his leg which had been injured, before returning to the Front in 1916. Promoted to Captain he was then attached to 22 Squadron, the Royal Flying Corps, initially a reconnaissance unit which became a fighter reconnaissance squadron when re-equipped with the new Bristol fighters and stayed with them upon the formation of the Royal Air Force on 1 April 1918. During one month alone, 22 Squadron became a highly successful fighting unit, accounting for over eighty German aircraft and one balloon.

Also in 1918 Captain Gill married, but it was destined to be a short union. On 23 October 1918 he died of wounds following an air crash in France.

Corporal 68982 Newman Henry BARTON
1 Buckingham Place, the Steyne, Bognor
1st Battalion, the Royal West Surrey Regiment, 33rd Division
Died of Wounds on 29 October 1918
Aged 19
Buried in the Cite Bonjen Military Cemetery, Le Treport, Seine-Maritime, France

Newman Barton was the son of Alfred, a timber dealer and his wife Anne, who lived at Streatham before moving to Bognor. He enlisted in Brighton into the Royal West Surrey Regiment and died of wounds less than two weeks before the Armistice was signed.

Sergeant G5427 Charles James BLISS MM
Council Cottages, South Bersted, Bognor
9th Battalion, the Royal Sussex Regiment, 24th Division
Killed in Action on 4 November 1918
Aged Unknown
Buried in the Cross Roads Cemetery, Fountaine au Bois, France

Charles Bliss enlisted early in the war into the Royal Sussex Regiment and served throughout the conflict, only to lose his life in the Battalion's last battle of the war. His wife received good news followed by bad:

'Mrs Bliss has just received the gratifying news, that on 16 September (1918) her husband, Cpl Charles James Bliss, has been awarded the Military Medal, for Gallantry in the Field and has been promoted to Sergeant', reported the *Bognor Observer.*

Three weeks later she was informed that her husband had been killed in action.

On 4 November 1918, the 9th Battalion Royal Sussex Regiment were ordered to take part in the taking and crossing of the Sambre Canal and lock and to join up with other British troops crossing further to the north and the French to the south. Sergeant Charles James Bliss and his men encountered heavy enemy shell fire, taking many casualties before zero hour. Their attack encountered very strong opposition and looked at one stage as if it might fail, but a crossing was achieved under very heavy fire. It is not known at which stage of the Battle of Sambre Canal Sergeant Bliss lost his life, only seven days before the Armistice was signed.

SALONIKA

British troops were sent to Salonika in the autumn of 1915 to assist in the prevention of Serbia falling into the enemies hands. However, they arrived too late and in insufficient numbers to succeed. They settled in facing the Bulgarian Army until September 1918 when, in a great Allied offensive, Serbia was liberated and Bulgaria capitulated.

Captain Alwyn Taytn PEPPER
Burngreave, Nyewood Lane, Bognor
100th Field Company, the Royal Engineers attached to the 22nd Divisional
Headquarters, Salonika Front
Died of Illness at the Salonikan Front on 6 November 1918
Aged 31
Buried in the Mikra British Cemetery, Kalamaria, Greece

Captain Alwyn Pepper was the son of William and Susan Pepper and was born in Surrey, where his father was a cheesemonger. Before enlisting Alwyn was a civil engineer. He met and married his wife Eleanor in Surrey and they appear to have set up home in Bognor. Captain Alwyn Pepper died at the Salonikan Front of dysentery, leaving an estate of over £1000.

WESTERN FRONT

Private G29491 Leonard Henry WALLER
Sefter Cottage, Pagham
1st Battalion, the Royal West Surrey Regiment, 33rd Division
Killed in Action on 7 November 1918
Aged 19
Buried in the Doullens Communal Cemetery Extension, Nord, France

Leonard was born at Boxgrove, Sussex, where his father Thomas was a farm horseman. Thomas and his wife Caroline bought up five children, Leonard being the second youngest. The family moved to Pagham and Leonard enlisted at Chichester, spending all his service time on the Western Front. He was the last local man to be killed in the war, just four days before the Armistice.

1919

Although the war had ended with the Armistice, servicemen continued to die. Below are some who passed away after the war, either from wounds, or illness, contracted as a result of war service. There may be others who should be included in this section, whose details have not come to light.

Corporal TF200744 Frank BICKNELL
1/5th Battalion, the East Surrey Regiment, 18th Indian Division
Died at Home on 3 January 1919
Aged 27
Buried in the Hollybrook Cemetery, Southampton, Hampshire

The second son of master decorator George and his wife Alice, who at one time 'had care of a tobacconists shop', Frank lived at the Moorings, Felpham Road, Bognor and worked as an assistant in a boot shop. He had joined up in the first few days of the war, his long service with the Royal Sussex Territorials standing him in good stead in his Army career.

His unit, 5th Battalion East Surrey Regiment, was immediately drafted to India, where it stayed for three years, during which time Corporal Bicknell saw a good deal of frontier fighting. On being transferred to Mesopotamia he went through a long campaign to Mosul, but was taken ill in October 1918. When it was realized that his illness was serious he was sent to hospital and was then hurried home to England, but died shortly afterwards in Southampton,.

Lieutenant Douglas Stalman DAVIS
Little Welbourne, Church Lane, Pagham
Honourable Artillery Company
Died at Home on 27 January 1919
Aged 27
Buried in the Arquata Scrivia Communal Cemetery Extension, Italy

'Many Bognorians will extend their sympathy to Major A J Davis, a former captain of Pagham Cricket Club, who lost a second son by death in Italy'.

Douglas Davis served in the Honourable Artillery Company, rising to the rank of Sergeant, before being commissioned. At one time he was the Aide-de-Camp to the Officer in charge of their lines of communication. Lieutenant Davis survived the conflict, only to be struck down by the influenza pandemic.

Petty Officer J/871 Henry Arthur COOK
Warfield, Spencer Street, Bognor
HMS *Lion* Royal Navy
Died at Home on 24 February 1919
Aged 26
Buried in Bognor Town Cemetery, West Sussex

Henry Cook was a telegraphist serving at HMS *Lion*, who died at home on 24 February 1919, possibly another victim of influenza.

Sapper Richard Theodore Montague ANDREWS
9 Elm Grove, South Bersted
Royal Engineers
Died at Home on 28 February 1919

Richard was born in Alton, Hampshire in 1888, the son of bricklayer William and his wife Eliza. The younger of two sons, Richard and his brother Frank both took up bricklaying, before Richard at some stage moved to South Bersted, where his home was named aptly named Alton Cottage. Here he lived with his wife and young son. Very little has come to light regarding his military service, except that whilst serving in France he contracted a serious illness in 1918 and was invalided home. Described as a 'highly esteemed and respected soldier', Sapper Richard Andrews' death occurred after the war following his discharge. His wife then moved back to Hampshire, where she ran the local Post Office at Holybourne.

Chief Stoker Frederick IDE
HMS *Victory* Royal Navy
Died 17 May 1919
Aged 45
Buried in St Peters Churchyard, Westhampnett, Chichester

'The funeral took place on Saturday May 24th 1919, of Frederick Ide, the second son of William Ide and the husband of Hanmetta Ide. Born in Bognor the deceased had served in the Navy for twenty four years and three months and had been all through the Great War and was a Long Service Naval Pensioner. After contracting Rheumatic Fever on HMS *Victory*, he was found a place at the War Office, where he served until his health failed again and he died of influenza'.

Private SS4200 S COSTER
Royal Army Service Corps
Died at Home on 1 September 1919
Age Unknown
Buried in the Bognor Town Cemetery, West Sussex

Private Coster is not mentioned on the Bognor War Memorial, his death occurring nearly a year after the Armistice. His headstone has been provided by the Royal British Legion.

1920

Private Henry (Harry) James Moulder JOHNSON
Died at Home 16 December 1920
Aged 32
Buried in the Bognor Town Cemetery, West Sussex, England.

Private Johnson is not mentioned on the Bognor War Memorial. His headstone states that he died of consumption (a wasting disease) 'contracted in the Great War'.

Private A IDE
Royal Army Service Corps
Died at Home 9 January 1921
Aged 40
Buried in Bognor Town Cemetery, West Sussex, England.

Private A Ide's name does not appear on the Bognor War Memorial; his premature death appears to have been attributed directly to his War Service. His headstone was provided by the Royal British Legion.

1921

Private William Levi TIPPER
1 Middleton Cottages, Brewery Lane, Bognor
2/9th Hampshire Regiment, 4th Division
Died at Chichester Hospital on 10 December 1921
Buried in South Bersted Churchyard, Bognor Regis, West Sussex
Not listed on the Bognor War Memorial

The youngest son of Charles and Charlotte Tipper of North Bersted, William had served as a despatch rider from 1916 until 1918. He contracted a serious illness and had to be sent back to England to the First Eastern Military Hospital, Cambridge for a major operation, after which he was medically discharged from the Army.

'For the next three years his health was a constant anxiety to his parents, who were summoned to his bedside on Tuesday, December 6th. They and his wife stayed with him night and day until Saturday evening when he passed peacefully to rest having been fully conscious to the last.

'His body was taken to the family home and then to South Bersted Church where he had been a lifelong member of the choir. He was given a military funeral'.

Corporal Charles Percy CLUER MM
Chapel Street, Bognor
4th Battalion, the Royal Sussex Regiment
Died in May 1921 as a result of War Service
Aged 32

A Territorial, Corporal Charles Percy Cluer, a son of hire carter and car man, Alfred and his wife Agnes, was born in 1889. On leaving school he secured the sought-after position of Post Office messenger boy, moving on to become a postman. A good sportsman, he also played football for Bognor. One of three soldier brothers, he was called up into 4th Battalion, the Royal Sussex Regiment and went with them to Gallipolli. Shortly after landing at Sulva Bay he contracted a fever and was evacuated first to Malta and then back to England, where he completed his service.

He re-enlisted into a Scottish Regiment and went to France, where he was in charge of a machine gun. He was wounded in the right arm, badly injuring two fingers and was awarded the Military Medal in July 1916 for 'Devotion to Duty' in this action at Armentieres. His citation read as follows:

'Whilst in charge of a mopping up party, he led his men with great dash into the enemy trenches and himself bayoneted several of the enemy. The remainder were bombed by his party and killed. He was severely wounded during the hand to hand fighting. He showed fine leadership'.

Percy Cluer survived the war and lived in Chapel Street, returning to the Post Office, where he was described as a 'popular postman'. He also resumed playing football for Bognor.

It was said that as a result of 'hardship and exposure he had suffered in France following his previous illness' he was taken seriously ill and died in May 1921. He was given a military funeral, his coffin being draped with the Union Jack, with his hat, belt and bayonet placed on top. As the coffin was lowered into his grave, which was lined with red and white flowers, three volleys were fired by twelve of his old comrades from the 4th Battalion the Royal Sussex Regiment, followed by the sounding of the Last Post.

Corporal Charles Percy Cluer's name does not appear on the Bognor War Memorial, although there is little doubt that his death was a direct result of his war service.

EPILOGUE

This book has concentrated on those men who paid the supreme sacrifice. However, we must not forget the many hundreds of local men who also fought and returned to their homes, families and employment. Sadly, amongst them were many who had been wounded, both physically and mentally, some so severely that they were unable to lead normal lives again. Let us not forget them - Heroes All.

Cliff Mewett

July 2014.

Printed in Great Britain
by Amazon.co.uk, Ltd.,
Marston Gate.